WHY I'M STILL MARRIED

"Artfully honest."   —*The Boston Globe*

"[Filled] with humor and compassion."   —*Newsday*

"To read [this collection] is to enlarge one's sense of what is possible in long-term love."   —Lauren Slater,
author of *Prozac Diary*

"Engrossing."   —*The Palm Beach Post*

"This revelatory collection offer[s] readers the unusual pleasure of looking inside other people's marriages to see what we can find there."   —Carolyn Parkhurst, author of *Dogs of Babel*

"The writing soars."   —*Ottawa Citizen*

"Funny, sad, hopeful, and honest." —*Richmond Times-Dispatch*

"In this groundbreaking collection, twenty-four ... women reveal secret truths about the ground rules of their most intimate interactions. You will be amazed at what you learn about your own experience."   —Suzanne Braun Levine,
author of *Inventing the Rest of Our Lives*

"Each of the twenty-four contributors to this thought-provoking collection has terrific stories and wisdom to share, and they all do it masterfully."   —*Publishers Weekly*

"[This book] should be required reading for anyone considering—or actively living—the plunge."   —A. Manette Ansay,
author of *Midnight Champagne* and *Vinegar Hill*

"Funny, passionate, fresh, and insightful, the essays capture the essence of what it means to be committed to another person."
—*The Advocate*

"This book is a must-read—I loved it. I have no doubt that every woman will find something of herself in these pages."
—Marlo Thomas

Why I'm *Still* Married

*Women Write Their Hearts Out
on Love, Loss, Sex,
and Who Does the Dishes*

**Edited by Karen Propp
and Jean Trounstine**

A PLUME BOOK

Some of the names mentioned in the essays contained in this book have been changed to protect people's privacy.

PLUME
Published by Penguin Group
Penguin Group (USA) Inc., 375 Hudson Street, New York, New York 10014, U.S.A. • Penguin Group (Canada), 90 Eglinton Avenue East, Suite 700, Toronto, Ontario, Canada M4P 2Y3 (a division of Pearson Penguin Canada Inc.) • Penguin Books Ltd., 80 Strand, London WC2R 0RL, England • Penguin Ireland, 25 St. Stephen's Green, Dublin 2, Ireland (a division of Penguin Books Ltd.) • Penguin Group (Australia), 250 Camberwell Road, Camberwell, Victoria 3124, Australia (a division of Pearson Australia Group Pty. Ltd.) • Penguin Books India Pvt. Ltd., 11 Community Centre, Panchsheel Park, New Delhi – 110 017, India • Penguin Books (NZ), cnr Airborne and Rosedale Roads, Albany, Auckland 1310, New Zealand (a division of Pearson New Zealand Ltd.) • Penguin Books (South Africa) (Pty.) Ltd., 24 Sturdee Avenue, Rosebank, Johannesburg 2196, South Africa

Penguin Books Ltd., Registered Offices: 80 Strand, London WC2R 0RL, England

Published by Plume, a member of Penguin Group (USA) Inc. Previously published in a Hudson Street Press edition.

First Plume Printing, January 2007
10 9 8 7 6 5 4 3 2 1

Copyright © Karen Propp and Jean Trounstine, 2006
All rights reserved

Pages 283–284 constitute an extension to the copyright page.

"Here" from *Begin Again: Collected Poems* by Grace Paley. Reprinted by permission of Farrar, Straus & Giroux, LLC.

Ⓟ REGISTERED TRADEMARK—MARCA REGISTRADA

The Library of Congress has catalogued the Hudson Street Press edition as follows:
Why I'm still married : women write their hearts out on love, loss, sex, and who does the dishes / Karen Propp and Jean Trounstine, editors.
p.   cm.
ISBN 1-59463-017-8 (hc.)
ISBN 978-0-452-28821-8 (pbk.)
1. Marriage. 2. Wives—Psychology. I. Propp, Karen. II. Trounstine, Jean R., 1946–
HQ734.W5787 2006
306.872'3—dc22   2005020754

Printed in the United States of America

CONTENTS

FROM SUGAR TO TIN

FROM PAPER TO WOOD

HERE

Grace Paley

Here I am in the garden laughing
an old woman with heavy breasts
and a nicely mapped face

how did this happen
well that's who I wanted to be

at last   a woman
in the old style   sitting
stout thighs apart under
a big skirt   grandchild sliding
on   off my lap   a pleasant
summer perspiration

that's my old man across the yard
he's talking to the meter reader
he's telling him the world's sad story
how electricity is oil or uranium
and so forth   I tell my grandson
run over to your grandpa ask him
to sit beside me for a minute   I
am suddenly exhausted by my desire
to kiss his sweet explaining lips

from *Begin Again: Collected Poems*

INTRODUCTION

We met for the first time at a reading in Providence, Rhode Island, where we both wore black and carried big bags. After we signed books, we went across the street to Starbucks and soon found ourselves in a looping, caffeine-inspired conversation. Somehow we got on the topic of husbands. Jean had been married for sixteen years and this was her second marriage. Karen, who'd married in her midthirties, had recently celebrated her eighth anniversary.

And then, as the espresso machine steamed and whirred in the background, the universe served up one of its serendipitous moments. We discovered we'd both recently written essays with the same exact title: "Why I'm Still Married."

We laughed at having struck, if not the uncanny, the coincidental. Or, maybe not all that coincidental. We began to deliberate. If we'd both written essays on this theme, there must be many other women out there with the same concerns.

Why *are* we still married? As independent, career-minded feminists, we felt oddly defensive to admit we'd settled into such an age-old patriarchal institution. In Jean's first marriage in 1970, she went to a lawyer to have a contract drawn up so she was able to have a credit card in her own name. Karen was practicing her version of the contemporary balancing act known as career and family. Could being long married also imply we were past our luscious prime and doomed for a future of unwelcome compromise? And when one of our husbands turned bedtime rituals into a health-care triathalon and one let loose his rage, we asked ourselves why we wonderful gals needed such behavior.

Implied in the question was, of course, something much deeper. We wondered what made us the ones who stayed. Why are *we* still married, we asked, when more single women than ever before in history are financially successful, eminently dateable, and leading full, independent lives? As ZZ Packer says in her essay for this collection, about her not-so-long-ago single days: "I'd always thought of marriage more like the weather: if certain atmospheric conditions occur, then rain will fall; if not, not."

Kamy Wicoff writes about her unexpected difficulty in giving up the freedom of her single life, worrying what happens to sex after marriage in her "Monogamy Meltdown." Contemporary marriages are inspired by expectations for individual happiness and romantic love. However, Susan Cheever reminds us in her essay, "Mrs. Married Person," that laws written on stones once deemed women the property of men. Marriages were arranged to keep liaisons within select families and to provide heirs. The first love poetry came later, during the Christian Crusades, creating the connection between love and longing that we now take for granted. But individual happiness and romantic love, as the poets know, are forever fickle. Perhaps that is one reason women coming of age today no longer assume they will marry and stay married.

Why are we still *married*? We know the dismal statistics: more than 50 percent of contemporary marriages end in divorce; married women are more depressed than married men and significantly more depressed than single women; married women with young children are the most depressed population. Aimee Liu, in her essay, "A Great Wall," speaks of a separation that completely "disassembled" her.... "In the therapist's office. Out of the therapist's office. Tears. Screams. Confession."

If there is so much pain in permanent coupling, what Maria Hinojosa calls "the long haul of love," why are the majority of us *still* walking down the aisle one, two, three, even four times? Julia Alvarez, in "Third Time Around: Snapshots from at Long Last a Long-Term Marriage," writes of her satisfying third marriage, which includes the challenge of stepparenting. Diana Abu-Jaber met her second husband "under the flickering, unfiltered ray of a computer screen," at a time when she wondered, "Do we know whom we're meant to love?"

Why do we keep getting married, and more importantly, what keeps us married? Is the answer as simple as Hannah Pine's confession about her passionate, open marriage: "At core, of course, *I'm still married because I still love being married to my husband.*"

We wanted to provide a forum for women to speak their truths, and we had a pretty strong hunch these truths could be found in stories—real stories about real marriages. Like everyone else, we knew about bad marriages that ended badly, or seemingly perfect marriages that succeed. But we wanted to know about the real marriages that survive, despite obstacles and struggles.

We wrote to writers whose work we admired and who we thought would have something valuable and important to contribute to the topic. We wanted people who were smart, articulate, funny, brave, and, above all, honest. We wanted diversity in age, background, cultural perspective, and geographic location. We wanted contributors whose insights grew from their number of years married. We asked to hear about the longings, losses, and betrayals in conjugal life that had tested their commitment. Sex is good, we said. Humor is even better.

Some writers we knew personally; most we did not. Many of the writers to whom we wrote responded with immediate, even urgent enthusiasm. Those who declined said they did so either because they were too busy or because they could not be as truthful as they'd like. "At the moment, I'm not brave enough to write this essay," answered one well-known author.

When the essays began to come in, we were struck by the range and variety of experiences that comprise marriages today. Anne Bernays, the longest married in this collection, recently celebrated her fiftieth anniversary. Her essay spans the historical changes that 1960s feminism wrought on the institution of marriage. Nell Casey, who describes herself in "Marrying Out of History" as a "thirty-four-year-old, happily married woman," is newly wed at one year.

We were moved by the range and variety of emotions at the heart of married love. Liza Wieland calls the pain from her commuter marriage, being separated for months at a time, a "hunger: to be held in my husband's large arms, to be kissed, to be carried up that flight of stairs." Susan Dworkin, in "The Marriage of Lost Fathers," courageously describes her husband after his stroke: "He did not recognize my face but he remembered that he had a wife named Susie, so when I walked in and said *I am Susie, your wife*, he held out his arms for me and I hugged him and kissed him." Eve LaPlante, in "18,260 Breakfasts," shows how important the regularity that marriage imparts can be to a child of divorce. Audrey Schulman, in "Murmurs," deftly describes the opposing parenting philosophies that struggle to coexist in marriage. And Jennifer Heath, in "The Two of Us," shows that marriage contains myriad moments where "we laugh, giggle, guffaw, chuckle, snicker, hoot, snort, cackle, and chortle until our sides hurt."

What surprised us was how many contributors staked the success or failure of their marriages around their growth as writers. Kathleen Aguero explains in "Koan" how she had to learn that a relationship can accommodate the writer's need for solitude. In "The Occasional Persistence of Love," Marge Piercy tells how she left a man who wanted her writing to take second place to domestic duties. Erica Jong tells, in "A Twenty-First-Century Ritual," how she agreed to marry her present husband only after he'd scribbled a written contract on a dinner napkin saying she was free to write whatever she wanted. And Bharati Mukherjee, in "An Experiment in Improvisation," says of her long, productive marriage to writer Clark Blaise: "Fiction writing brought us together and kept us together." Perhaps it's no coincidence that *four* contributors mention Jane Austen, who of course never married, though she is our genius in portraying the psychological and societal journeys young women experience in order to *get* married.

It's fitting that two people working on a marriage book as closely as we did for the better part of eighteen months should perceive their working union as a kind of marriage. We met every week at a café and continued our caffeinated conversations, first about the individual essays and later about the book's development. We talked at least once a day on the phone and sent countless e-mails. When we opened a joint bank account and ordered checks with which to pay our contributors, we joked that now we were "really married." We negotiated, complained, and stretched our imaginations. We had our first fight and made up. We discovered little quirks and different strengths. Karen had a talent for dealing with delicate interpersonal situations; Jean was brilliant at creating useful lists and organization out of chaos.

It was Jean's idea to shape the book around the number of years each woman had been married. Wouldn't it be interesting, she thought, if the essays engaged in conversation with one another, a kind of coffee klatch through the pages and the ages? Karen thought to title each section based on the quaint lists meant to guide anniversary gift-giving—wood to celebrate a couple's fifth year, china to celebrate their twentieth—reminding us savvy wives of the world that not only is marriage an inherited institution but one that's rooted in things domestic.

Once we began to sort through the glorious stack of essays we'd

received, we found they fell naturally into four groups. "From Silver to Gold" contains essays written by contributors who've been
married twenty years or more, several long enough to have experienced historical changes in marriage. "From Steel to China" has essays by women married from ten to twenty years, many having
made it past the most difficult places. "From Sugar to Tin" is written by women married five to ten years, still struggling with the
knowledge that comes with commitment. "From Paper to Wood"
contains essays by women just starting out, some in the throes of
adjustment, others still in the honeymoon glow, all married one to
five years. Readers may simply want to read essays by writers who
speak to their specific experience. But those who choose to read the
book in sequence will, we hope, gain a delicious sense of the rich
complexities and rewarding challenges that long-term marriage
confers.

While we were working on this anthology, marriage wars were
raging across the country. Staunch leftists found themselves defending marriage just as heatedly as they had once criticized it. "All
I wanted," says Meredith Maran about her ecstatic marriage to Katrine Andrée Simone Thomas, "was the same things every lover
wants: for it to be good, and for it to last forever. Like love, marriage, and the baby carriage, I thought, one led to the other, and
only in that order."

Perhaps it's no coincidence that we began to work in earnest on
this book shortly after May 17, 2004, the day the Massachusetts
courts began to issue applications for marriage licenses to same-sex
couples, and the day that Elizabeth Graver writes about in her
moving essay, "Gathered." "I had taken advantage of that right before I'd known that they would have it, and so my lessening of guilt
was spurious, and so the easy answers continued to refuse to
come," she says. On the other hand, Helen Fremont, with characteristic wit, remarks that Massachusetts' legal support "was both

annoying and exhilarating. After all, Donna and I had been married for eight years already, without an ounce of help from the state."

This collection went to press at the same time as thousands of gay and lesbian couples celebrated their first-year (paper) wedding anniversary. We like to think one of the reasons the essays in this anthology are as vital and engaging as they are is because they were written during this historical first year.

As we proudly turn you over to these wise and loving writers, it is our wish that they spark your own well-earned stories.

From Silver
to Gold

FIFTY YEARS IN THE
BONDS OF MATRIMONY
Anne Bernays

When I think of my life before I married, I see another person, a child really, although I was almost twenty-four when I became a bride. I see myself the creature of my mother, a feminist beyond the front door but a Victorian mouse at home. She warned me, among other things, that "all men sleep with their secretaries." Some women do have to deal with their husband's girlfriends or their gambling or too much whiskey or a little slapping around. What I had to deal with, first, was my husband's success. And if that were not enough to create waves in our marital sea, the women's movement flooded our sweet little ship and threatened to toss us in the drink. It's always something.

By the time I met Justin Kaplan in the fall of 1953, I had been around the block a good many times. Having gone to an all-girl school and then two women's colleges—Wellesley, then Barnard—I knew almost nothing about males except that they weren't anything like girls. From the moment I hit puberty, I went from one boyfriend to the next so rapidly that within days I had forgotten names and faces. We didn't go to bed with guys back then; we did what was called heavy petting. It was great fun and persuaded me that married life was mostly about sex.

Justin—whom I call Joe—was almost off the charts on the reticence scale. Unlike my father, whose powerful personality emerged in verbal barrages hard to resist or challenge, Joe was deliberate, measured, slow to react, quiet. I figured he preferred thinking to talking. But I sensed that underneath was a man of immense brain power, goodwill, humor, near-perfect instincts, and a touch of self-doubt to keep him from getting obnoxious about his brilliance. It took him a while to admit that he had entered Harvard at fifteen. A prodigy! Just the opposite of me, who struggled academically and had no goals in life other than to turn into a married lady [sic].

My mother was a founding member of the Lucy Stone League. This was a handful of professional women—one of them was Jane Grant, the ex-wife of the *New Yorker* editor Harold Ross—who had refused to take their husbands' names after marriage. They wanted every other woman to follow suit and wrote articles about "loss of identity" and so on. I failed to see what all the fuss was about. From the moment I was a wife, I was delighted to be Mrs. Kaplan. I sent Miss Bernays into exile without a single tear. The fifties were like that, a kind of postwar moratorium; no one did much of anything by way of protest, not about names, not even about civil rights.

During the early years of our marriage I felt about fourteen years old. As the daughter of extremely rich parents, I had never shopped for or cooked a meal. Joe had to demonstrate how to shop for food, prepare it, wash up after eating. He was amazingly patient. Tying on an apron, I thought, Look at me, I'm a bride in her own kitchen. Still, I deferred to him in most things that involved the two of us: where to go on a two-week vacation (Montauk), when it was time to move (from East Thirty-seventh Street to Nineteenth), whether we should buy a car (no). We loved being with each other and rarely quarreled. We stayed in bed until noon on Saturdays doing what newlyweds do, playing childish games and listening to records—long-hair stuff, Mozart, and Bach. The spinster who lived on the floor beneath us complained to the management about our noise. After lunch we put on our Saturday clothes and visited auction houses like Sotheby's, where we watched and never bought anything.

Weekdays, Joe worked at the art-book publisher Harry N. Abrams. I was the managing editor of *discovery*, a literary magazine published by Pocket Books. We spoke to each other on the phone a couple of times a day, at the end of which Joe picked me up and we walked back to our tiny apartment together. Hearing that "marriage takes a lot of work," I didn't know what people were talking about. Our honeymoon lasted a long time.

Around the middle of our third year together I woke up one morning desperate to have a baby. Joe and I—partly, I suspect, because we believed ourselves sort of Peter Pan–ish and not that far from childhood—had never once mentioned having any children together. When the maternal urge took hold, it was fierce. Within months I was pregnant and visiting my mother's ob/gyn, a natty person with an office on Park Avenue. He made me starve myself— "No more than seventeen pounds, please." I used my pregnancy to quit my job and took a writing assignment from Joe, who was now a senior editor at Simon and Schuster. The assignment meant rewriting a manuscript he had bought but that needed several runs through my Olivetti typewriter.

We had already moved once, from his tiny bachelor pad to a somewhat larger place. Now we moved again, this time into a five-room apartment on Riverside Drive. It was when Susanna, born in May 1957, was about two months old that I began to write fiction. The origin of this urge was as mysterious and subterranean as the urge to produce a child had been. Maybe they had something to do with each other, the creative floodgates having been released in a torrent. Whenever Susanna slept in the daytime, I put the phone in a deep drawer, piled pillows on top of it, and closed the drawer. I wrote ten short stories in one year, the words pouring almost, it seemed, unbidden. The stories were awful—humorless, tedious— but my agent, whom I had acquired from knowing him while at *discovery*, managed to sell one of them for twenty dollars. It was about a young pregnant woman (guess who?) who meets an old beau on the street who upsets her by asking what she's doing to make the world a better place. She runs to her husband for comfort. By the end of this overlong, overwrought story, we learn that what really upsets her is childbirth; how does the baby get through such a tiny opening? I published this story—in an obscure literary magazine—under the name of Anne Kaplan. Who was this stranger whose name was printed under the title of the story? Kaplan hadn't written it—Bernays had; it occurred to me that maybe my mother was right about keeping one's name. In spite of its subject matter, the story embraced far more of what I had learned while single than what I had experienced as a married person. I told Joe I wanted to bring Miss Bernays back out of exile. A look of doubt crossed his face, not, I think, because his manly pride was bruised but because he thought that maybe this meant I didn't love him anymore. But he didn't make a fuss. From then on, Joe always introduced me by saying, "This is my wife, Anne Bernays." I've been Anne Bernays ever since—except on my driver's license, my passport, and my Social Security card.

When Hester, our second daughter, was two months old, we moved from New York to Cambridge, Massachusetts. By this time Joe had quit his classy job in publishing to write a biography of Mark Twain. We chose Cambridge mainly because of Harvard's library—and besides, I was tired of waiting for the elevator in our apartment building. A silly reason for leaving New York? Probably. But it was Joe's imperative: he needed the library; I could write anywhere, I could bring up the children anywhere. Cambridge seemed to offer a calmer—not to say stupefying—place to work: few distractions, no elevators, relatively fresh air. We settled into a large house on a groovy street not far from Harvard's famous yard.

When Hester was three, Polly was born. The day after her birth, my obstetrician came into my room at the Lying-In Hospital and said, "Well, Anne, when are you going to try for a boy?" I said, "I like girls." I couldn't stand his macho smugness.

About this time people—mostly women—began to ask me how I managed to write and do all the things a wife and mother is supposed to accomplish. My answer: "Having money doesn't hurt." We weren't filthy rich, but we weren't poor. We could afford live-in help—which we had for the first couple of years, graduating later to a student to whom we would give bed and breakfast and dinner on the nights she babysat for us. In 1962, the year Polly was born, I published the first of my nine novels. During the sixties I published three more. Thinking about it now, seventy-four years old and the grandmother of six (five boys, one girl), I can't believe this was me. I've grown lazy—though not complacent. I must have been incredibly focused, not wasting a minute, leaving dishes in the sink, the beds unmade; in fact, not doing any domestic chores until I had done my daily quota of pages—two. (My first desk was in the bedroom, my next in an unheated back room, my third at the end of the hallway on the second floor. When Polly went off to college, I finally got a nice big room on the second floor.) Not answering the phone, making no morning dates or even doctors' appointments unless I was bleeding from the ears. I must have done this, but I find it hard to remember hewing to such a regimen. It had to be more obsessive than the way folks today go to the gym and work out.

And where was Joe all this time? He was downstairs in his book-lined study, working, for seven years, on his Mark Twain biography. We spent one summer in Berkeley, California, where he went to the university's Bancroft Library, depository of Samuel Clemens's papers. When his book, *Mr. Clemens and Mark Twain*, was published in 1965, it won both the National Book Award and the Pulitzer Prize. It was his first book. By that time I had published two novels and was working on my third. Suppose that, having given up his job, moved away from New York, and worked that long and hard, his book had dropped into the void that so many others fall into? His third book, a biography of Walt Whitman, won another National Book Award. He has been awarded a Guggenheim and membership in two august academies. My envy of his triumphs was not softened by the knowledge that he deserved the praise and the awards. For years I felt like a ballet dancer with one mangled foot, watching her partner fly around the stage. And even as I burned in silence, I burned with guilt. How could I be envious of him when he worked so much harder than I did and was touched by brilliance? There were times I wished I'd married a dummy like one of my pre-marriage boyfriends who was as sweet as a ripe watermelon but who hadn't read any books, knew no history, had never gone to a concert, and, half the time, didn't know what I was talking about.

For years I suffered from the psoriasis of envy. When it began to morph into resentment, I decided to tell him what I was going through. "I don't understand," he said. "You've done fine. You've published novels with good houses, you were on the cover of the *New York Times Book Review*, people like your work . . . blah, blah, blah."

"Compared to someone who can't get her book published, I'm okay. Compared to you, I'm a sixth-grader learning what a paragraph is."

"What are we going to do about it?" He asked me if I wanted him to stop writing. I don't actually think he would have stopped if I had said yes. But I had the sense not to require him to make a major sacrifice.

"Of course not," I said. I suppose, at that moment, I forced myself to recognize what, in a short story, is called a turning point. Which meant I could either get out of a situation that made me miserable from time to time or swallow it and move on. It wasn't his problem, it was mine. And after all, he could have had a girlfriend, a thirst for whiskey, or an uncontrollable temper. He was—and still is—remarkably easy to live with. He does a lot of the food shopping (he claims he enjoys it!) and he cooks. When the children were small, he took his turn carpooling. He sometimes took them to the dentist. It's not his fault if he outshines me.

When we had been married nearly twenty years, Jean Baker Miller published a book called *Toward a New Psychology of Women*. By this time the women's movement had built up an impressive head of steam; females were rattling the bars of their cages. A psychiatrist with sociological underpinnings, Miller understood all too well the moves of the oppressed/oppressor choreography. Reviewing her book in the *Boston Globe*, I wrote, "This small book may do more to suggest the range and scope of female possibilities than anything since Women's Suffrage." I don't think I was exaggerating. Miller's book changed my life. She did this by persuading me that a marriage in which the man calls most of the shots is about as healthy as a master-slave combo. A couple of nights before I got married my mother had given me some wonderful advice, namely, "Remember, Annie, whenever you argue with your husband, he's always right." Now Miller comes along and challenges me to "renegotiate the marriage contract" and change the lopsided arrangement of husband and wife. Before I read her book I hadn't been aware that Joe and I even had a contract. Miller warned that, along with change, there would inevitably be conflict. If Beta dog doesn't feel like being Beta anymore, Alpha is certainly going to find out about it in a dramatic—and maybe bloody—way. I looked around me; many of the women I knew who were about my age were divorcing their husbands. This is what prompted me to write my third novel, *Prudence Indeed*, a book that takes its title from the Declaration of Independence. The story involved a woman married to an emotional tyrant. She just manages, at the end of the book, to escape from his clutches. It was a novel only a few people read, but a couple of years ago I saw it mentioned in a piece about feminist fiction as the first contemporary feminist novel. Miller's challenge was a test for me: Isn't it much easier to give in than to fight?

For starters in the new regime, I no longer picked up Joe's clothes from where he had dropped them outside his closet to signal the laundress—me—that they needed washing. I told him I wasn't going to iron his shirts any longer. His solution was to pay one of our daughters to do it, thereby unwittingly awarding her wages for housework, something women were making noise about. These may seem like small acts of defiance, but Joe got the message: "I'm not your servant, I'm your partner." Slowly, I worked my way into making joint decisions: how much to spend on a car, where to go on vacations, even money matters. Until I told him I needed to be in on whatever dealings he had with his investment person in New York, I knew zip about how much money we had, how and where it was allocated, what to do in case of emergency. I think it was hard for him to have me ask so many questions, and question so many transactions. It meant he had to educate me, and that takes time and forbearance.

It's inevitable that, after you've been married for as long as we have, folks want to know how we accomplished it when close to 50 percent of marriages bite the dust or the husband and wife end their days together not talking to each other. There are so many ways for two people in the same house to be abrasive that unless you find strategies to avoid being hurt you'll go crazy. It took a while for us to stop accusing and yelling during an impasse, but we finally learned how to defuse an explosive situation by humor and by making fun of it. One night when I was especially nasty, Joe looked up from the book he was reading and said, "You creep!" How can you stay angry at a man who calls you a creep?

Temperamentally, we are as different as a racehorse and a turtle, yet we get along so well that one of our friends calls us "Bobbseys," after the fictional twins who were rarely separated. We've managed to accommodate each other's natures and the occasionally dicey habits that emerge from them because . . . well, I'm going to have to admit that I haven't the foggiest idea. Maybe it's because we just plain like each other. He makes me laugh, I make him laugh. I like the way his mind works—he's a true original. Neither of us gets bent out of shape when the other is annoying. Sometimes I tell him to "shut up" and he either does or he doesn't, but nothing terrible results. We both like the same things: mindless movies, neighborhood diners (rather than posh restaurants with linen nappery), talking about books and food, playing verbal games (some of which are our own invention, like "Debate on Wheels"), not going to large parties, and comfortable clothes. We tend to like the same people. While Joe's literary god is Proust and mine is Jane Austen, two authors from opposite sides of the spectrum, we do a pretty good job of not getting on each other's nerves.

Besides, he's my love bug.

THE OCCASIONAL PERSISTENCE OF LOVE

Marge Piercy

By the time I was twelve, I promised myself never to marry. Looking at the lives of married women around me in the working-class neighborhood of Detroit where I grew up, I could see brutality, tedium, frustration, and misery of all shades and types. It looked to me as if a woman put her head into a halter when she married, and I wanted to be free. The few working single women I knew were pitied by the wives, but I thought they had a better deal going. They were far more independent, although in those years many still lived at home. They dressed better, talked more boldly, carried themselves with a confidence that some of the married women acquired when their men were away at war, but lost when the husbands came home.

Who has not experienced dealing with a woman known only as part of a couple, a nice woman, sure, but rather meek and self-effacing? Bland, even. Then her husband goes out of town and you have lunch with her; suddenly she's alive. She has opinions, she tells raunchy jokes; she laughs spontaneously. She's an animal let out of a cage. Often women lose more than their names; they may lose their ambitions, their power, sometimes even their personalities. I don't think a lot of marriage as an institution, but in some ways it is a convenient compromise between comfort and pleasure.

Yet as it turns out, from twenty-one to the present, I have been married three times. I have been in my present and, I hope, last marriage for twenty-two years. Being sexually active at a time when girls were not supposed to experiment, by the time I hit twenty-one, I was scared for myself. My first husband was a French physicist, a Jew who had spent the war mostly in Switzerland as a young child separated from his parents. He was and probably still is a gentle and kindly man, but he had very rigid ideas of what marriage should be. He was unable to take me seriously as a writer, a woman with a central agenda equivalent to his. He took for granted that I would always put his needs, his desires, and his pleasures before my own. I had assumed, since I had been writing seriously already when we married and had won several prizes for my work, including the money on which I went to Europe with him, that he would understand how important writing was to me. But I realized by the second year of marriage, my poetry and fiction would always seem a hobby to him, something to fit in on the side once I had carried out my myriad duties as a proper French housewife. This was not a compromise I could wedge myself into. I began to have dreams in which I was dying. We could not communicate about sex roles; he simply kept saying that was how things had to be. I left. I walked out with my typewriter, my books, my few clothes and moved into a rooming house.

My second husband was a systems analyst. He was much less conventional and more accepting of my writing and offered, after our second year together, to give me five years of support to establish myself as a novelist and poet. By the time we got together, I had decided I did not want to have children; he agreed. It did not take another five years for me to begin to make a living by writing, but it did take four. By that time he had insisted we have an open relationship—he wanted to be free to pursue affairs with other women. It was a time of great sexual freedom and experimentation. In my experience, open relationships work only in specific circumstances: *both* parties are willing and able to have other people in their lives. Jealousy is not a major issue for any of those concerned.

The other people with whom the husband or wife becomes involved do not passionately wish to have a monogamous relationship. Neither husband nor wife is given to uncontrollable infatuations. If everybody likes each other, that helps a lot.

Our open marriage worked fairly well for nine years. The freedom helped me since my husband was a fairly cold and uncommunicative man, unable to give emotional support. We could communicate intellectually and politically, but the language of emotions was foreign to him. I was able to form strong bonds with other women and with men who did give me what my husband couldn't. It was a time in which relationships with a number of friends and lovers were very important to me.

A traditional marriage can be an inconvenience when a woman is younger, giving her less mobility through society and consuming time and hard work in its upkeep that she might better put to use in her career, in educating herself, in making and keeping friends. I took full advantage of my freedom, often pursuing teaching stints or conferences that kept us apart for weeks or months as a time, as did he. I was able to have intense friendships as well as lovers. But having multiple relationships is time consuming and energy intensive. Finally, the other relationships became more important than the supposedly primary relationship, which frayed until it ripped apart. While I became sexually and emotionally less important to him, I was still the wife responsible for home maintenance, food preparation, budgeting, and all those unglamorous daily tasks that comprise life support. Thus I was constantly reminding him of chores, bills, and repairs while the "other woman" represented pleasure. Not much fun in that division of labor.

Also as I got older and the women my second husband was involved with got younger, they began to treat me with contempt, which rubbed off on him. If this exciting new nubile girlfriend did not respect me, why should he? I endured a constant stream of acid criticism spattering me from women whose sole virtues, as far as I could see, were youth and the fact that they liked to have sex with him. I felt betrayed. I had believed that he could and would want to remain strongly connected to me while he pursued his other adventures, but over time I learned I could no longer trust him. I was devastated and torn. I felt as if the center of my life had gone. The only support or encouragement I got came from outside the marriage. When that happens, you know it's not working.

My third husband, Ira Wood, is also a writer. I had been enamored of men who were very different from myself, being physicists, mathematicians, systems analysts, all those fields I did not understand; but then, of course, they could not understand what I did either. Having been involved for five years before we married, Ira and I had a thorough sense of each other's virtues and faults, our stress points, our strengths as a couple. We decided we wanted to be monogamous and have remained so. We are each other's best friend, and we communicate about everything, endlessly. When you've had as many adventures as I have had over the years, there is little temptation to stray. I have no curiosity about others sexually. I can pretty well guess what it would be like, and I've been there, done that. Love, love of me as I am, as I do, what I do is the thing I most craved and can now find in my marriage. I have an ally, not a competitor, not a client. We have a certainty that the other is not looking to trade up; that we respect each other's work. That trust—that the other is on your side and wants you and what is best for you—is terribly important.

Although we are both involved with writing, we are not competitors. We rejoice in each other's successes because we believe they enhance our life. We try to refrain from blaming the other for our failures. Ira and I had worked together writing a play and seeing it through its first Equity production. Working together is a great if hazardous way of really understanding each other. You see different sides of a person than you do just seeing them for playful things, for pleasure. Since then, we have collaborated on a novel,

Storm Tide, and a how-to book, *So You Want to Write: How to Master the Craft of Fiction and Personal Narrative,* now about to go into its second edition. One of the most valuable things we do for each other—and the hardest, most painful, and most hazardous—is critiquing each other's work. We are each other's best but also most stringent critics. It takes a strong emotional commitment and connection to endure this on either side. One thing we share is a work ethic: we respect each other's work and try to structure our lives accordingly so that each of us can and does work.

One difference that strikes other people is that Ira is considerably younger than me—thirteen years younger. Now this probably is less jarring to me than to most people since my mother was at least seven and probably more (she did not have a birth certificate) years older than my father, and my Aunt Rose was married to an even younger man. Many of my affairs during my second marriage were with younger men—they were more comfortable with the notion of an open marriage. Since I'm a strong feminist, I often find men my own age antagonistic to my politics. Sometimes my outspokenness offends or even frightens them. Many younger men have grown up with the concept and images of strong women and may even like the equality; they are sometimes less threatened.

When we women were little, we got used to stories that ended with marriage: the prince and the princess wed and lived happily ever after. But getting married begins real work. You have to stay connected. That sounds easy when you're romancing each other. It's much more difficult six years later when the water heater breaks down and you have ten people coming for Thanksgiving. It's hard when one of you gets sick and stays sick for two months. Ira had to help me through a period in which I was enduring painful eye operations, one after the other. I was legally blind, and when we went for walks, I had to follow him and could only proceed by seeing the white of his socks. I tripped and fell a great deal. My cats were stepped on so many times they hardly bothered to cry out. I looked awful and felt worse. My pain was almost incessant. It takes tremendous commitment to ride out a long period of difficulties. Ira is prone to depression. We have gone through his down periods dozens of times. I do my best to stay connected, and we work our way through the bad times.

The hardest thing in a long love is not to begin to take each other for granted, somehow to keep finding in the other what you can and do love, and to express that. To remain loving, you have to keep your eyes on what you care about and cherish in the other person, through a choppy sea of distractions—bills, household problems, minor quarrels, all the myriad tasks and worries of every day, and, if you have children, their woes and needs and problems, and the money to give them what they need and what they passionately want. Keeping in love is not that different from being able to focus on sex when you get into bed. If you are thinking about the grocery list or what's wrong with the furnace, you will not get much pleasure from the sex. If you hold grudges or let the small nuisances and failures accumulate, love will suffocate. The love that matters in marriage is not that jolt you felt when your eyes met in the early days, that obsessive gnawing of desire. It is akin to friendship but deeper and more rooted in your identity. Sex is important to some of us; to others, it couldn't matter less. I find a strong sexual connection keeps me motivated to work out problems and helps heal breaches that occur. It won't do that if you get out of bed and go right back to the same argument you had before.

Nobody is a perfect match, and we have to accept that. I am insanely punctual; Ira is only careful about time when he has a plane to catch. He believes that being late is being polite. Ira hates anyone picking food out of a serving dish with their fingers; I have learned to use a serving spoon or fork and put the food on my plate before I eat it, in order not to set him off. He is phobic about the smell of fish; I hate dirty laundry left on the floor. It is not that we have worked out these foibles, but we have learned not to blow them out of proportion and—much of the time anyway—we are careful not to trip each other's guy wires. You cannot choose what annoys you. Perhaps that spot was sensitized in childhood. You can't stand when someone cracks their knuckles or talks with their mouth full. But you can choose what to express of your annoyance and what to tell yourself: Don't be a child about that. Let it go. Does it really matter that he always forgets to hang up his coat? So you spend five minutes a day putting it on a hanger; big deal. Is that worth a fight?

We are both high-maintenance people. We come from difficult families where we felt unloved, unappreciated. I'm a loud opinion-ated pushy woman. I care immensely about equality in relation-ships. If I cook, he does the dishes. If I do the laundry, he does the shopping. Ira is emotionally high-maintenance. He broods. He wor-ries. He ties himself in knots. He takes seriously insults that slide off me. He needs a lot of daily reassurance.

At the same time, we both need a measure of independence. He is very involved in local politics. I am more globally focused. I need quiet time more than he does; he requires more stimuli from out-side than I do. I need one evening a week to myself without having to deal with anyone at all, so he has to fill that evening time every week. We both have friends we see independently of each other and friends we see as a couple.

We create rituals—not only observing Shabbat, but that one evening I have to meditate; big celebrations of Passover; a Fourth of July garden party; Thanksgiving and Rosh Hashanah; little rituals like him taking the car to be serviced the day before Thanksgiving, picking up a fresh goose and having brunch with an old friend of his; planting peas as close to St. Patrick's Day as possible; ordering seeds together in early January from eight catalogs, always too many seeds. Rituals mark time and affirm the couple.

I have learned what I can comfortably—or even somewhat uncomfortably—compromise on and where I cannot give way. A couple of marriages that went bad quickly or slowly have taught me a lot about what I need. I must have a situation with whomever I live with that enables me to write. I need some privacy and much intimacy. I am the kind of fussbudget who hates when anyone moves things on my desk, not out of neatness—I am hygienically obsessive about my body but when I am working, blind to the mess I am creating—but because it's my work and nobody touches it without my permission.

I need to know that my partner has my back, is on my side, can be trusted out of my sight; Ira needs that also. He needs me to avoid situations that trigger his jealousy, jealousy that in other relationships has eaten away at his sense of self-worth. I have to put up with his teasing; he has to put up with my ever encroaching mounds of papers. He had to learn to live with cats in order to live with me. I had to learn to follow and understand football in order to live with him (all credit to *Football for Dummies*, which has probably saved other marriages beside my own).

You learn where your real boundaries lie as you work your way through a marriage, where you can give way and where you cannot. When you are young, it's no particular advantage to be married unless you're having a baby and want help and support. When you're older, it's much more valuable to be in a good marriage. Who has time or patience to date after forty unless you absolutely have to? We need each other more as we age, not less. Growing old together is, in part, not forgetting to grow.

THE MARRIAGE OF LOST FATHERS

Susan Dworkin

Our mothers raised us and taught us how to live. But it was our fathers who caused us to marry each other, who made us go on loving each other even when our marriage fell ill, made us stay married even when our love grew old. We used our long union to fill in the blanks where our fathers should have been. For our fathers were never there, you see. They never visited our house. Our children never said "Grandpa" to them. Fathering was a just a fantasy to us. A cautionary tale. A discipline. Our aspiration.

I.

When I was a young woman, I was quite alone. My family members all belonged to other people. They were gone from me; had been gone for years. I tried to get my friends and my job to substitute for my family, which placed an unbearable load on my job and my friends.

My evenings were full of dates. Talk talk talk talk. Dinner dinner dinner dinner. Men kept proposing to me. I was shocked because during all that torrent of conversation I had never taken even one of them seriously. I forgot the men I was with while I was with them, so vague and daffy was I in those times. Once I called my boyfriend repeatedly by the name of one of the characters in a novel I was writing. He raged, convinced I was cheating on him. How could I explain to him that it was really much worse than that?

I never cleaned; never shopped. I often passed mirrors in which I noticed no reflection. I was a cloud, a nothing. I lived as Galway Kinnell's poem says, half alive in the world, the missing half of me wedded to "a wild darkness." My work was filled with dreams of power and safety. My main characters were men.

When I met my husband, I remembered him instantly. He had a herculean handshake. A good old car. A big nose. He knew how to stand up to bullies and how to make a living. Every word he uttered pierced my mind like great literature. I slept with him immediately and married him without a second thought.

My husband had some books that I had never seen before, books that probably belong to many leftist families. One book I liked particularly. A graphic novel called *God's Man* by Lynd Ward. The story was told in woodcuts.

An artist comes to the great city. He is a gifted painter, a pure spirit. The satanic forces of greed and ambition seize him, use him, corrupt him. A scarlet woman tells him she loves him. A power broker offers him fame and riches. Hypocrites fawn upon him. Soon he is an empty shell, his work turns to shit, his fortune is stolen, the woman leaves him, he is alone and penniless and abandoned and resurrected only when he stumbles into the haven of true love.

One night, before we were married, my husband cuddled me into our little bed in my apartment above the Stage Deli and read Lynd Ward's book of pictures to me. I rested my head on his right shoulder. He held me with his right arm that reached all the way around my upper back, and the fingers at its end traced the shape of my right ear as he read. My right ear still feels the touch of those long fingers. My left ear still feels the warm, soft, hard haven of that shoulder, and it was more than forty years ago. I curled against him, insubstantial as a cloud, but so secured and supported by his long right side that I could not float away. A cloud against a marble curb.

I felt that if I married him and loved him always, I would never again float away. I could be the artist I longed to be and not always feel lost in the city of dreams, like the hero of Lynd Ward's book, and I and my children would be always secured and supported and anchored in the void.

Will you take care of me, my love? Will you be on my side?

Yes, I will. I am here. You don't have to be afraid. I will not leave you. I am right here.

I still feel the caress of that commitment, and it has been more than forty years.

II.

He spoke little about his father, Louis. I knew only that he was a retired physician and a Communist. He had been married twice to my mother-in-law. The first go-round produced my sister-in-law. The second, my husband. Clearly, my mother-in-law, a feisty, bright woman, could not live with him and could not live without him, either.

The second marriage ended when my husband was eight. From the paucity of his talk about Louis, I assumed he never saw his father again and even wondered if the old man might have died without us knowing. Turned out he was alive and not well, living in Toledo, Ohio.

Pushing and insisting, I finally heard a few stories about Louis. Impossible to know how much of the truth they represented.

He never paid child support although he made a good living as a doctor. His children were chronically strapped. My husband went to Fresh Air Camp. The community had to take up a collection to get him a pair of sneakers.

When my husband was a little boy, Louis would occasionally collect him from my mother-in-law's tiny house and take him out for an anti-kosher Chinese dinner, with Louis's current girlfriend along for the meal. My husband became adept at answering the inevitable question *How was your dinner with your father?* with greater and greater circumspection.

When my husband got his license as a teenager, Louis gave him a car. Since he had no money to buy gas, he told his friends that anybody who could fill the tank could drive the car. That car was the plaything and practice vehicle for a whole gang of teenagers in Detroit.

Some years passed before I was allowed to know that the second divorce had occurred while Louis was in jail. His propensity for social agitation had always landed him in trouble. While serving in the army on a base in Alabama, he deliberately sat in the back of a public bus with the African American passengers. As a result, the local Klan burned a cross outside the army base. The army was not pleased. In later years, he was frank and forthright about his Communist affiliation. In 1944, the feds arrested him—ostensibly for supplying morphine to a patient. It was a trumped-up charge, to mask a political detention, not uncommon for self-avowed Communists in those days.

My sister-in-law eventually acquired the trial records under the Freedom of Information Act. So much was blacked out for security reasons that they were hard to read, but one fact emerged clearly. It was the girlfriend who had served as a snitch for the FBI. She testified against Louis in court. A public scandal.

My mother-in-law said in later years that she divorced him because he was a Communist and a jailbird. But I figure she divorced him because of the terrible humiliation that befell her as a wife because of the trial. My sister-in-law dropped out of school for a while. My husband turned to stone.

Let's go see your father in Toledo.

There are more important people for us to see.

If we are going to be married, I have to meet your father.

We found Louis a cripple in a wheelchair, living alone, unable to get to the toilet, unable to wash his dishes or himself. The story I heard was that he had fallen and sustained some fractures, and although he was cautioned not to get up and walk, he tried to do so anyway and had refractured his leg. Too embarrassed to report that he had neglected his physician's advice, he immobilized the leg and hoped it would heal properly. It did not. So now *he* was immobilized. Trapped. The place stank of piss and sour milk. If he had anything clean to wear, it was because my husband's sister journeyed down from Cleveland to do his laundry, schlepping her kids.

My husband had not been to see his father for a long, long time, and the state of the old man obviously upset him.

Louis could hardly talk coherently, for his teeth had rotted and the few survivors clacked and wobbled in his mouth. He wanted to make us welcome, but what could he do? We had to wipe off our chairs to sit. He babbled about his education and his hometown, pretending that he still had father status and the keys to our history. I pretended those things too and told him about my family as any prospective daughter-in-law might, respectfully. My husband-to-be said nothing.

He did not hold his father's hand or meet his father's flickering, blearing eyes.

When we left Toledo, I seriously considered breaking off our engagement.

What kind of a man would leave his father in such a condition? I thought.

Then I explained to myself: a man who is really mad at his father.

It was my very first close encounter with the wages of divorce and the rage of abandoned kids. A bitter lesson, it lived on in my mind.

I lied to my mother. Told her that Dr. Dworkin was a charming and interesting man, very friendly, but too disabled to travel to the wedding.

Finally, a social worker was enlisted. Louis went to live in a nice nursing home. There the godless old Red sat all day in the little synagogue, reading holy books. We went to visit him with our babies. The pictures I sent him were always displayed on his dresser when we arrived. My husband continued not to hold his hand or meet his eyes, and the visits were largely conducted between Louis and me.

When he died, we had a tiny graveside funeral. Some elderly black people showed up, having heard, they said, that Dr. Dworkin had passed. For them he had cared, never charging a fee, with an open hand and an open heart. His own children and his twice-abandoned wife received no support and rarely a kind word.

What philosophy produces this morality? Is it easier to embrace social justice than to love your wife and your kids?

Apparently so, said my husband with a sigh.

My mother-in-law, too old and sick to attend the funeral, wept so piteously for Louis that I knew she must have loved him truly, and I believe that all his sins were washed away by her tears.

However, I do not know of any baby in the family who was ever named for him.

III.

My husband learned several unfortunate lessons from his father. He learned to ignore his health, to blow off his doctor's advice, to medicate himself. He learned not to believe in the possibility of true love, even though the evidence for its existence lay before him like the promised land for decades. He learned how to humiliate a woman so thoroughly that she would have no choice but to seek anonymous refuge in a strange town.

However, in the main, he defined himself (and made himself a hero to his wife and kids) by determinedly becoming everything that Louis *was not.*

He rejected extremism. The righteous Right and the loony Left both left him seething with contempt. He hated stinginess and was the soul of largesse. He doted on his mother, brought her to live with us, paid her bills, employed me (I willingly acquiesced) as her aide and her personal shopper and her transport manager. His family was always welcome in our house. He loved to put all the leaves in the table and have giant dinners for everybody.

A different sort of social activist than Louis, he preferred not to make trouble but to make peace. Macro-peace between the races; micro-peace among the cousins. He always worked within the community, immersing himself in programs for young people. The fatherless boys in the homeless shelter stayed up late pitching pennies with him and talking about the future, while their exhausted mothers slept. Friends of his children, who were studying in Israel, came hitching and hiking from Galilee and the Negev to have lunch with him by the sea in Tel Aviv.

But he never chose the community over his own family. His children were his treasure. He drove them everywhere, always left work to attend their games and shows, moved heaven and earth to pay their tuition, never rested until they were home safe. They were living proof for all the world to see that, as a father, he had not turned out like his father. And as the instrument of that triumph, I had—it took me a lifetime to understand this—an ineradicable place in his heart.

About twenty years into our marriage, my husband began to enjoy some success in business and rewarded himself for his triumphs, as so many men and women do, in ways that broke my heart.

Not knowing how to hold my head up in the community anymore, I decided to leave him and go to Los Angeles, which is always a good idea. (If only my mother-in-law had thought of that!)

An actress friend met me for lunch in the sun in Venice. She told me that she too had walked out on her husband and had left her children behind, and when it came time to divorce, she had been labeled the abandoning parent and had lost custody.

I took the red-eye that night and packed up my youngest and moved him West with me. My husband, having fun in his new midlife life, seemed relieved for a time. But soon, the terror of becoming Louis kicked in, and he came flying out to see us, scared that his children would be mad at him for not loving me. He remembered his own anger, how perfectly content he would have been to abandon Louis in his old age, and he couldn't bear to imagine himself in that position, feared that he too would be an old man sitting in his own piss in a dirty house alone alone all alone.

So he said: *Come back to me.*

No way.

I was doing well by then in L.A., supporting my boy in style, living the great Helen Gurley Brown lesson that success was "the best revenge."

Come on Susie, I miss you. Come back to me.

No.

He gave me money. I didn't need it but I took it anyway. Stuck it in the bank. Told myself that money meant nothing but money so I might as well.

But in my heart, I knew the truth. He wanted to support us because he still wanted us to be his. Support was a symbol of his commitment. Support means you are the father of the house; that you are pulling your weight, meeting your obligations. Even if you are a woman, it means that. Which was why I felt it was so important to live on my own and support my son.

This lesson I had learned from my own father, whose name was Ben, whom I had never known. When I was thirty years old, he reached up from the grave and surprised me with a matured insurance policy, bought when I was born. *Happy Birthday, Susie*, it said, *with love from your father.*

IV.

My father was a myth to me. He died when I was three. I was lied to about his death.

Your father went away on a business trip.
Your father is still away on a very long business trip.
Okay. Your father is actually dead. He died of a heart attack.
Okay okay, he died of cancer.
Didn't you know? Cancer of the jaw.

This last piece of news, delivered inadvertently by my big sister when I was nineteen years old and smoking two packs a day, sent me rushing madly to the dentist for the first time in years.

Our family's obsession with concealing bad news made me suspicious of the stories my mother told me about how terrific my father was. I spent my life looking for corroboration from disinterested sources and plumbed the memories of my cousins on my father's side.

I heard that Ben was a charitable person, deeply involved in providing recreational opportunities for disadvantaged young people, and that he built a youth center in crime-ridden Brooklyn. He veered toward politics. The fabled liberal Paul O'Dwyer became his good friend and mentor. My mother said Ben might have been borough president—except that he got sick. I figured she was exaggerating, but dreamed she might not be, and we went ahead and named our firstborn son for him.

In the twenties as a single man my father went to Europe. He hung with artists in Paris. Bought books in London. He journeyed to the newly revolutionized Russia to visit an aged aunt and uncle who had remained there when all the rest of the family moved to America, and left some money to help them out. After he was gone, the locals murdered the two old people and took the money.

This terrible event left Ben disgusted with Communism and doubting its ability ever to alter traditional Russian anti-Semitism. He became a Zionist. My big brother once told me that before the war, Ben came into his room, took his baseball bat, and went out with a bunch of guys to break up a meeting of the Nazi Bund.

He never looked at another woman, Mom said. Never.

Go corroborate *that*.

I met this mythologized man only through his library, which was filled with books by authors slightly more centrist than Lynd Ward. Novels by Upton Sinclair and Lion Feuchtwanger. Pleadings for the Jewish national homeland by Pierre Van Paassen. A book by Walter Lippman called *A Preface to Morals.*

What's morals? I asked my big sister when I was a little girl.

It's what you think is the right way to behave.

What's philosophy?

It's what you believe that makes you think you know the right way to behave.

I looked for Ben's philosophy in the thick yellowing pages. I looked for his morality in a world without conscience. I looked for him in synagogues, in political science classes, in soup kitchens and orphanages, on collective farms in Israel. But with every year that passed, he seemed to disappear a little more. I despaired of ever finding him. I understood that the loss of my father was the making of my own invisibility, that cloudlike vagueness, that daffiness that haunted my relationships, confounded my boyfriends, and irritated the hell out of my husband. So I tried to make myself more real by inventing fictional fathers in plays and stories. I called them Charles and Misha, Abraham and Angelo. They were all dreams of Ben.

V.

One night we decided to go to the theater. At the intermission, my husband went off to the bar to get us a ginger ale. I was hanging out in the crowd waiting for him and suddenly I saw a woman I had known many years before when I was a little girl. Her name was Sheila. She had married the son of a family friend. His name was Bobby.

My mother had told me that back in the forties, when Bobby was a kid, he became very angry at his father, and engulfed by adolescent despair, he decided to run away and join the navy. Ben was home a lot because of his illness, and available to the young boy. He talked Bobby down from his anger; convinced him not to so very hastily blow away his life.

Bobby did join the navy in the end—and saw action in the Pacific—but not until he had finished high school. My father's doing.

Eventually, Bobby married Sheila. Now she is standing before me. She remembers our family and greets me warmly.

Then Bobby appears. And he's got my husband with him.

"Sheila!" he calls. "I met this man on line at the bar and we started talking and you know he reminds me so much of Ben Levine, you remember Ben, he was like a father to me, saved my life, wonderful person, and this man is just like him, it's amazing, it's like Ben walked into the theater . . ."

My husband was laughing. Bobby looked at my face. I didn't need to tell him who I was. He knew.

Here it was. The real deal. Corroboration.

I realized in a flash that the reason I had married my husband without a second thought was that, like Bobby, I recognized my father the instant I met him.

How can you leave the man who has brought your father back to life, who inhabits his philosophy as no library ever could? How can you stay separate from a man who is your anchor in the void, whose commitment is proof that you exist, who wants to be a great father, who wants you to love him forever because he is such a great father, how can you not go back to such a man?

Again, he flew out to Los Angeles.

Come back to me.

I don't know.

Please. I love only you. I can't stand sleeping without you. Please.

Okay, I said.

You think everything was perfect after that? No way. Perfect is for kids, and we were—finally—grown-ups. But a certain reality set in, and the cloudlike time ended, and that was certainly a pleasure. The years after our reconciliation were among the best of our long marriage. We loved the trips we took and the house we bought and the way our children grew into adults whom we both felt proud to know, and to be honest, I greatly enjoyed the respect he had for me because I had left him.

My husband began to tell me new stories about his father. We drove up to Canada to see the medical school that had accepted a gutsy immigrant kid when the American institutions were too anti-Semitic to let him in. We planned a trip to Russia, to visit Louis's hometown. We began to spend some time with my husband's cousins on his father's side.

VI.

He was at the Helen Hayes Hospital in Rockland County after his stroke.

He had lost his sense of himself. He could not fathom that he was ill. Could not understand where he was. He did not recognize my face but he remembered that he had a wife named Susie, so when I walked in and said *I am Susie, your wife,* he held out his arms for me and I hugged him and kissed him.

They got him up out of bed into a wheelchair. They were busy and set him in the middle of the floor while they attended to other people. He sat in puddle of sunshine, turning his head from side to side the way Stevie Wonder does, only he was not blind, he was rather lost. Blind from within.

He felt thirsty, but because of the tube in his throat, he could drink nothing by mouth. I went down the hall to get him some ice, to wet his lips. So suddenly he didn't see me anymore. He thought I had left him.

I could hear him calling: *Susie. Susie. Susie!*

His voice was filled with panic. My marble curb, my anchor in the void, he was afraid! It was impossible! Unbearable! I raced down the hall with the paper carton of little ice cubes, shouting: *I'm coming, Moish, I'm coming!* The ice cubes flew around me, scattering on the floor.

I ran into the puddle of sunlight and held him close and rubbed the last couple of cubes on his dry lips.

I am here. You don't have to be afraid. I love only you. I will not leave you. I am right here.

And he believed me even though he didn't recognize my face because he knew that we adored him, that in his life he had become the father he wanted to have, that wonderful mythlike stories would be told about him and children would be named for him, and that his wife, who had also become the father she wanted to have, would secure him and support him and be on his side no matter what happened and would take care of him forever.

A GREAT WALL

Aimee Liu

*W*e met on the Great Wall of China. This is our marital myth, the line we unfold like a party trick, to show and tell why we're together. Without this myth, we make no sense. The fourteen-year age gap's the least of it. M. was bar mitzvahed in the Bronx; I was confirmed in Connecticut. He makes movies; I write books. He plays basketball three times a week; I consider sleeping a sport. But for the Wall, I'd be hosting literary teas in Darien, and he'd have a real trophy wife.

"Of course, it's not true," I say, as M. fills our dinner guests' glasses with wine. "I never even saw him on the Wall."

"That pile of rubble would no more protect the Middle Kingdom than I would come to China to find the woman of my dreams. That's what *I* was thinking that day," says M.

"It was nineteen seventy-nine." Steam spirals over the table as I start serving the pasta. "Courtesy of Nixon and Kissinger, the Chinese had opened the door to American tourists for the first time in thirty years."

One of our guests taps a glass. Did we or did we not meet on the Great Wall?

M. raises his palm. "Hold on. These are critical details. My merry band of showbiz juveniles—"

"Juveniles in spirit anyway," I say. "The Writer, the Director, and Mr. Producer here were all pushing forty. You weren't techni-cally tourists, either."

"*Technically,*" he says, "we were scouting movie locations. Ours was supposed to be the first Chinese American feature film coproduction."

The wistful lilt of his voice sends a frisson around the table of eight that has nothing to do with our myth. We live in L.A., where even poets know the term *turnaround* means a chance to profit from someone else's abandoned opportunity. Our guests want the details of M.'s erstwhile project. He runs down the plot: American woman in pre–World War II China searches for her missing big-game hunter husband, instead brings back the first baby panda in captivity. True story. The women present send up a collective "Awww."

"Seems a lot of people go to China, bring back a surprise," M. observes.

"Like Marco Polo and pasta." I wave my hand over the lasagna. With all the tomato sauce, béchamel, mozzarella, and ricotta, it doesn't exactly look Chinese, but it's the closest I come to ancestral cooking—other than heating up take-out dim sum.

"At any rate," my producer husband tells the opportunists at the table, "the project passed through at least five other production teams and twenty more years before IMAX finally made the panda story." He kisses the top of my head as he passes into the kitchen for another bottle of wine. "Your turn."

My reasons for being in China were infinitely simpler than M.'s. I point to the sideboard, a framed photograph of my parents, who bore a strong resemblance to Katharine Hepburn and Ray Milland in the fifties, except for one detail. "My father's half Chinese. He was born in Shanghai, lived in Peking, but moved to America in the thirties and hadn't been back to the mainland since before the Communists. He, my mother, and I were making a roots trip, revisiting the scenes of Dad's boyhood and wartime adventures."

"Tell the truth." M. comes back in, corkscrew and bottle in hand. "Your parents brought you along because you were broke, jobless, and about to get booted out of that closet you called an apartment back in Greenwich Village. They planned this as a bonding trip that would reel you back into the family fold."

In fact, I had a grand sum of $110 in the bank, as well as a string of heartless lovers all in the past tense and a year of my life sunk into a first novel that my agent had advised me to burn.

"I was at a crossroads," I admit. "But all that was a million miles away that day on the Wall. Beijing was our first stop in China. I was still fighting jet lag and could barely keep my eyes open, let alone worry about the rest of my life."

M. reclaims his seat across from me. "My group, on the other hand, had been in the country for three weeks by that point. On the train out from the city to the Wall they'd decided to vent. I was the Producer. It was my job to jolly the boys, so that left me looking for girls." He spreads his hands and gives a little push in my direction. "There directly in front of us stands an indisputable girl who is not only delectable and young, but also, Chinese heritage aside, *American*."

His lecher's grin is cute, but two decades out-of-date and skewed by his horn-rimmed glasses. I point my knife right back at him. "If you hadn't sicced your wolves on me so fast, I might have had a chance to notice *you*."

M. shrugs. "It's the Producer's job to do the needful when his crew's in testosterone meltdown. What else could I say, but, 'Go get her, boys!' "

One of our guests makes a rude remark about pimping in the People's Republic. I pass the bread. "The Writer looked like Elmer Fudd—balding, nearsighted, dressed for safari. He never stopped talking. The Director was closer to Abbie Hoffman—lots of curly hair, black, beady eyes, lumpy T-shirt, and stand-up dirty jeans. They were both several inches shorter than me and nearly twice as old. So I said hello. I said good-bye. And my parents and I moved on to our next stop of the day, the Ming Tombs." I instruct our guests to visualize an enormous cave with an army of life-size clay soldiers standing in formation to escort the emperor to the next life.

M. grins. "My guys were more than willing to stand up and escort you, babe." I roll my eyes. "I couldn't get away from them. Here I am half-blind from stumbling around in this underground tomb, and as I come blinking out into daylight, who's standing directly in front of me but Elmer and Abbie. I thought I was hallucinating."

"The Tombs are just down the road from the Great Wall." M. gives a dismissive shrug. He never has liked this story beat as much as I do. "In those days the government made sure every Honored Guest in Beijing was taken on the same combo day trip, but my guys insisted this 'second encounter' was kismet. Then they remembered the local film studio was hosting a banquet for us that night, and nobody had a date—until now." He leers at me.

"When I balked, Elmer called over the elder members of the scouting mission, two gray-haired vegetarians wearing matching L.L. Bean hats—"

"Our Lawyer and his Wife," M. says.

"—to convince me I'd be well chaperoned."

"Whereupon your mother cleverly summoned you for a photograph." M. scans the images clustered around the frame of my parents—wedding photos of us trading gazes of mock adoration with M.'s then five-year-old son giggling between us. "Where did you put that picture?" M. asks.

I check our company for flagging interest, but they urge me on. I fetch the snapshot in question from our bedroom and am humbled and a little appalled by the youth it contains. This once-me wears a man's tuxedo shirt from a thrift store on the Lower East Side. A multicolored Guatemalan sash cinches my twenty-six-inch waist. My hair, parted dead center and dark as mahogany, falls straight past my shoulders, and my makeup is smudged in a way that makes me look deceptively wide-eyed and innocent. I'm not exactly Suzie Wong, but the Temple of Heaven rising behind me sets the appropriate atmosphere.

"Fresh for the plucking." M. passes the picture.

"Unencumbered," I correct him. "The exact opposite of you, I might add. You had a two-year-old at home, a relationship on the rocks, and elderly parents in residence."

"I was not the one making a play for you. As you're so fond of pointing out, you didn't even know I existed that day."

That does it. Our listeners want to know: When *did* we meet?

I toss the salad and send it around. "I did not accept the invitation. The next day my parents and I flew fifteen hundred miles to western China."

"The Hollywood contingent headed south, meanwhile, to spend a week in the Yangtze gorges."

"Two weeks later," I continue, "my group flew back across the country to Shanghai and checked into the Peace Hotel. The next day I was on my way into the main dining room for lunch when I noticed this familiar-looking woman sitting in the lobby eating raisins out of a plastic Baggie. It was the Lawyer's Wife!"

M. picks the sprouts off his lettuce. "Vegans. For six weeks, while the rest of us diplomatically sucked up sea cucumber and bear paw, the two of them lived on trail mix—"

"The point is," I cut him off, "we'd traveled umpteen thousand miles in opposite directions. Two weeks had gone by, and—"

"You hadn't cleared the door before the boys started drawing straws for you."

"Forget them," I scold him. "You're supposed to say 'That's when you finally saw me,' and I say, 'I did indeed.'"

As I came down that hallway he was sitting sideways directly in front of me. Thirty-nine, fit from the six miles he was then running each morning, he wore his shirtsleeves rolled to the elbow, his dark hair curling into his collar. Pink. The shirt was pink that day in a room painted pastel green. He lifted his chopsticks to make a point to someone sitting across from him out of my line of sight. "I thought, Hmm, if I can wangle another dinner invitation, this time I'll accept."

He seizes a couple of spoons, bangs them together against his knuckles, and yowls—his Chinese-opera sound effects. One of our guests, laughing, gets up and says, "No comment on his performance, but where's the bathroom?"

"I was late getting there," I jump ahead. "The streets were jammed with bicycles. Back then nobody in Shanghai drove a car. Only half the city even had electricity, and the signs were all in Chinese. I had to take a cab from one end of town to the other with a driver who spoke no English. I'd lied to my parents to get out of that night's opera, and I had absolutely no idea where I was going."

"She was going," M. sets the stage, "to one of Chiang Kai-shek's former mansions. Built by the British, complete with ballroom, grand staircase, red carpet, and a porte cochere straight out of *Cinderella*."

"My Prince!" I open my arms to him, but our guest returns from the powder room, ruining the effect. Everyone has finished eating. I need to get up and make the coffee, but this is our Big Moment.

I pause, thinking how much more romantic the truth is than the flip version we always tell. In reality the night was humid, sooty, and throbbing with cicadas, the smell of jasmine and diesel, bicycle bells soft in the distance—all this pouring through the open window as my cab rolled to a stop. The grounds of the mansion were walled and unlit, the gardens dense with foliage. There were none of the usual hotel attendants, not another car in sight, and from what I could see through the glass doors, the lobby blazed with mirrors but was as deserted as a scene from *The Twilight Zone*. I started to panic. What was I thinking? I'd never exchanged a word with the man I'd come for, had no guarantee he'd even be there. Suddenly, I saw movement inside. Someone was coming down the grand staircase. A civilian. Khaki pants, a crisp yellow shirt, no Mao jacket—tall and dark and American.

M. reached the bottom of the stairs, pushed open the door. I was out of the cab now, reading his face as his expression changed by degrees, from concern to relief to something else, something very different as our eyes met. Everything slowed way down. He took my hand.

"Lightning struck," I say, as if it's a joke. "We stood there in this palatial lobby. He did not ask me to dance, but it was that kind of room, long and wide under a crystal chandelier, lots of red and gold. We had the whole floor to ourselves. If either one of us knew how to waltz, that would have been the moment."

I get up and dance into the kitchen with an armful of dishes. M. laughs. "There she was. My very own Miss America. I stuck out an arm and showed her up to the grand ballroom."

I bring in the decaf and pass around mugs. "Do you even remember what we talked about?"

"I remember," he says, "you wore a fetching black ensemble that you'd somehow cobbled together out of your suitcase. I also remember that every few minutes somebody would make a toast. *Gan bei!*" He lifts his glass in demonstration, and downs it, bottoms up.

"Try that with mao-tai." I grimace. "No wonder we don't remember what we talked about. Chinese lighter fluid."

A couple at the end of the table helpfully stack their dishes.

"Not so fast," M. says. "The night was still young. The Chinese had arranged a screening for us back on the studio lot. Elmer and Abbie insisted our Honored Guest join us."

"By the time they let go of me it was after midnight. Shanghai was dead to the world, and I had to get back to my hotel—"

"Which, of course," M. says, "was out of the question. They had it all worked out. We'd bring you back to my room, since I obviously wasn't in contention, and after a couple of drinks, you'd choose one of them."

I remember what they plied me with. "Chinese red wine. Now there's an aphrodisiac for you. A vintage blend of plum sauce and turpentine."

He scowls at me. "And you ignored them both!"

"I kept waiting for *you* to make a move."

"The only move left was yours, hon."

It's time to wrap this up. The dregs of dinner are starting to congeal, and we're not even done with the first night, the first kiss in the cab, the clerk we roused from under the front desk back at the Peace Hotel. We could tell about the second night, too, the walk down the pitch-black alley where Shanghai's young lovers went to kiss and grope, their sighs quivering out from under the silhouettes of parked army trucks. Darkness so dense you could squeeze it. That's how I remember China.

I rise and walk around the table to kiss my husband's cheek. "It finally dawned on me, all I had to do was ask you to take me home."

The morning after our latest retelling, we take turns waiting for each other's eyes to open.

"Remember when we used to seize the day?" I kiss him good morning. "Carpe diem, and we'd haul out of bed and run five miles before breakfast."

"That was twenty years ago. We've graduated to Pat the Day." His hand travels down my body.

I smile. "Remember Plan A and Plan B?" Our crossroads conversation the second night in Shanghai. Choices I didn't know I had he'd sketched out for me: life according to my parents' expectations—marriage to a diplomat or Wall Street tycoon, a dabble in the high life of Manhattan, followed by my filial duties and a handsome home in the suburbs; or, alternatively, unnamed choices for which I alone would be accountable.

"Your parents were right, you know."

"About what?"

"You never should have married me."

I throw my leg across his back. He cups my heel in his palm.

"I'm too old for you," he continues. "I just want you for your body."

"Thank God." I turn him to find his eyes. They're hazel with subtle variations of green. He has severe astigmatism. I know I see him better than he sees me. "I want you for your hair." I do. It lies like thick, brushed silver now against the white pillowcase.

"Good thing you didn't marry Elmer, then." He grins.

I lean down and whisper in his ear, "It's all right, hon. I was never even tempted by anyone but you."

"Poor you." He glances at the clock. "Are we going for our record?" A few days ago we lay in bed talking past nine.

"It's only seven twenty!" But I peel myself off him. Who's kidding who? I threw my back out two days ago. He strained a muscle playing basketball yesterday. I groan as I stand up. My hips are shot, too.

"No fair," he says. "You were supposed to take care of me in my dotage."

"A quarter century with you would age anybody."

"You had your chance."

"Believe me, I enjoyed every minute of it," I lie. Our six months of separation, just five years ago, completely disassembled me.

"Best days of our lives." He's standing up now, walking toward me.

"Can you believe how I regressed?" It's true, I think. In the therapist's office. Out of the therapist's office. Tears. Screams. Confession.

"I regressed further than you." He puts his arms around me. Flight. Betrayal. Fantasy.

"Good thing we had the Wall." I inhale his soft, dark, sweet scent. Maybe it's not his hair I love most.

"Homeland security," he quips.

The Ch'in emperors who originally envisioned the Great Wall snaking across the face of China believed they could unify their civilization by constructing a barrier that would at once keep invading barbarians out and restless subjects in. They spent centuries proving the plan didn't work while simultaneously creating one of the Seven Wonders of the World. The Wall was never completed. Attacking hordes easily scaled it. Vast sections fell into ruin. The beauty of that serpentine line today lies as much in the audacity of its inception and echoes of voices stilled in its rubble as in the concrete details of geography and structure.

It may be a mistake to overromanticize such an imperfect symbol of wholeness. The Middle Kingdom was never actually the middle of anything other than its own illusions, and the Wall marked neither the beginning nor the end of civilization. But when astronauts spot the Wall through their windshields in outer space, they don't think about the imperfection. They don't fault the line for being too short, or too old, or irrelevant. They speak of the sighting with awe and pride, as if the Wall is their own. From that great distance it marks where they come from, and where they belong.

KOAN

Kathleen Aguero

I don't sleep with my wedding ring on, as my fingers often swell at night. One morning, while I was working on this very essay, I was putting my ring back on when it slipped out of my hand, fell to the floor, bounced, and disappeared through the small crack between the chimney and floorboard in our attic bedroom. It happened so quickly that though I darted forward I couldn't stop it. I panicked. My wedding ring! My mother's diamonds in it! I shouted for my husband. We peered through the narrow crack with a flashlight but couldn't see anything. "Could we fish for it with a hanger?" I asked. "If we put a piece of chewing gum at the end of it?" I wondered how far it had fallen. Was it somehow in the furnace?

"No," Richard reassured me. "We have a subfloor."

"Okay," I said, "we'll pull some floorboards up."

"Not so easy. This is an old floor. The boards are tongue and groove."

That evening I asked him if we couldn't fish for it with a magnet. Would a magnet pick up gold?

"Hmm," he said. "I could run a current through a wire. . . ." He proceeded to describe some Rube Goldberg–like invention.

"Great," I said eagerly.

Later I came to my senses. Richard is no Thomas Edison but a writer and English teacher like me. I called my oldest friend, whose ingenious son, now a freshman at MIT, had learned from the Internet how to pick locks. "I've got a problem for Joe," I told her. But Joe was too busy studying. I was ready to tear the floorboards up with my teeth. This is it, I thought. I'll have to die here. I can never move out of this house while my wedding ring is under the bedroom floor.

When I was seven or eight years old and reading mysteries— Nancy Drew, Judy Bolton, Cherry Ames—my favorite series was Vicki Barr, stewardess. I longed to live alone like Vicki and organize rooms just the way I wanted them as much as I longed to stumble upon mysteries to solve. Even at that age, I alternated periods of intense sociability with complete solitude, sometimes telling friends I had to leave our game of tag to help my mother with the housework. I liked the dreamy state that solitude afforded, the chance to repair myself from the sharp-tongued nuns at school, and as writing became more important to me, solitude became even more tied to my sense of self.

Independence, reverie, writing, a true sense of self—all inextricable from being alone. No wonder at the first opportunity I moved by myself into a funky studio apartment in the basement of a large building. I hung blue fishnet between the kitchen area and the living-room area, refusing to be discouraged by the fact that heavy rains had caused the city's sewers to overflow, so I couldn't use the bathtub for weeks. Over the years, I progressed from that studio to one run-down one-bedroom apartment after another, thrilled with each one, despite cockroaches, poor heating, pipes that froze. My apartments felt so like a second skin that entertaining friends in them was almost too intimate. I cleaned before guests came to hide traces of my secret self and again after they left to scrub away the feel of "strangers."

It's a wonder that I married. I don't particularly believe in marriage as a civil institution. I'm well aware of its history of oppressing women and its origin as a business transaction, a way to gain and consolidate property. Though my husband-to-be wasn't particularly oppressive, and although, as an adjunct professor and a prep-school teacher, respectively, we had little business to transact—no property, no life insurance, no retirement benefits—I was wary. Let's just live together, I countered, when he first mentioned marriage. That seemed the most practical choice. But since my adjunct teaching positions had no security, we'd be moving to the private school at which he taught. Unmarried couples living together would be anathema, and he wasn't willing to lie, although I suggested it.

"You know why I'm here," Richard told me, when he came up from New Jersey one day in March. "I want us to get married."

"Okay," I said quickly, "but why?"

"Marriage is a public commitment. It ties you into a community of support." I must have looked dubious. He leaned across the kitchen table to touch my hand. "Besides," he said in an effort to reassure me, "we can always get divorced."

"Right," I snorted.

But in the end, his confidence won me over. I have a hard time making up my mind about anything, and he seemed so sure. Though I still loved living alone, I feared that if I kept at it I could become the kind of person who couldn't stand the sound of someone else brushing his teeth, the kind of person who walked after other people putting things back in their place. Marriage, I reckoned, would be an adventure that would keep me from shrinking into my smallest self. Why not marry? I thought. If I'm lucky enough to find someone I love, someone who loves me, why not?

Richard is a magnificent sleeper. That, oddly enough, is one of the things that won me over. I, who sleep so fitfully, was charmed by his ability to sleep and sleep and sleep. Often, I would lie in bed an hour or so after I'd awakened, basking in the aura of Richard's sleep. And when he finally rose, he was, well, still asleep. He seemed to me like an animal emerging from hibernation as he sat there with his coffee, patiently waiting for consciousness to surface. Something about this proposed marriage felt as solid and comforting as Richard's sleep.

So, ten years after that first studio apartment, the one I'd wanted since fifth grade, I found myself sitting in the Laundromat with the man I'd just agreed to marry watching our wet clothes spin round and round in the dryer—my socks and his socks, his briefs and my panties, my bras, his undershirts, rolling together in a blur of white. I might get a quick glimpse of some item I suspected was mine, but I couldn't really be sure whose was whose. When they came out of the dryer, they'd have to be carefully sorted and folded into separate piles. My heart sank a little. This is what it's like to be married, I thought—all jumbled together with another person. I wanted to open the dryer door and snatch my clothes.

The morning after our wedding, I lost my voice. So inaudible was I that I had to point out my dinner choices on menus so Richard could order them. "I have to use the bathroom," I'd mouth, and he'd ask the waitress where the ladies' room was. Surely this was the quietest honeymoon on record. Worst of all, I was totally dependent on my husband to make my wishes known, and a writer literally without a voice. This laryngitis symbolized my nightmares of what could happen to a woman in marriage. Even at the time, I saw the perverse humor in this.

Nearly every adult at the small New Jersey prep school where Richard taught seemed to be married, as if the campus were some kind of Noah's Ark and all the animals came in twos, us included. My alienation was compounded by my unplanned and nearly immediate pregnancy. I would walk the country roads around the campus more and more slowly as my belly swelled, wondering what on earth was happening to my life. How had I wound up living some-

place where our host at a dinner party actually told me I should
support my *husband*'s writing, ignoring the fact that I was a writer
myself? Where everyone just assumed I'd taken Richard's last
name: "Oh, you must be Kathi Hoffman."

"No," I'd say sourly and leave it at that.

Although Richard and I were both in our thirties when we
married and should have known better, to some degree we each
married the person we wanted to see rather than the complex individual we'd chosen. I don't know who Richard thought he was marrying, but I thought I was marrying a calm, easygoing guy, able to
soothe my always present anxieties, someone who might stir my
passion but not my fury and selfishness, someone whose needs I
could satisfy while keeping myself primarily for myself—separate.
His beard, prep-school clothes, slow way of moving and speaking,
at least compared to mine, all reinforced that impression. It's not
that I didn't get direct information to the contrary—one of his students referred to him as the moodiest man she knew and one of his
colleagues told me Richard was always in better spirits when I was
around—I just chose to ignore these comments. They didn't fit the
picture I was composing. I thought Richard's habit of drinking
bourbon before dinner was amusing—something people our parents' age did. One day, before we married, we had been sitting at
the kitchen table in my apartment. "My baseball coach abused me,
sexually, when I was eleven," Richard told me in an offhanded way.

Part of me registered, this is a big deal—but also, he's not saying
this as if it were a big deal. "Oh," I responded.

"It's okay," he said and shrugged.

I saw his pain but not his rage at his abuse, at his two brothers'
untimely deaths from Duchenne muscular dystrophy. These trau-
mas, I thought, accounted for his compassion and sensitivity. In
fact, the abuse had occurred just as Duchenne's was making
Richard's brother Bobby, until then his closest friend and playmate,
less and less able to keep up. How naive I was to accept the way he

downplayed this. However, marriage, like motherhood, eventually makes you face your worst self.

After our son's birth, my parents invited us to house-sit for a year. They planned to travel extensively (at least that's what we heard), so we could easily share their large home in the Outer Banks of North Carolina. That way we both would have time to write and to spend with our new baby, as our expenses would be minimal. Perfect, we thought as we accepted their offer. Only, as it turned out, they didn't travel nearly as much as we expected. If it was difficult for me as a new mother and relatively new wife to juggle these roles and to build a new family in the midst of the old; it was excruciating for Richard, who felt like a guest in my parents' home and had to change his habits to adapt to their rules. A man who every morning settled into a comfortable chair to drink his coffee and read the paper now had to sit on a stool at the kitchen counter because my mother didn't allow eating in the living room with its Oriental rugs and antique furniture. In addition, the cough that had delayed his mother's visit when the baby was born turned out to be lung cancer.

Our clashes seemed violent in a household where my parents argued without shouting. More than once our loud, angry voices brought my father downstairs, his face tight. "Don't slam those doors," he'd hiss, barely controlling his own anger. "You'll break them." How awful for him, I think now. As if his children were back, fighting, but not cute, not pretty.

Other scenes I remember include sitting on the deck with the crying baby while Richard stormed out of the house shouting up at me, *"Nurse that baby"*; his deciding to leave me, taking the sleeping baby out of the crib to bid a tearful good-bye, and my begging him not to go. I remember wheeling the carriage along the dunes thinking that by the end of the year I'd be divorced and my parents wouldn't be speaking to me. What held me together was the time I had to write and whatever other solitude I could muster. I took long walks on the beach; I ran six to ten miles a day. I don't know how Richard—struggling to comfort his father, to care for his mother, for his new baby and postpartum wife, all the while living in his in-laws' home—survived that year.

Richard's mother had been thrilled to have a grandchild, so we wanted her to see the baby as often as possible, a bittersweet comfort. We spent a lot of time traveling between North Carolina and Pennsylvania, and since I was breast-feeding, where the baby went, I went. I felt engulfed in the drama of a family I barely knew. "I feel like a wet nurse," I said to Richard, infuriating him.

Christmas morning, 1983, with Richard's family, I was upstairs trying to get the baby and myself ready. "How's it going?" Richard's father called up the stairs.

Let him get the baby dressed, I thought and called back down, "I'm doing the best I can," in a curt tone.

Richard was angry with me. I was embarrassed. His mother was walking around attached to an oxygen tank, and I was the one feeling put-upon.

Sometimes driving from North Carolina to Allentown, Pennsylvania, to visit his dying mother, we'd try to talk about our anger at each other. "We need to go to couples' therapy," he'd say.

"I'll go, but only if you admit that some of our problems are your responsibility. It's not just me."

Silence. I knew from previous conversations that he didn't see it that way. He wanted me fixed. I was aghast at his arrogance. "Then there's no point." Only now do I wonder, was he frightened his drinking would be discovered?

Later that week in a gift shop he bought me a card saying he'd change. Back and forth we teetered, fight and forgive.

* * *

By the time we'd been married two years and were in our own apartment, we were in rough shape. Richard's mother had died, the third untimely death in that family. During those same years, Richard began to experience in a new and more immediate way the impact of his childhood sexual abuse by his baseball coach. I struggled ineptly to hold on to a sense of myself, vacillating between trying to make things right for him, then, overwhelmed and resentful, angrily pushing him away until guilt started my part of the cycle over again. His drinking accelerated. I managed to ignore this through an ignorance that had to be willed.

We were sitting on the banks of a river one day, picnicking with a friend. "So, you're coming over Tuesday night?" she asked.

"Tuesday?" said Richard. "I didn't know. I'm busy that night."

"I left you a note on the kitchen table asking you to tell me if it wasn't okay," I said.

"I didn't see the note."

"I guess I should have taped it to the front of the liquor cabinet."

On the way home, Richard tore into me for my comment about the liquor cabinet. Unbelievable though it seems now, I wasn't conscious of the implications of my remark. "Don't get mad," I protested. "That's just where you'd see it."

I sometimes suspected our marriage provided Richard a situation secure enough to fall apart in, but I, who'd married with the confused notion of having intimacy when I wanted it and dismissing it when I didn't, wasn't able or willing to contain him while he came to grips with his past. I began to realize I couldn't make up for a childhood in which he'd been raped and had lost two brothers, and, at some point, in what felt like self-preservation, I refused to try. Selfish? Perhaps. Definitely ironic—I, who feared being swallowed up by marriage, had ended up in a relationship that seemed designed to swallow me. In addition, as writers working full-time outside our home, with two young children, we competed ferociously for time. When he told me he realized he had a drinking problem, I thought, great. Another problem. Another reason to center our lives on him. Although in the long term addressing his alcoholism was the most pressing matter for all of us, I had no long-term vision left.

Our individual needs felt so urgent at times that neither of us would budge. One evening we both had to go out. We'd arranged for a neighbor to babysit, but one of the kids was sick.

"It's my meeting for survivors of sexual abuse," Richard said. "I have to go."

"But I'm introducing the speaker at tonight's English Department lecture."

"Someone else can do it."

"No one's prepared. This is a big event."

"I'm going."

I couldn't believe his selfishness; I'd just gotten this teaching job and to introduce the speaker was an honor. He went to his support group every week.

We both went out. I felt terrible leaving the baby with a neighbor, but still I went. When we got home, the neighbor told us the baby had run a temperature and cried all evening.

More often the nature of Richard's needs—to go to AA meetings, to meet with a support group for men who had been sexually abused—trumped mine, and I resented it. I remember finally having the opportunity to get away for the weekend with friends. As I was packing, anticipating relaxing at the shore, Richard came to me saying he felt suicidal. I turned around to study his face. Was this for real?

"Call your friends. Someone from your support group," I said, deciding it was just a ploy to manipulate me. What a chance I took! I both cringe at and sympathize with my own behavior. By then, I was suspicious of his every move, trying to figure out what he was trying to gain and what I had to lose. He'd say, I need the car

Saturday because I have dorm duty, and I'd think, Terrific, that leaves me stuck in the apartment with the kids. I wish I had dorm duty. I began to look furtively at apartment ads, wondering how we could support two households.

The thing is, we wanted to do better. Once one of us had a job that offered health insurance, we went to marriage counselors, several of them. Not until one therapist told us, "No one should be as unhappy as you two are," did I feel the relief of having someone understand how miserable I was.

"I want you to do something that will help me quickly get a sense of what's going on," the therapist told us. "Each of you stage a scene showing what you want from the other person."

In Richard's scene, he had just come home from work.

"Richard, how are you?" he directed me to call. "Did you have a good day?" Then I was to walk over and give him a hug. This is it? I thought. I haven't been doing even this?

On the drive home I asked him about it. "No," he told me. "I come home and you start in with a list of complaints."

A few sessions later, I made an appointment to see our therapist alone. My usual tendency would have been not to confront her for fear of hurting her feelings, but there was a lot at stake. I was determined to stand up for myself. "You're much harder on me than you are on Richard," I told her. "You call me on everything, but when he starts claiming he knows my motives, what I really think, the very thing I've said I won't put up with anymore, you let it slide."

She nodded and apologized. "He's just much more hurt and vulnerable than you are."

I was startled. My anger dissipated. I hadn't seen it this way. The rage that made him swell like a blowfish, his insistence that if only I changed, everything would be fine, the stony silence when he discovered I'd been looking at ads for apartments (What on earth did he expect, I'd thought at the time, that I'm just going to live like this?)—they were just ways he was protecting himself?

I thought of the time while we still were dating when I'd gone to Martha's Vineyard to visit Richard, who was attending a conference for writing teachers. We were walking on the beach when Richard stopped, turned me to face him, and put his hands on my shoulders. "I'm going to change your life," he told me.

Inwardly, I rolled my eyes. Where does this guy get off? I thought. I like my life. But, as it turned out, he was right. He had changed my life. Perhaps in that moment with our therapist when I began to see the connection between his fear that I would leave him and his anger, I also began to understand that it was okay that he had changed me. He'd given up drinking, worked hard to come to terms with his history; maybe I could stop fighting so hard to protect myself. Because in thinking about getting married, I'd also been right. Marriage had meant the end of a self, that falsely separate self I'd constructed to protect myself from scrutiny. And I'd been right about something else, too—neither of us was the type to get divorced. In the end, we couldn't face leaving each other.

The birth of our son had been difficult. Complications from a cesarean had kept me in the hospital for ten days, with a nasal-gastric tube for many of them. When I got pregnant again four years later, I was determined not to repeat that experience. I went back to them to read up on vaginal births after cesarean, or VBACs, as they're commonly known. I'd figured my first labor would last about seventeen hours. It lasted thirty-six, and during most of those hours Richard had stood by the hospital bed holding my hand, stooped over at an angle that must have sent his back into spasm. Twelve hours for this one, I calculated. After all, it's a second child. It should be easier this time.

"Whatever you want, I'm game," Richard told me. We found an

obstetrician who seemed willing to give me a chance, unlike others who examined my pelvis and dismissed the idea. Together we met with a labor assistant who was experienced in assisting with VBACs and who herself had had one.

Our hospital had an enlightened labor-and-delivery unit with a wonderful hot tub to soothe labor pains, but being in labor can do strange things.

I panicked when the tub began to empty in preparation for my getting out. "I'm going to be sucked down the drain." I caught a look between Richard and the labor assistant as they hauled me out, trying to calm me. How did they keep from laughing? A one-hundred-forty-pound pregnant woman going down the drain?

When I started to push, the nurse suggested Richard climb onto the bed and sit, legs apart, to function as a sort of birthing chair for me. Good-naturedly he complied. Grunting and sweating, I lumbered onto his legs. "Yeah, you smelled pretty bad," he told me later.

This labor lasted even longer than the first one, but I got what I wanted—birth without surgery. During the entire forty-eight hours, Richard encouraged me, never once letting on that the nurses were telling him I should give it up.

Describing the tender disciplines and pleasures of marriage is difficult for me. They're not embodied in catchy anecdotes or startling moments. The pleasures of our relationship are mundane—shopping together for kitchen linoleum at the Home Depot, reading together in bed. No matter how much we get on each other's nerves—must you leave dirty coffee cups in every room? Fill every closet with thrift-store clothes?——we also laugh together. He buys me flowers for no particular occasion. I buy him espresso beans covered with dark chocolate. I admire and respect Richard for turning his trauma first into memoir, then into social analysis and activism. All that anger and shouting, all those tears had bound us together in good ways as well as bad. We'd seen the worst of each other and still on balance wanted what we saw. After making each other both dream and nightmare, we now had to face the less dramatic reality. How paradoxical that reality can be richer than fantasy. We love each other. But that's not it, not enough. In the end I can't explain why I didn't divorce any more than I can explain why I married. I wanted to/I didn't want to. At the core of my deepest commitments is something mute, a koan.

A few days after I lost my wedding ring, I called a contractor. He understood. "We'll get that back for you," he promised. A carpenter arrived the next day, determined to recover the ring. He pulled up the floor near the chimney, but apparently the ring had also managed to slip through the narrow crack between the chimney and the subfloor. Richard and I went with him to the basement, but there was no way it could have fallen straight through to the floor. The carpenter removed the baseboard next to the chimney in the second-floor bedroom. No luck. He pulled the baseboard off the chimney in the dining room. Nothing. Next he made a hole in the plaster farther up the wall. Together Richard and I sifted through chunks of plaster and horsehair, coughing from the dust. No ring.

"There's no way it could get past this ledge," the carpenter told us. "It's got to be here somewhere. It must have bounced and rolled to the other side of the chimney. Someday, get this entire casement taken off—it's not such a big job. You'll find it. I really wanted to get it for you. I know how important a ring is." He seemed at least as disappointed as I.

Richard turned toward me. "It's okay."

I'm still determined get that ring back. And yet . . . somehow it's fitting; there it is safe, a riddle deep in the walls of our home.

AN EXPERIMENT IN IMPROVISATION
Bharati Mukherjee

I was born in Kolkata (formerly Calcutta), the second of three daughters in a Bangla-speaking, staunchly patriarchal Hindu family. Growing up in Kolkata in the forties and fifties, I took it for granted that my father (who fancied himself a benevolent autocrat) would find me a suitable husband and that my husband and I would stay married until death parted us. The chosen bridegroom would belong to our caste, Brahmin, and subcaste, Kulin; be an ethnic Bengali from an upper-middle-class family much like ours; have completed a medical or engineering degree (preferably from a respectable institution abroad); have demonstrated his potential as an above-average provider; be of good health and free of inherited physiological and psychological disorders.

In our community, a father's sacred duty was to marry off his daughters, for an unmarried woman could not attain salvation. The ideal Kulin Brahmin wife worshipped God by worshipping her husband. Nineteenth-century instructional verses reminded wives: if husband is pleased, pleased is god / husband is life / husband is pride / husband is the sole jewel.

There were no unmarried adult daughters in my dutiful family. Nor had I encountered any in the families of our neighbors.

As a child, I didn't think of marriage as a legal contract between two individuals. In my parents' generation, marriages were performed by priests in front of a sacred fire and witnessed by as many wedding guests—relatives, neighbors, village luminaries, Brahmins and beggars—as the bride's guardian could afford to feed at the wedding banquet. The wedding rites were designed to symbolically *fuse* the bride and the groom into a new entity. A Hindu marriage could not be annulled by a priest, though (through my two grandfathers' generation) tradition allowed the Kulin Brahmin husband to send his wife back permanently to her father's house under specified circumstances (such as barrenness or failure to bear a son), and to take co-wives. Until divorce laws were passed in my girlhood, a Hindu marriage could not be dissolved by a judge either. Desperately unhappy wives sometimes drowned themselves in wells or burned to death in "accidental" cooking fires.

My formal training in what I should want of marriage and how I should foster conjugal contentment was based on my paternal grandmother's version of an ancient Hindu how-to handbook on womanly deportment attributed to Manu the Lawgiver, and was reinforced by bedtime retelling of Hindu mythological stories of the wifely ideal. The training, however, was undermined by personal examples set by the many squabbling married uncles and aunts who lived with us in a crowded household during my first eight years.

I did not formally study Manu's book until I was nineteen years old and preparing for a master's degree in the fields of ancient Indian culture and English literature at the University of Baroda. Nor was I aware until then that Manu's laws had been well-known in nineteenth-century Europe in English, German, French, Portuguese, and Russian translations. Manu set down in formidable detail all laws, duties, and taboos that should guide a good Hindu's social, political, marital, religious, and moral conduct. My father's concept of the suitable groom, I discovered, was derived directly from Manu's caste- and class-related laws.

My paternal grandmother, Thakuma, concerned herself with making us bride- and wife-worthy. Manu forbids a decent man to choose for his wife a woman who has red hair or thick body hair or dark complexion or physical flaws, such as deformities or scars. Thakuma interpreted "red hair" as Manu's coded way of describing either a mixed-race person or a peasant with sun-bleached hair from having to work long hours outdoors. To counteract the slightest possibility of sun damage to my waist-long black hair, she gave me a daily hour-long head massage with hibiscus-scented hair oil, then braided my hair and wrapped the braids with lengths of cloth. To lighten my complexion, she suggested I wash my face with a turmeric paste instead of soap. I had cut my forehead badly in a fall when I was a toddler. My entire family worried that the one-and-a-half-inch-long scar would make me unmarriageable. For years I was made to rub the scar with butter and with the soft flesh of green coconuts, which were said to have scar-fading properties. The lesson I learned was that, when the time came for marriage negotiations, my family's history and status, and first impressions of my physical appearance, would matter more than my intelligence or character. I accepted my elders' fear that my father would have to wear out the soles of his shoes in his pursuit of a willing bridegroom. The aim of marriage was to bring honor and happiness to the clan. Finding a spouse required team effort, and the team would not allow itself to be sabotaged by any impulsive individual.

Manu also had much to say about power relations within a marriage. By nature, women were mean, devious, avaricious, and lustful. A stable household required the householder to establish absolute authority over his wife. She had to be forced to obey her husband's every wish, and kept financially dependent. Her role was to bear her husband sons, act cheerful, and master homemaking skills. A wife who failed to provide sons or was ill too often or was sullen should be sent back in disgrace to her father's home.

Thakuma's favorite mythological role models for us were Sita and Savitri. One had willingly undergone an ordeal by fire as proof of purity at her husband's request; the other, through the force of wifely devotion, had moved the God of Death to resuscitate her husband's corpse. But I was growing up at a tilt time in national history and was witness to the battle between nostalgic traditionalists like Thakuma and reformist visionaries like my mother. Thakuma advocated pliancy and self-effacement; my mother, who had been married off at seventeen and denied permission to get a college education by my father's reactionary family, championed women's literacy and women's right to inherit the property of fathers or husbands.

"I'll make sure that my daughters are not the chattel that I'm forced to be," was her daily chant. Pursuing that goal, she sent us to an English school run by Irish nuns for high-achieving young women from Kolkata's elite families. In that school, in addition to science, math, English and French literatures, European history, moral science, and sports, my sisters and I were exposed to ballroom dancing and too much Jane Austen. As a result, our ideal fantasy bridegroom became a Bengali Brahmin version of *Pride and Prejudice*'s Mr. Darcy.

There was no question of us meeting our Mr. Darcys on our own. My father disapproved of coeducational classrooms and permitted us to attend, with chauffeur, chaperone, and private bodyguard in tow, school friends' birthday parties only if we could extract a guarantee from the host that no male guests would be around. The bodyguard was my father's effort at protecting us from possible violent explosions of class tensions. During my girlhood, we had begun to feel the first shudders of rage of the dispossessed. Over the next decade, after my immediate family had left Kolkata for western India, and my sisters and I had installed ourselves in schools in the United States, that rage swelled into an organized and violent Maoist-style revolution.

My father started bridegroom-scouting for my older sister when she turned sixteen. I was twelve at the time, and our youngest sister, nine. We would have to wait our turn. Protocol protected seniority.

The oldest Mukherjee sister was considered a "catch" in our community. In the Kolkata of the fifties, my father, the cofounder of a successful pharmaceutical company, was a prominent figure in corporate circles. He was expected to be generous in dowry-giving. My sister was pretty, and the only one of us three accomplished in traditional womanly arts, such as singing, dancing, painting. I dreaded the time when I would have to be "interviewed" by a series of prospective bridegrooms and their nosy, critical families. Meanwhile, the hunt for my older sister's husband dragged on. Marriage was about the permanent merger of two compatible families, requiring complicated precautions and transactions.

My father solved his immediate bride-marketing problem in an inspired, if unexpected, way. He offered each of us the choice of taking the money he intended to spend on our dowries and lavish weddings and investing it in an American education. While we were abroad, he would continue his bridegroom-scouting. All three of us opted for school in the United States.

I had known from when I was three years old that I would be a writer of fiction, and had begun my first novel at age nine. At school the nuns praised me for having "a gift of the pen." My parents, too, always encouraged me in my writing. They were ecstatic when two short stories that I'd written as school exercises were published in Kolkata's English-language magazines. I think they'd convinced themselves that during future marriage negotiations, they could present my portfolio of stories the way parents of bridal candidates with more conventional accomplishments showed off dance diplomas, music certificates, needlework, and painting. A respectable married woman could have a successful career as a novelist without leaving home. They would not have countenanced my wanting a career in law or medicine. We learned of Iowa and the University of Iowa's MFA program quite accidentally from an African American academic traveling through India in the summer of 1960. That one could get a university degree in creative writing and, in my case, a scholarship, seemed to us a well-timed boon.

The night before I left for Iowa City by way of New York (my younger sister was a sophomore at Vassar) and Detroit (my older

sister was a graduate student at Wayne State University), my father gave me some advice. Don't move out of the women's dormi-
tory. Don't date. Don't let a man pay for any meal. Be wary of love.

I had just turned twenty-one. Until then I had never spent a single night on my own. I should have felt desperately disoriented; I
knew from my sisters' weekly letters to my parents how lost and
homesick they were, how anxious to return home. I shocked myself
by feeling happy instead at being alone, at making friends (all of
them women) on my own, at getting my voice heard during workshop discussions in a coeducational classroom. And I, who had been
exposed only to expurgated editions of novels and textbooks,
shocked myself by not being shocked by Henry Miller's *Tropic of
Cancer* and *Tropic of Capricorn*.

My social life in Iowa City revolved around the international
students' center, which was a block away from the women's dormi-
tory I lived in. The center had a Ping-Pong table in its basement.
Ping-Pong was my only sport, and for a demure sari-clad woman, I
played an aggressive game. I like to think that it was my Ping-Pong
playing that attracted nightly crowds of international students,
especially admiring Indian men. The Indians were mostly postdoc-
toral research assistants in fields such as nuclear physics, engineering, medicine, and dentistry. I enjoyed the attention they paid
me. I especially enjoyed being free of bodyguard and chaperone.
But none of the attentive men was a Bengali Brahmin. I received
their admiration, but did not consider them potential husbands. In
my weekly letters home, I turned their courtship into amusing
anecdotes in the manner of Jane Austen. When one of these admir-
ers pressed his case too boldly and reacted to rejection too harshly,
requiring a counselor's intervention, I recast it for my parents as a
melodrama in the manner of Bombay films.

My father hadn't given up on the idea of finding me a bridegroom. It was my turn, because in the fall of my second year in the
MFA program, my older sister had found a bridegroom on her own
in Detroit, an Indian graduate student from a prominent Bombay

family, and a Brahmin. My father asked for a photo, and I sent him one that my Singapore Chinese roommate had taken of me in front of our dorm. But I wasn't ready to return to the safe, circumscribed world that, just a year before, I'd unquestioningly accepted as my permanent home. In fact, I was so reluctant to go back that I applied for, and won, a full scholarship for doctoral studies in Victorian literature at Bryn Mawr College.

And then, late in the summer of 1963, about two weeks before I was to leave for Bryn Mawr, love hit me like a tornado, wrecking beyond repair my culturally conditioned discomfort with caste-crossing and my scientist-entrepreneur father's distrust of liberal-arts graduates with poor salary prospects as bridegrooms.

Only two weeks before, I had been proud (on behalf of my mother, the champion of education for women) that I had won a scholarship, covering my tuition, room and board. I had been eager to jump-start my life's next phase. My trunk had already been shipped to the college and a ride to Philadelphia arranged. Now I began to fantasize about throwing that scholarship away and staying on in Iowa, somehow, anyhow. It *was* a fantasy. My American women friends in love, and in a bind like mine, could have found themselves jobs. The local bookstore and the diners near the main campus were always advertising for help. But I was in the United States on a student visa. Dropping out of school was not an option; nor was applying for jobs without a work permit.

"I can't let you go," my lover said. "Marry me."

I scrambled for late admission into the PhD program in English at the University of Iowa and pleaded for a teaching assistantship. My mentor, a Restoration scholar known for his wryness, eased my way through bureaucracy. But he couldn't keep his disappointment to himself. "That's the trouble with you women students. You are unreliable. You throw away a great scholarship, and for what? Why can't you wait two or three years?"

How could I explain to him that, for the first time in my life, I had let foolish, maybe destructive, passion trump bourgeois common sense?

So a wedding took place, though not the kind of wedding to which brides in my family felt they were entitled. My maternal grandmother, the daughter of a Bengali Brahmin landowner with progressive ideas, was married off at age seven in her ancestral home on a night at the turn of the twentieth century deemed auspicious for weddings by Hindu priests and professional astrologers. The bridegroom, the son of a prominent Bengali Brahmin doctor in the provincial city of Dhaka, was ten or more years older. The wedding ceremony, performed by a Brahmin priest in front of a divine fire, lasted many hours and was witnessed by a thousand guests. My mother, the daughter of a lawyer with nationalist ideals, was married off at age seventeen in the metropolis of Kolkata in a ceremony that is legendary for my maternal family's extravagance and my paternal family's dowry demands. I was married at age twenty-three on a lunch break in a lawyer's office above a coffee shop in Iowa City. My husband was a twenty-three-year-old, blue-eyed short-story writer. It was the first day of classes in the fall semester of 1963.

A married fellow student had planned for us to have the wedding and reception in his home over the weekend. We had been having lunch in the coffee shop and chatting with friends, a printmaker and a writer, about the class that I had taught as a teaching assistant that morning, my first ever.

"Why wait till the weekend?" my fiancé said.

We called the law office and got an immediate appointment, then picked up our rings from the jewelry store a block from the coffee shop. The printmaker and the writer volunteered to be our witnesses. "Give us fifteen minutes to get you a present. You can't have a wedding without a wedding gift." They ran to the nearest department store and bought an artisan-crafted tea set while we made sure we hadn't lost our marriage license and rings, and then we all clambered up a steep, narrow staircase to the lawyer's office. In a ceremony that felt as though it lasted fifteen minutes or less, I became the wife of a twenty-three-year-old, Fargo-born, half French Canadian, half English Canadian short-story writer and fellow student named Clark Blaise.

I'd first met Clark in the home of Paul Engle, the then director of the workshop, on a snowy January evening in 1962. He had hitchhiked in from Massachusetts earlier that day. Bernard Malamud, his writing teacher at Harvard that summer, had recommended him to Iowa's MFA program. Paul Engle had invited him to stop by that evening and pick up his coveted scholarship check. I was Paul's only other guest. Though I didn't know it at the time, the workshop rumor was that Paul liked to play Cupid, especially for his few women students.

Clark had arrived in Iowa City penniless and careless but not friendless. I was fascinated by Clark's blue eyes. A Kolkata fortuneteller had once read my palm and predicted that I would marry a man with blue eyes and live in exile. Clark made jokes, not all of which I caught, and chatted with Paul about Bernard Malamud, whose works I had not yet discovered.

At the end of the evening, Clark and his friend invited me to go out for a pizza with them; I declined because I could visualize too graphically my father's horror if he came to hear that I'd been seen out at night with two American guys in a pizzeria.

I saw Clark twice a week in the workshop classes. I envied his lyrical stories about a displaced Canadian child trying to "belong" among settlements of moss pickers in a central Florida wild with snakes and alligators. But Clark didn't ask me out on a date until late in the summer of 1963. None of the men in my classes asked me for a date. A woman student later revealed why: Americans knew little of what would offend an Indian woman, especially me, a Brahmin woman whose father was said to have bodyguards in place in Iowa to kneecap inappropriate suitors.

* * *

Immediately after the wedding, before teaching my afternoon class, I sent a cable to my parents to tell them that by the time they received it, I would already have been married. In my father's cabled response, I read shock (that I had had it in me to make the most important decision of my life without consulting him), resignation (what was done was done), and counterintuitive hope (check out the boy's lineage).

For fifteen years I didn't disclose to my parents that Clark's parents were divorced; that his mother was the second of at least five of his father's wives; that the only picture I'd seen of my father-in-law was of a handsome man with a bandaged head recovering from a blow to the head delivered by one of his ex's as she had walked out on him and filed for divorce. Instead, I made much of the biographical facts that would persuade them our families were socially compatible. Clark's mother came from a prominent, prosperous Manitoba family and had trained in the decorative arts in the Bauhaus. She had worked in Montreal as a professional interior decorator and as a schoolteacher in Winnipeg. His maternal grandfather, a physician and horticulturist, had founded an insurance company that was still flourishing across Canada. His father had owned two furniture stores in the suburbs of Pittsburgh.

Why disconcert my anxious parents with minor details, such as that Clark's father, the youngest of seventeen children, was streetsmart but barely literate? That he had boxed his way out of the ghetto, winning the Golden Gloves championship? That he had worked as a day laborer in New Hampshire in his youth and as a liquor runner for a major Canadian bootlegger during the Prohibition era? That he was a compulsive philanderer? I no longer believed in the tyranny of genes.

There was so much of Clark's personal history that I felt I had to catch up on in order to understand the man I'd married so impulsively. When his parents divorced, Clark had dropped out of Denison University for a semester, drifted back to the Deep South of his childhood working odd jobs, and joined a group of Nashville students as a Freedom Rider, all of whom had been hauled off to jail and placed in police custody. He mentioned a cell mate named John Louis.

I'd known of Joe Louis back in India, but not John Louis and nothing about Freedom Riders. My mother raised me on tearful bedtime stories about Joe Louis and segregation, but at home we held on to conservative social attitudes and class distinctions. My father was a committed and generous patron of the disadvantaged, but not Clark's kind of a civil libertarian. I'd have to reassess my values without choosing disloyalty to either husband or father.

It also shocked me that Clark had dropped out of school for a semester. Ambitious young Indian men, the kind of men my father had hoped I would marry, would have decided on a profession in elementary school and pursued it without distraction. Dropping in and out of school, changing majors or careers, struck me as an American luxury or folly.

Clark is the ultimate sports fan and needed me not only to understand all forms of ball games but to share his extreme enthusiasm for them. In the early years of our marriage, before each football game he would pop popcorn, sit me next to him on our lumpy thirdhand sofa, and draw diagrams so that I would get the most out of each play. Baseball was his favorite sport, though, and during the fourteen years that we lived and taught in Montreal, Canada, he dragged me to every game, every doubleheader played by his favorite team, the Montreal Expos. My vocabulary swelled with new words and phrases that, over the years, have found their effortless way into my fiction. "Downfield blocking!" "A West Coast offense!" "Short passes under the coverage, pauses to running backs and wide receivers!" "Flood the secondary! A scrambling quarterback!" "It's about the width, using the whole field, connecting in the flat, no interference. . . ."

Clark, in his turn, embraced India. His half of *Days and Nights in Calcutta*, our joint book on the first of our two yearlong stays in India, is more enthusiastically received by Kolkata residents than is mine. "He may be a sahib, but he is so sincere," readers have said. "Clark-babu is finding and loving the real us."

Our friends, in India and in the United States, anticipated an early breakup. A school friend visiting from Kolkata asked, "Don't white people do everything differently? Don't they even brush their teeth in a different way than we do? How can you stand everything being so topsy-turvy?" My American women friends had other concerns. It was the sixties: wives, empowered by their "consciousness-raising" groups, were leaving their husbands, experimenting with sexuality, busting suburban taboos, and finding themselves by throwing pots and through performance art.

We had no time to worry about doctrinaire emancipation as dictated by *Ms.* magazine. I was in the doctoral program, and a teaching assistant; Clark was a graduate student. Our first child (much to my parents' joy, a son) was born in the first year of our marriage. (At home in Kolkata we had never discussed family planning or, for that matter, any physical consequence of marriage.) While our friends were drawing up formal contracts specifying which partner should take out the garbage and which should cook or clean and on what days, Clark was teaching me how to boil water for instant coffee. I had never lit a match. "How will I know the water's come to a boil?" I'd asked Clark. In Kolkata, we had four cooks, and the cooks wouldn't have taken kindly to invasion of the kitchen. The first week of our marriage, Clark had caught me storing eggs in the freezer.

Clark had also to get accustomed to my not knowing how to drive and not intending to ever learn. I have a deficient sense of direction, including telling left from right. Since there was no driver's education classes in Indian high schools, I hadn't been forced to get over this lack. Besides, a driver involved in an accident on a Kolkata street ran the risk of being lynched. Those who could afford a car, it was assumed, could also afford to hire a chauffeur. Being a nondriver in American cities without public transportation, much to my feminist friends' horror, I was dependent on Clark for getting me wherever I needed to be.

Clark and I survived because we held no assumptions in common; because we were forced to improvise. We were students, teaching assistants, parents without forethought. Each of us did what housework needed doing when we had time. As writers we were perfectionists; as homemakers we were blithely sloppy. We juggled our classes and teaching schedules so that one of us could be home for child care. Our two sons cooperated in their own ways: the older one was born during the summer vacation, and the younger one on the first day of Christmas break. We kept our roles flexible. There were no rules other than "do the best you can and stay relaxed." We trusted our sense of humor to carry us through catastrophes.

Fiction writing brought us together and kept us together. We understood each other's *visions* and could help each other as we grappled with the right narrative strategy for each novel or story. Our "fictional worlds" are so disparate that we can be canny commentators on each other's works without being personally competitive. If I had married a doctor or engineer of my father's choosing, I would probably not have enjoyed equality of power sharing.

The closest we came to a breakup was in Canada. In 1966, when we were looking for our first jobs, we applied only to universities in Montreal. For Clark, whose English Canadian mother and Quebecois father had met and married in Montreal in 1937—we're talking Montague-Capulet ethnic hostilities in that era—that city was the longed-for home. Canadian literature was just emerging from the stranglehold of British and French domination. And Clark was among the small group of influential writers, among them Margaret Atwood and Alice Munro, exploring Canadian identity through fiction.

But in the midseventies, I learned through painful experience that Canadian policy was hostile to its nonwhite citizens, and that because Canada did not yet have a Constitution, victims had no legal redress for racial discrimination. In governmental policy papers about immigration, nonwhite people like me were being described as a "visible minority," threatening predominantly white Canada's "absorptive capacity." The society made routine, humiliating assumptions about me and my "kind." By 1978 the race-related, anti-immigrant incidents had become frequent and turned physically violent.

I wanted to move back to the United States, without Clark if necessary, because I wanted to live in a country that had a Bill of Rights and a Constitution. Clark chose to move with me, even though it meant uprooting himself from his adoptive homeland and tearing himself away from the scenes and the peoples that fueled his fiction writing. No marriage should be put to such a test of loyalty.

In 1980, we returned to the United States.

For Clark, the writer, the price paid for the move has been steep. He who founded the creative writing MFA program at Sir George Williams University, nurturing the next generation of anglophone Montreal writers, and who was at the center of the Canadian literary scene, now finds himself on the margins of the U.S. one. He has published over twenty books, but the majority of his readers remain Canadian.

Since then, we have not found suitable jobs in universities in the same city and have had to improvise the how-to of a happy commuter marriage. We've paid our dues; we've kept our sense of humor through the desperate times; we've always seen ourselves as a team. We have survived, I am convinced, because ours is a literary marriage. The novelist Bharati looks on the relationships, scenes, and events being acted out by the real-life Bharati as a continuous, dramatizing narrative.

Our marriage started out in heedless passion in the heart of the American heartland. We've stayed married for forty years, and expect to stay married for forty more. It is a new American love story.

From Steel
to China

A TWENTY-FIRST-CENTURY RITUAL
Erica Jong

Ten years after we were married, my husband and I burned our prenup. We burned it in a wok at the end of a dinner party to which we invited our dearest friends—and our lawyers. Either that's the most romantic gesture ever made or the stupidest. I prefer to see it as romantic.

Marriage is about trust, and trust takes you quickly to the matter of money. Money matters demand total transparency—even admitting to your husband how much those designer clothes cost—the ones you hid in your closet hoping he wouldn't notice. It is very hard to trust someone and share all your worldly goods with that person, but the alternative is worse.

During the better part of a decade when I was single and recovering from the bitterest of divorces, I usually felt fine until I saw the term "next of kin" on a form. These three little words shook me up more than "I love you." Leaving the space blank meant there was no one to look after my daughter if something happened to me, no one for doctors to consult in case of emergency, no one to bury me if I dropped dead, no one to decide which manuscripts to burn and which to sell. Leaving the space blank meant I was an orphan from the human family.

Marriage fills the blank, but it does more than that. A good marriage replaces monologue with dialogue, enhances your life expectancy, and gives you somebody to blame for whatever is wrong with your life. If you want to stay married, you don't hold the grudge. You realize that whatever you gave up in order to join your life with this other person's was more than compensated by the things you got. But that doesn't mean you lose the right to complain. Healthy complaining—even the occasional unhealthy rage— also keeps marriages together. It's the angry silences that torpedo them. I always know that a marriage has a good chance of lasting when both members of the couple can openly complain, bitch at each other, even scream. Good marriages are noisy.

When Ken and I met, each of us had been married—twice in his case, three times in mine. We stamped the phrase A TRIUMPH OF HOPE OVER EXPERIENCE in red on our wedding announcements right over the line "Erica and Ken are astonished to announce their marriage." We joked a lot because we were terrified. We both thought we had come to our last chance. We didn't want to blow it. Not long ago, I learned from a cousin that at our wedding celebration in 1989 people were taking bets on how long it would last. Sixteen years later, they've thrown in the towel.

My own marital history made great copy but was hell to live through. My first husband went crazy and thought he was Jesus Christ. My second was the psychiatrist I married to protect myself against madness. My third was my dearest soul mate until he became my bitterest enemy. No wonder I never wanted to marry again. When I met Ken, I had figured out how to have men in my life without making a commitment. Either they were terminally commitment-phobic or they were otherwise committed. I tried to have two or three at once so as never to have to depend on one. I quickly learned that three men add up to less than one. But I thought the system worked just fine for me. Until I met Ken.

On our first date, I insisted on bringing a car and driver so he wouldn't be able to drive me home. (It was spring break and my daughter and I were ensconced in the country house.) After our second date, I devised a business trip to Los Angeles to get away from him. (But then I called him as soon as I arrived and left my number.) After our third date, I escaped to Europe—supposedly to attend a cooking school in Italy—though I never cook. Of course there was a boyfriend in Italy—one of those otherwise-committed charmers who liked to drop in unannounced and then flee back to home and hearth. While I was waiting by the phone for him to call, as usual, Ken kept calling instead. Ken was on his way to Paris and sending me a ticket to join him. Meanwhile, Signor Dolce Far Niente hadn't been heard from. By the time he slithered into the dining room of the cooking school, I had made other plans. (Which didn't prevent me from having a farewell tryst with him.)

I am reporting the events but leaving out all the anguish. In the midst of these opera buffa arrangements, I was in turmoil. Often I think the turmoil enhanced the passion. Unless you are a cold-blooded psychopath, it's not easy to juggle partners. My life often felt like a French farce.

Ken had lived his own version of this comedy—through two marriages and one long-term cohabitation that was much like a marriage. Instead of feeling free as a result of his escapades, he often felt trapped. Instead of feeling sated, he often felt lonely.

During that first weekend in Paris, we talked so much we never slept. We also fought, but it never ended the conversation. We discovered we always had more to say to each other. When sex also entered the equation, I became so scared of this intimacy that I went home early. Left to my own devices I would have sabotaged the relationship. But even at our darkest moment, Ken was optimistic. When we had our first fight, he ventured out for a walk and brought me back a first edition of Colette's *La Fin de Chéri*. He presented it to me as a farewell present. I was so touched by his knowing it was one of my favorite books that it became a hello rather than a good-bye. It was his generosity and risk-taking that constantly won my heart.

When we got back from Paris, we had dinner every night. We used to look up from the table at one in the morning and be surprised to find restaurants closing around us. Everyone's deepest hunger is to be known, and we were determined to know each other. The more we learned about each other, the more connected we felt.

When we had been together two months or so, we went to Vermont for a weekend. We stopped at the Putney Inn for dinner and I blurted out my worst fear.

"It seems okay now, but pretty soon you'll be telling me what to write—and threatening me if I don't write what you like. And I can't live with that."

Ken grabbed a paper napkin and scrawled on it, then handed it to me to read: "I trust you completely. Do whatever! Write whatever you want! I release you! Ken!"

I folded up the napkin and kept it. I still have it. A month later, we decided to get married.

Why did we write a prenup? Ken, who is a divorce lawyer, wanted to waive it, but I felt I needed the protection of a legal document. I had worked hard for my fuck-you money in a very unstable profession, and I had no intention of jeopardizing it. Also, I had no faith in my own judgment. I had been so wrong about men in the past. I fully expected to be wrong again. So we both prepared net-worth statements. And we both agreed to keep our monies separate. If we walked away from this marriage, we'd both take our marbles and go home. I hired a lawyer to put all this in writing.

But here is the strange thing about marriages: either they get better and stronger or they wither away. With every year that passes, the matter of money seems less important. Inevitably funds get mixed and commingled. Eventually you buy things together and you write wills protecting each other. Prenuptial agreements little by little go out-of-date. Do you sit down and renegotiate after ten years—or do you quietly agree that the document has served its purpose and let it lapse? Because a prenup does serve a purpose. It says: "I hope I'll be able to trust you, but I'm not sure yet." When we discovered after ten years that we trusted each other more, not less, we decided the prenup was obsolete.

"Will you still be happy to have revoked it if he runs off with a twenty-five-year-old next year?" my lawyer, Ellie Alter, asked me.

She was right to ask that unanswerable question. But I was pretty sure I hadn't married Donald Trump.

It's in the nature of life that we protect ourselves against things that never happen and utterly fail to contemplate things that do.

About a week after we burned the prenup, Ken collapsed with what at first appeared to be a mild heart attack. When it proved to be a potentially fatal dissection of the aorta, the first thing I thought was: We should never have burned the prenup. The prenup had gone from being a legal document to being an amulet. I think it was an amulet all along.

During the hours I sat outside the operating room and the weeks I spent in the hospital waiting, I realized that my life was irrevocably bound with Ken's—prenup or no prenup. We had crossed that invisible barrier between being two people and being one. I had failed to protect myself against grief and loss. I had failed by succeeding in building the real marriage I had always wanted.

The matter of the prenup seemed like very small potatoes compared to what I had discovered. If you join your life with someone's, you become a hostage to fortune in a way that no legal document can protect you against. Marriage is primal stuff—two people confronting their own mortality. It is not for the faint of heart. It is not for beginners.

When I first saw Ken after his open-heart surgery, his body temperature was twenty degrees below normal and he wore a ventilator. He didn't know I was there. My daughter was so upset that she ran out of the ICU. Somehow, I stayed. I never considered the possibility that he would not recover.

"I didn't see a long tunnel with a blinding light at the end and my mother and father waving," Ken said when he recovered from his near-death experience. "I didn't see my body on the operating table connected to a heart-lung machine and hear angels choiring in the background."

But he is different and so am I. (And it isn't only because of his new Dacron aorta.) The time we spend together is infinitely more precious. We are arranging our lives to have more of it. After Ken recovered, we bought a sailboat and called it *Vivamus*, or "Let's Live." The endless hours we spend sailing are a response to his near-death experience. We are also giving ourselves more and longer vacations.

I would not be telling this story honestly if I did not admit that I feel in grave danger revealing all this—as if I were tempting the gods by admitting that things are good. Early in my life, I got married without having an inkling what marriage meant. I was lucky to survive my marriages and even to survive writing about them. Now I want to protect what I have with discretion. I really don't want to expose even this much of what passes between us. I am fiercely superstitious.

"I hope you're taking notes," my husband always says to me when we go through a hard time. He relies on me to be his chronicler. He was mostly asleep during his crisis and I was awake. I am supposed to be his Boswell and he my muse. Marriages have been based on worse contracts.

Marriage is, of all human arrangements, the chanciest. We know all the things that can go wrong, but we are still delighted when they go right. We never tire of hearing how couples met. We never tire of stories of lovers and the obstacles they've surmounted. We pride ourselves on being hard-boiled and pragmatic, but deep down we long to be gooey and romantic. Burning the prenup has become the commitment "I do" was for our grandparents. It's a new ritual for the twenty-first century, and it's probably fated to become a trend. Vintners will create special wines and bakers will devise special cakes. Priests and rabbis will be asked for new vows. As prenups become routine, burning them will become the true test of love.

"Darling, do you love me enough to burn the prenup?"

THIRD TIME AROUND:
SNAPSHOTS FROM AT LONG LAST
A LONG-TERM MARRIAGE

Julia Alvarez

I didn't seem to have a problem getting married. But staying married was my problem. "Happily ever after" was a phrase that eluded me.

By age thirty I had been married and divorced twice. These were not long-term marriages: the first lasted a year; the second lasted three years, and then, only because it took two years after leaving my husband for us to agree we should divorce. I admit that for years I sort of collapsed these two former husbands into one and said I'd been married "before." Technically, I wasn't lying. Mostly, I was embarrassed to tell people the truth. Divorcing once in my generation wasn't such a big deal. But twice? And after such short marriages! What would folks think? Wow, she must be a horrible person to live with! Of course, what folks didn't know is that unlike most of my contemporaries who were coming of age in the sexually liberated America of the post-sixties, and who by age thirty had had numerous lovers, I had only had sex with two men, and like a good Latina raised Catholic by my *mami* and *tías*, I had married them. When in later years I would describe my former husbands, nice enough fellows but so obviously incompatible, to my friends, they would ask, "Why on earth did you marry them?" I'd tell them the true reason why—I thought I had to. I'd had sex with them.

Okay, by the second time around, I knew better. But I had to redeem myself to my family for the first marriage: I had dropped out of my last year of college to elope with a folksinger, who had dropped out of high school. My second husband was a businessman, older, established, rich, British. (There was a title in the family, an uncle who was Sir Something or Other. "Lady Julia," my sisters teased me.) Mami, who had disowned me after my first marriage, fell in love with this second husband-to-be who very winningly asked her and my father for my hand in marriage. (He did ask me first.) Mami was thrilled. How could I not marry him?

After the second divorce, I decided, enough! I'd never marry again unless I was really sure. Even Mami hinted that it might not be a bad idea to get to *know* a man a little better before I married him. The way she said "know," I took as a nod and a wink to the biblical sense of the verb. Know him, as in carnally, as in live with the guy a year or two, before you bring him home as someone who is going to join the family.

And so, fast-forward, through ten years of loneliness, celibacy, a few getting to knows, and enter, my third and present and "perfect husband," Bill. At least, that is what my sisters started calling him soon after we married and he joined the family.

I don't know what's worse: getting teased about being Lady Julia or about being married to a perfect husband. What can I say? I have three sisters; the first three of us are a year apart. We are close, and not just in age; we love each other fiercely and that gives us the right. The gray areas of tact and restraint in other families are hung with green lights in my family. We stomp where angels fear to tread, comment and tease and get away with murder because down deep we all secretly believe we are the same person. Which means you'll never find such loving, passionate, and true *hermanas*. So, you pay your dues. I've paid my share in the husband-teasing department.

So yes, for the first few years of my marriage, my sisters teased that I had married the perfect husband. There was some jealousy involved, the way we are jealous when the people we love become happy and stable enough not to need us the way they did before. How was my perfect husband? What did my perfect husband advise, and so on. Where did they get this idea? I wondered.

Well, he sure looked good, and not just on paper. The oldest in a poor sharecropping family, Bill took over a lot of the chores at the farm at nine, in order for his dad to work the night shift at Continental Can. Meanwhile, Bill also studied hard, graduated first in his high-school class (it was a one-room schoolhouse, I reminded my sisters), went to medical school, ended up buying his parents the farm they never owned, having farmed other people's land all their lives. He did get divorced (a fact my sisters seized on as proof of his humanhood), but he stayed fully involved in his daughters' lives. A devoted doctor, he answers calls at all hours; his number is in the book. But farming is his first love. He comes home from the office, dons his work clothes, goes out on his tractor. He grows most of the food this vegetarian eats. He cooks and cans and freezes, too. He even wrote a cookbook for his daughters when they moved away from home, a book that I take credit for making him write out of not-disinterested motives. (I learned to cook from it as well.) He has taken excellent, patient, loving care of my own parents. When Mami took exception to my writing and disowned me after my first novel came out, and then again after my third novel came out, Bill stayed in touch (she wouldn't talk to me); a couple of times, he even drove down to visit Mami in New York City, the second time taking his parents, to intercede for me. ("It's fiction, Mami, that's why there are so many 'lies' in her books." "Then why does she have to make the characters Dominicans? Why can't they be Scandinavians?") Bill reported that he sat for several hours while my mother told him all about what an impossible, imperfect woman he had married, who would someday write a book about him. (Here I am proving Mami right and writing an essay about us!)

But my sisters, savvy girls that they are, know there is no such thing as a perfect man or a perfect husband. Over the last sixteen years that they've gotten to know and love Bill, they've seen what's wrong with this perfect husband of mine. Now any mention of "perfect Bill" is always accompanied by aerial quote marks, and I'm glad. This way I don't have to continue to feel guilty that I'm happily married to a perfectly wonderful man.

By now, this epithet for Bill is one that I myself use to tease him and pretty consistently get a rise out of him. (I said I wasn't perfect.) What I've discovered from staying married this last time around is pretty much what I learned from writing novels: You have to work at it page by page, day by day. And if you stay with your story and characters, if you give your passion and talent and faith to the writing, and if after the bad days, you still come back to the writing, well, you're going to end up not just writing a novel, but learning and growing by doing it. So, with marriage. And like the novels that get finished and end up being wonderful books because you tapped a subject and characters that deeply hold you and intrigue you, the marriages that last and are fairly successful are probably the ones in which you've found someone with whom the roots can go deep and the space can open wide and surprises can happen.

So, I've come to give myself some credit as well for this good, third, charmed marriage. I work hard to make it work. And so does Bill. We've had rough times and hard periods where we're on what I like to think of as a learning curve as a couple. One or the other or both are growing in ways that shift the balances and challenge us to come up with new and interesting ways to be together. Otherwise, we have to cut off all the richness and possibility in our selves to stay married to each other.

Here are some glitches on that learning curve, moments when we could have broken up and didn't ... because we kept learning and growing and surprising ourselves and each other.

*   *   *

How we almost didn't get married: It happens so serendipitously, it seems that it is meant to be. I am a new person in town. I have an eye condition that has been giving me trouble for years. It flares up when I arrive looking for a place to live. I go to the eye doctor. He is surprised to find this condition in someone in Vermont, as it is rare here, but common in the tropics. Oh, but I'm originally from the tropics, I explain. Really? From where? he asks. The Dominican Republic. Really? he says, I was just there with an organization doing Third World ophthalmology in a free clinic. Wow, I say. Then, he tells me where the clinic is, who it's run by. My cousin I grew up with! I tell him. Wow, he says. Yeah, I say, wow.

That's it. Eye condition improves. No reason to go back to see the eye doctor. Except I'm looking for an apartment in town and can't find one and so the Realtor suggests I think of buying a condo. Only problem is the condo is in the process of being built, but I could look at a finished condo. Call this number and ask if the owner could show it to me. Name seems familiar. I call the number. It's my eye doctor! He remembers me, too. Sure, stop by this evening, he'll show me around. When I drop by, Bill and a woman who obviously lives there show me around their condo. I assume this is his wife. I thank them both and leave.

A few weeks into the school year, I am in the grocery store and I bump into my eye doctor. We chat. He learns that I didn't buy the condo. I tell him where I am living. Before we part, he asks if he can take me out to dinner sometime. I give him a sharp look. You two-timing sleazeball, I think. No, thank you, I tell him. This is a new job. I'm working toward tenure. I have to write a book to get tenure. For the next few years, I am going to be very busy. But that same persistent, sometimes righteous quality that will later drive me batty doesn't get deterred so easily. Fine, he says, but you're going to have to eat dinner sometime; here's my home number, give a call, okay?

Home number? So maybe the woman wasn't his wife, after all?

Maybe she was a live-in girlfriend and they broke up and she moved out?

But I'm too embarrassed after the list of excuses I gave him to call him up. Too proud. Too stupid. So, thank goodness for the sweet and lovely persistence of the man: One day when I come home from classes, there is a bouquet of flowers in front of my door with a little note. *Welcome to your new hometown.* And his number. I call to say thank you. And sure, I'd love to have dinner with him soon, like how about tomorrow?

I love you, but I love being without you . . . at least part of my day. I used to think that I couldn't be married because I liked being alone so much. I'm a writer. I work in solitude. But it's not just that. I love solitude. Don't get me wrong, I love people, love being part of my noisy, impossibly crowded extended *familia* in the D.R. But solitude is my bread and butter. My sisters call it "working." Do you ever take a day off? they wonder. A day off from what? Does a nun take a day off from her vocation? Do mothers take a day off from being their children's *mamis*? It's a calling, a way of life.

I always tried to keep this part of me secret from people I became intimate with, even girlfriends. It seemed antisocial, a testament to how in a pinch I wouldn't be "there" for them. Or even if I showed up, I was going to want to get away after a while. In my very social Latin culture, a person who went off, even with a valid excuse like reading a book, was considered *rara*. "*Se va enfermar,*" my grandmother used to say about my solitary, bookworm cousin Juan Tomás—"He's going to get sick."

But what I didn't know until I married Bill is that you can be solitary together. Come to find out it's not just writers who love solitude. Farmers do too. There is nothing Bill loves more than working on the land, letting the wind take him where it will. Sometimes as I sit at my writing desk and look out the window and see the tractor going by, Bill mowing the back pasture, I smile to myself. We're each doing the passionate work we love to do. Tonight at supper, he'll tell me what he got mowed, what is coming up, what he plans to do next year in the upper garden, and I'll tell him about what I'm working on, what I'm having trouble getting down on paper, and ask what he might advise for a farmer character who is not him, I promise, as the guy is Scandinavian.

I am not going to make myself over into a beautiful woman to please you: I worried that to keep a man you had to be beautiful. If you weren't born beautiful, well, you'd have to work at making yourself attractive in order to keep your man. So long to not shaving your legs all winter. So long to never putting on makeup except for special occasions. I had read those articles waiting on line at the Grand Union. Women worrying about wearing mascara to bed. Getting dressed up in something sexy for when he came home. How to never have a bad hair day. How to always be sexy.

Since I was an independent, liberated woman, I could not openly worry about any of this stuff. But it was there under my bluff. I had to be attractive to him. Or else he'd lose interest in me. And so, when he came home with gifts, little dresses and sheer tops I would never have worn pre-him, I dressed up in those clothes and felt like Halloween. I did it to please him for about a year, and then I asked him, what was wrong with my old way of dressing? Your one-size-fits-all jersey period, he called it. Everything was black and looked like a hand-me-down I hadn't grown into. "You have a nice figure; you should show it off."

Vanity made me stick with it a few more months. And then one day we were in a shop together. Bill and the young saleswoman were emoting over some slinky, little dress with spaghetti straps and practically no back. "She would look fabulous in this!" the saleswoman said, holding it up in front of me. The dress was also super-expensive—in the not-too-distant past this would have been my food money for a month. Besides, where on earth would I wear this thing in small-town Vermont? I shook my head, no thanks. But the woman persisted and Bill chimed in. I had to get this dress. It was made for me.

I turned to my perfect husband, and I said, "I am not your Barbie doll! If you don't like my black jerseys, marry somebody else!" And then I stomped out of the store. A local store. A few days later, a close friend of Bill's asked if everything was going all right for him. There was a rumor going around town that our marriage was on the rocks. We were getting divorced.

Bill's friend was right. There are a lot of little divorces that have to occur for a good marriage to last. Barbie Doll and Fantasizing Hubby didn't last. We did because we were able to discard them. I get to wear my comfortable, inexpensive jersey line of clothes. And sometimes, I dress up in one of those old sexy numbers he paid too much money for.

Being the only step in the family: Coming into a marriage in which you're outnumbered by blood kin ain't easy. My problem was that I thought it would be. You see, when I married Bill, I thought of it as a plus that he came with two girls. I would get not just a husband, but daughters. I imagined them as younger versions of my sisters. We'd stay up nights gabbing. We'd share everything, tease Bill together, green lights left and right.

The problem was these girls already had a mother. They didn't ask for me to be in their family. Already it was not a clean transaction. But like old Goldilocks, I stepped right in and made myself at home and then wondered why the stepdaughters were not overjoyed that this interloper was sitting in the Mama Bear chair and sleeping with their father.

I used to get so hurt and unload on Bill when we were first married. Couldn't he make them take off their boots and not come in leaving muddy prints all over the house? Couldn't he make them at least acknowledge I had a birthday, a job, a newly published book . . .

All these questions boiled down to one question: Couldn't he make them love me?

He could not.

Bill is a father, and he and his former wife are the parents of two beautiful daughters I wish were mine. My jealousy and loss have been hard to acknowledge, to him, to myself. On the other side of that admission comes, I think, the possibility of a cleaner transaction: mutual respect, acceptance of whatever we can be for each other, a shared love for a lovely man who has not always been a perfect father, and a new shared love for their babies now being born, whom I claim as my full grandchildren. After all, I started out with everyone else from day one, cooing over their cribs.

"*Mía*," Naomi, my oldest grandgirl, calls me. That's Spanish for "mine." I'm hers, all right. And she is mine.

How we get over a fight: I didn't come into this marriage with good fighting skills. I learned two ways of fighting growing up: threats (Mami) and departure (Papi). I didn't know until I was with Bill, and the time of pussyfooting around each other was over, that I didn't know how else to fight. Early on, I'd threaten divorce. And then, I'd leave, and then have to sheepishly come back home to threaten to leave some more.

And my husband would greet me at the door, not smug and ironic, but stern and paternal. As soon as I stopped acting like a child, he would discuss the issue with me, he'd scold. Discussing the issue involved him telling me what was rational and right about his opinion and what was childish and unworkable about mine. If I was upset about something hurtful he'd done or said, I was told he hadn't done or said anything mean. I had misunderstood. But he was sorry that I had gotten upset. That was supposed to end the fight, and yet, what I felt was anger I'd forced myself to tamp down. The man had apologized. Why did I have to hold a grudge? And so fighting would "end" at this muddy, unsatisfying place, where one person was right but sorry that the other person had gotten upset.

Then, I got to see it from the outside. It happened that one of my stepdaughters got furious at her dad. We were at her apartment, and she departed to her room, then came out a while later and told him why she was upset with him. (I could see her point, but of course—I'm not that slow a learner—I kept my mouth shut.) She was crying as she went over what she was angry about. Out of the mouth of my beloved came that phrase I hear all the time: "I'm sorry you got upset at what I said. All I meant was . . ." And he proceeded to very rationally explain how what he said was nothing to get upset about.

"So you're not sorry about what you said, just that I got upset? What kind of an apology is that?" my stepdaughter cried.

I stood there in the middle of their fight with a huge lightbulb going on inside my head. *What kind of an apology is that?* Exactly. All these years I knew down deep that he wasn't apologizing. No wonder I never felt the issue was really discussed, understood, resolved.

Next time we had a fight, when he fed me that line, I told him straight out: "What kind of an apology is that?" The fight with his daughter had been recent enough that a certain synergy happened in his brain. I could see it on his face. He got it. Something was wrong with his way of apologizing.

So, how do we get over a fight? We now have ground rules: Nobody leaves the house. Threats are not okay. We're going to stay together, and more important than one of us being right is both of us feeling understood. And you can only apologize for what you did, not for the other person being upset.

Of course, these rules go out the window when you get really mad, but hopefully, incrementally, they do start making a difference.

Our most recent bad fight took place in the Dominican Republic. We have a project there in which Bill is modeling sustainable farming methods with the help of some local NGOs and in conjunction with a group of local campesinos. The farm also hosts a school where adults and children learn to read and write. You can see our two passions coming together here. A perfect project for us. Well, not always. Like all perfect things, there is always something wrong with it.

So what's wrong with this picture? A pokey lawyer. For ten years we've been waiting for the local *licenciado* to acquire the titles to the land. Recently, as we turned over the farm to three NGOs to build a national green center there, acquiring those titles became important.

I have been at this lawyer's office countless times before. Since Bill was not willing to change lawyers, I had finally given up and said, okay, then you handle it. This time, Bill asked me to go with him. I am fluent in Spanish, so I could state our case in no uncertain terms and we could finally move on.

"Okay," I agreed, thinking that after ten years Bill finally believed me that this lawyer was taking far too long.

And so I again found myself sitting inside the small, overly air-conditioned office, restating our case. The *licenciado* smiled graciously, asked after my writing, asked after my health, told me he'd seen the film version of *In the Time of the Butterflies* on cable TV, all smarmy and not getting to the point, Doña Julia this and Doña Julia that. I persisted. The lawyer then brought out the chart he always brings out, the wheel of the titling process, thirteen points, and he began to go over them. "*Licenciado*," I interrupted, "you've already explained this before, and we are going on ten years. We want the titles now."

The *licenciado*'s smile froze. "Oh, but Doña Julia, it sometimes takes much longer than that."

"It's taken long enough," I shot back.

Into this moment of reckoning, my beloved husband, who'd asked me to come and be the barking dog, turned to me. "Honey, he's right. Remember how long it took us to get our permits in Vermont?"

"Don Bill understands," the lawyer beamed. "He is becoming a real Dominican."

I kept my temper until we had left the office, and then I got furious at Bill. Why had he set me up and, instead of covering my back, betrayed me by jumping on me in front of the lawyer?

"You misinterpreted," Bill said. "I just stepped in because I didn't want to see you getting upset with him."

"Who are you taking care of?" I confronted him. "Him or me?"

We were in the pickup headed down the mountain to my parents' house. We had an hour or more of traveling together. I wanted to jump out of the truck and walk the rest of the way to the capital. To show him. To make him feel sorry. But I couldn't. A deal's a deal. No taking off during a fight. Instead, we fell into sullen silence.

Finally, Bill said, "I'm sorry that you got upset about what I said."

"There you go again," I pounced. "What kind of an apology is that? It's like you're not really sorry for what you did, you're sorry that I got upset. It's like you're perfect and never wrong, and it's always the other person's fault."

"I'm not perfect," he said, offended.

"Then act like it!" Sixteen years of marriage and I finally said it.

We were coming around a curve in the steepest part of the mountain road, a place where there have been a lot of accidents, and where, therefore, a little roadside altar to *la Virgencita de la Altagracia* has been built. Every time I pass her, I have to stop either on the way up or on the way down. We hadn't stopped on the way up in our hurry to get to the farm before darkness fell. But now I was in the middle of a fight and I'd be damned if I was going to remind Bill to stop so I could say good-bye. Most times when I ask, I get a sigh of indulgent impatience and a little lecture on how Dominicans chose the worst places to set up their roadside shrines.

The pickup slowed, and Bill pulled onto the narrow shoulder.

He remembered, I thought, as I climbed out of the cab and headed up the steep steps. At the shrine, I touched the grate and asked *la Virgencita de la Altagracia* to help me not be so mad at this man in the pickup. This icon of *la Virgencita* is one in which she appears not as a solitary virgin, but with Joseph behind her, the baby Jesus in a crib in front of her. I love it that my *virgencita* is a woman in a partnership. She understands what I am going through. She had a perfect son. A perfect, long-suffering husband. Please, help me be a better person, I pleaded, then headed down the steps, feeling a lot less angry at Bill. He had remembered to stop and he hadn't even lectured me about the bad planning of Dominican shrine-building.

"Did you ask her to help me be a better husband?" he asked as I climbed back in the pickup.

"Yeah," I said, trying hard not to smile.

A bus roared by on its way down the mountain. The pickup shook. We reached for each other at the same time. And all I could think was, he's right again! This is a bad place to build a shrine.

THE FINISH LINE

Jean Trounstine

I'd been married six years when I met Gary at an audition. He
was almost a cliché, tall and muscular, with the kind of sexiness
that defines racehorses, the obligatory sheaf of dark hair grazing
one eye, seven years younger than my thirty. He had a bottle of
Coke with him, and every so often he'd take a swig, throwing his
head back so that he had this Greek-god thing going, all angles and
smooth curves. In those days, I was trying to imagine myself the
girl in a Coke commercial, long hair swirling around my face, wearing almost nothing under a sheer blouse, ready to run toward my
Coca-Cola mate on a beach and abandon everything as I tumbled
gently into his arms. Art was the highest good, and I was on my
way to fame. Marriage seemed like an afterthought.

As we stood opposite each other, both holding scripts, in a small
room with a long table between us, I wondered how to breathe nor-
mally to conceal the pounding in my chest. Lines flew back and
forth across the room. I laughed. He laughed. *The Owl and the
Pussycat* came alive, me in the Barbra Streisand role, throwing
come-hither looks at Gary with my eyes and hips. When the director said, "Good, good, this is what I'm looking for; this is chemistry,"
I should have turned and run from the energy that was collecting in
my thighs, bounded out of that room and onto a bus, made my way
home to the safety of Delores Street's palm trees. But being an actress meant going toward the feeling, not away from it. And so I

stayed, glued emotionally to the moment, watching Gary take gulp after gulp of Coke, eagerly waiting for the director to make his choices. When he told us Gary and I would be spending a week together in a small town in California as the two leads, Gary turned to the director and said, "She's a keeper."

In Mill Valley, rehearsing every day made me forget that at twenty-four I'd married a man with heart problems. Mt. Tamalpais seemed to surround our minds with craggy beauty, and dramatic sunsets lit up the sky. On evening trail walks, Gary and I would go over lines. By the time the play was over, I'd spent most of my nights in Gary's bed.

When we came back to San Francisco, I left my marriage. Lured away by my urge for excitement, enticed by the rush—head to toe, warm, tingly, at times pulsating—I followed longing and moved in with my Fantasy Man. Illusion—the meat and potatoes of theater—took us together to Hollywood. Breathlessness lasted for a year. I stayed for two. Gary and the flimsy world of film wore off about the same time. Broken, asea, it took me almost five more years to pick up my life and put myself back together. I could be an artist, but I promised myself I'd never again fall for the role instead of the real person. I'd be someone who kept her vows.

I fled the California coast and got a teaching job in Boston.

Bostonians walked on cobblestone streets, and everyone had good shoes. It didn't matter that the shiny penny of my acting career didn't seem so shiny. I was a teacher now, in a life that valued the mind above the body. Now, I drank Diet Coke.

Enter, Bob.

Bob's credentials were impeccable. He lived in Cambridge, had protested the Vietnam War, and earned sixteen hundred on his SAT. He'd majored in philosophy, literature, and mathematics at MIT. He listened to Bob Franke's folk music, liked to dance, and enjoyed Garrison Keillor's radio show, *A Prairie Home Companion*. On an early date, Bob asked me to "cuddle," and when we got to my apartment, he actually unpinned my hair in the hallway and kissed me, pushing my body against a wall. There was no lack of breathlessness.

Sixteen years later, when we finish dinner, he still says, "Let's go into the living room and sit down together." Sometimes I'll put my head in his lap, and sometimes he'll put his head in mine, asking me to kiss his eyelids. Often I get into bed first and watch him come into the room, padding along in his briefs. They make a vee against his skin, surrounding a crescent of tummy. When he turns to sit on his side of the bed, just before he gets naked, I love to stare at the hairy place in the small of his back.

But as for fantasy, the notion of two lovers running toward each other on a beach, filled with desire, the wind blowing around them, with something like the theme from *Dr. Zhivago* in the background? Bob can hardly walk for long on the beach, much less run, now that his back and feet are bothering him. Every morning and every night he sits on the living-room rug and does a half hour of stretches, pulling what looks like a long sash around his feet to stretch out his aches, rolling around on the floor so that his back is untensed, caressing a tennis ball with his toes. I have empathy for him—the nips and tucks of aging have not passed me by—but the image of Bob perched with one leg across the other, icing his feet with water frozen in half a Dixie cup, just after he's brushed his teeth with an electric toothbrush, flossed ferociously and taken all his vitamins, gets in the way of the Coca-Cola fantasy man.

Which brings me to sex. We're the types who have to have time for it, and there's no time during the week what with working and all. And Bob is just not the kind of guy to get sexy before he does his hour of bedtime rituals, which also includes blowing water into his nose—this is not really worth imagining, trust me—so that he has some relief from clogged-up breathing. Then there's putting on an ice mask that makes him look like the Blue Man Group, in the eyes only; delicately positioning a nose strip on his nose to breathe right during the night; taking Lipitor to lower cholesterol, St. John's Wort for depression, and an occasional megadose of Advil. So by the time he's done, Bob resembles some sort of Pod Person who can't be touched too quickly or too intensely. It's not like sex is out of the question but mostly so until Sunday morning when he's disarmed.

Bob rented five movies when I went to a conference in England, and he watched none of them. He buried himself in paperwork and chores, eating mostly tofu and tomato sauce. When I saw him at the airport with hair that had started to curl up on the nape of his neck and index cards in his shirt pocket, I knew it was good that I was gone only a week. It was good that I had returned so I could keep him from a full pod transformation. Marriage is like that. Reminding the other person occasionally not to turn into a complete idiot.

Bob was dear to me that first day I was back. He listened to every story, took me out to eat, sat around while I yabbered in the bathtub about currency rates and the new Globe Theatre, and let me fall asleep during *60 Minutes*. But since it was Sunday, we had to wait a week for sex.

Expectation. Disappointment. Adjustment. Sometimes marriage feels as if there's no spontaneity. In spite of nurturing intensity with my morning coffee and enjoying a dash of impulsiveness, I'm not consistently what you would call a throw-caution-to-the wind, run-on-the-beach type. Descending from Germans on both sides, I always know what time it is. I get up at 6 A.M., exercise almost every day, and pride myself on the fact that I never miss work. Bob says I have my own particular set of showstopping quirks: I continue to eat—no, not just eat, but crack my teeth on—hard candy, in spite of root canals, crowns, and other major dental work; and my acrylic nails have been known to come off in bed, causing a nail alert in the most compromising of moments. In spite of such moments, we have had some spectacular sex. But it hasn't been on mountaintops with sparklers or like in the days before commitment, when I'd take a forbidden lover, say a chef at a restaurant where I waitressed, and we'd have sex crowded up against some cement wall in a South Boston parking lot. No, marriage doesn't have the excitement of the illicit or the thrill of the daredevil. It's more like the quiet hum of the everyday and the occasional surprise of the sunset.

Seven years into my marriage with Bob, I found myself on an airplane heading home from a professional conference. I was surprised when a dark-haired man in jeans and a tweed jacket seated in front of me turned around to talk. He looked like a runner, but dreamier and more dangerous, the likes of nighttime romance novels, dark and brooding, and like Gary, he had hair falling over one eye. We'd first noticed each other at that wonderful moment when he put the baggage in the overhead compartment. I'd looked up from reading my *Vogue,* his body straining just enough for me to see chest muscles under his shirt, and he was staring into my eyes. I loved his leather belt with the big silver buckle, and somehow that saved him from cliché. But I told myself to forget it, I didn't do affairs anymore, and gave him an oh-if-only-I-weren't-married smile.

After liftoff, he inquired if the seat next to me was taken. I was startled to hear myself say no, to be inviting him with every bit of my body to sit down next to me. He was young, maybe thirtysomething, certainly younger than my forty-seven years, and so much Al Pacino that I could hardly breathe. He slid by my aisle seat and sat down next to the window. On earth, I might have remembered my vows, but there, thousands of miles above my husband, I wanted seduction, and more than that, I yearned for something I could wrap my mind around, something to take me away. I noticed the way he strapped in his seat belt, secure and certain. I caught a glimpse of the laptop he tucked under his seat. I noticed he had no wedding ring. And without turning my head, I knew the exact moment he would lean across the armrest and put his hand lightly on my forearm, asking, sotto voce, "If you weren't married, would you have had dinner with me?"

The stranger and I talked for hours, or rather, he talked and I listened—he told me about the one who hurt him, the one he couldn't love, the money that meant nothing without a warm sensual woman like me—before we introduced ourselves. I even took his card before I got off the plane, imagining some secret rendezvous in a Boston hotel. However, this was not exactly a desire to make real love. I knew where that road went. And God forbid Pacino would see my aging body; he, too, probably looked better in clothes. Where would we do it, anyway? Crammed into one of those awful airplane bathrooms, or turned sideways under a frayed blanket? No, it wasn't the flesh that I craved; it was all that passion in my mind.

A year or so after that experience, I started thinking a lot about longing. I was plagued by attacks of pre-fifty jitters, and I was worrying that after fifty I'd never have another plane experience. Even though I didn't need to run off, I certainly didn't want to stop imagining it. And frankly, like other midlifers who take off in airplanes, bungee jump, skydive, and buy new cars, I was yearning. I was yearning for more than unexpected passion. I wanted to fling myself into the illusion that I would live forever. If we can feel all that alive, we can't get old. If we don't get old, we'll never have to die. As Shakespeare says, "Put on my crown; I have immortal longings in me."

On a certain level, longing seems easy to understand. Don't we all yearn for something beyond what we have? Snuggled beneath the low-hanging boughs of a giant weeping willow, I knew enough at seven to push my lips up, pointing toward the sky, toward some invisible hope that I felt, even as a child, waiting for Johnny Cohen to kiss me. I was Snow White, pining for my prince to "wake me up." I have to admit, there still are times I feel like Lizzie in *The Rainmaker*, wanting a Starbuck to swoop into my life, whisk me away, and bring rain. But I also have to admit, in light of who I am today, a feminist, a person who sees herself as assertive and who centers her life on work, I am the one who swoops. I dive into activity much the way I dove into making angels when I was five, throwing myself into the snow, grabbing handfuls of white stuff, legs and arms awash, wild.

Just after I turned fifty, I realized I'd actually stayed married for almost ten years. Had I lost the need to run off, turned into one of those housewives who gives up and settles for the humdrum, doomed to insignificance?

My husband reminded me, the morning I brought this up to him, that I was not exactly a housewife, at least not the type who stays home. "And you're hardly doomed," he said, slipping me the shampoo. We were taking an early-morning wake-up shower, all practicality, each regrouping under separate sprays of hot water. I began waxing poetic over my new Saturn, a shiny racy green with new-car smell and deep plush seats. It had a stereo with twelve FM stations, antilock brakes, and red lights that flashed TRACTION ACTIVE on the dashboard when we took sharp turns in the snow. With this car, I could go anywhere, be anyone. Bob commented that "Saturn" means "planet of limitation." As I reached for the Kiss My Face soap, I sputtered at Bob, reminding him that "saturnalia" means "wild spree." He suggested to me that in limitation there is discipline, perhaps even hardship. I wasn't thrilled.

But he had a point. I'd lost interest in longing; well, not exactly, but I'd found more interest in trying to figure out what it is that keeps me married and insists I not run off with Fantasy Man. Besides, I had run off once before. Who cares, I'd thought then, if longing's companion is often illusion? Or if it doesn't take long for illusion to wear off, probably about the time it takes to pull the sheets to his side of the bed? Longing engulfs, fills us up like a dry well, has its own life, and can attach itself to the unexpected: a man's large hands curled around a newspaper; the sound of peepers mating on a summer eve; a sliver of sand across a tanned back on a beach in Maine. I didn't seem to need the out any longer, and in a way it was a relief, but I worried what I had lost.

Just when I'd decided that saturnalia belonged to those under fifty, a furniture refinisher appeared at our house to help me take apart beds that I'd inherited and fit them into the guest room. I was feeling a little lonely, missing my parents, more aware than ever of my mortality. I was feeling a little vulnerable about all the possessions that were soon to arrive from my family, reminding me of my heritage, my gains and my losses.

The furniture refinisher was a kindly man, with sons and grandkids, and he arrived in a utilitarian van marked THE FINISH LINE. He brought a young assistant and talked to him while he examined the beds and took out tools. He was the ultimate father figure, wise with ideas—these hundred-year-old beds with old bolts were better made than any on the market today, and even though the bolts were hard to remove, it was worth saving the beds. He was the knowing craftsman—gently prying apart the wood frame, without hammers and without drills. When I took him around the house, excited to show this man all the pieces of furniture that meant something to me, he was the gentle lover—stroking the beautiful glass-top table with handmade needlepoint, explaining in words plain and simple how hand-carved inlays were created in the antique secretary. He was capable of delight, laughing at an old trunk that creaked when opened, tickled by the humidor for cigars located in one side pocket of the antique buffet. Then we went together into my bedroom.

No, I know what you're thinking, and it wasn't true. I didn't want him to make love to me. Unlike Gary and Airplane Pacino, I was not entranced by the furniture man's outward appearance. It was the way he looked at the dresser that got me. Here, in the bedroom, when I pulled open the top drawer to show him a sticker my grandmother had put in the left-hand corner, revealing that her grandmother had purchased the dresser in Cincinnati in 1860, his eyes glinted. He put his hand on the dresser top, just one hand, gently. "This is a beautiful piece. Be sure to give it lots of oil." I loved him. He understood the value of permanence.

Permanence had never been my mantra.

Then, at fifty-three, I got breast cancer. Every ounce of whimsy seemed to disappear as I buckled myself in. It was the flight that most breast cancer patients take, filled with surgery, chemo, and radiation. What dominated was my need to be, a yearning for survival, for whatever could root me to the real—hot baths, a bowl of soup, daily tears, a nap. Bob was there. He sat next to me in the doctor's office. He came with me when I shaved my head. He curled up and cried with me on the couch, and he made love to me, bald and with a bandage on my breast.

What makes many of us stay married might be called another kind of longing. A longing for what's irreversible, for what we find while looking for the Holy Grail, some quest for the everlasting. Maybe the deepest satisfactions pull on us like anchors, grounding us whenever we feel the urge to slip away like ships at sea. Maybe what keeps us married is the hand that reaches across the abyss to comfort, a moment in darkness that outlasts all the fleeting brilliance of daylight. It takes us through the tough spots—illness, job loss, our broken hearts.

When I did get cancer, I'd wake up night after night, crying, with that awful ache in my stomach, realizing nothing would ever be the same. Again, Bob lay next to me without complaining that it was one or two or three in the morning. He'd stroke my back. He just let me be scared. "I'm afraid, too," he'd say. And then he'd stroke my bald head as if I had just been born.

No doubt, marriage wounds us. And no doubt, the bonds that link us are not as pure as we would like to believe, or without endless annoyances. But marriage has the potential to make us better people. It challenges us beyond what we can imagine, demanding us to hold on, to bear up, to learn. While fantasy is a warm wind in the night, with marriage, I climb to higher ground during a storm.

That's my grown-up answer for why we stay married, the one devised for new-age yoga magazines if they ever come to interview us. But when I asked Bob the question, he said that the best answer lies in the parable of the lost sock.

In every load of laundry there is one lost sock. Let's just imagine it's a blue one. After the laundry is washed and dried and the socks are sorted, you search furtively through the washer and dryer, trying to find that sock, to no avail. Meanwhile, new laundry accumulates and you use up all your blue socks, except for the loner. That poor sock starts to look pretty shabby. In fact, you're sure that you've had that sock forever. You think about going out, maybe to Marshalls or perhaps even to Saks, to buy new socks. You fantasize about their plushness, how good they'll feel on your ankles, your sore feet. You might even go to the store, run your hand over rows of socks—blue, brown—ones with little airplanes on the stretch part. In the midst of all this, you have to do the laundry again, and lo and behold, the blue sock turns up. It has lint on it and God knows where it's been for the past week. But you're happy. It really is the only one that could match that worn old sock.

The other night, just minutes before bedtime, I was in the kitchen and had taken out a plastic trash bag, the kind that we save from the grocery store. For once, I'd decided to follow Bob's direction and do something I think is stupid, but he says works. I shook the bag open and blew in it, in order to make sure there were no holes in the bag. And even though I usually snicker when I see him standing in the kitchen with his mouth inside a piece of plastic, this particular night there I was, almost as though I'd absorbed his method, blowing for my life to see if there were any holes in the bag. I did this before I lined our trash can with a holey bag, one that allows leaks, which Bob says is my usual modus operandi. This time I saved Bob, the garbage-emptier, from the very unpleasant chore of cleaning out a garbage-encrusted trash can.

That same night, Bob and I made love and he didn't cough once. I realized, somewhere around the cuddling-up-after part, that it wasn't Sunday, and I felt this sort of joy, a kind of satisfaction deep in my bones. It was the feeling that I'd always run from, searching instead for the thrill of the moment, the first blush of fantasy, the Pacino on the plane. I had one leg outside the covers and one under, and Bob was curved sideways next to me, his foot strewn over my ankle. If the commercial people had come knocking on our doors for middle-aged models, our sagging and pudgy bodies wouldn't have been their first choice. But the joy was an extra, a sort of wow-I-can-still-be-surprised-by-my-husband. We were sixteen years married; we knew each other; we had lived through fires. I was glad to have my mate.

MRS. MARRIED PERSON

Susan Cheever

I have loved being married. A marriage proposal suffuses me with a sense of belonging that increases over time. I am accepted; I feel bathed in security and nourished by the subtle sense of protection marriage provides in this uncertain world. It's delicious to be so intimate with someone that you can report on whether or not the dry cleaning was delivered or whether you are grilling fish for dinner, and they're actually interested. A marriage provides a sounding board for the important questions: *Should I take the job? Should our kids go to private schools?* It provides a listener for the unimportant questions: *Does this essay sound good to you? Do these jeans make me look fat?* "The apt and cheerful conversation of man with woman is the chief and noblest purpose of marriage," wrote the poet John Milton.

As a couple we have more assets than I would alone. Married to a handsome man, I feel beautiful. Married to a wealthy man, I feel rich. But the best thing about being married is companionship, the sense that there is someone else on this earth—even though you sometimes hate him, even though he's sometimes infuriating—who is sharing the texture of your life. My experience of marriage is a wonderful one, but am I the poster girl for modern marriage? Not exactly. I have delighted in being married three different times in three different marriages.

Our first laws as a civilization were marriage laws, posted on stele, carved stones, in the Babylonian marketplace by the ruler Hammurabi around 2000 B.C. "If a man has taken a woman and has not drawn up a contract for her, that woman is not his wife," Hammurabi wrote.

What a culture needs, it will try to get through marriage laws. Warring peoples modify marriage laws to produce sons for their armies. Dwindling cultures modify marriage to increase the population—in such cultures young marriages are encouraged, unmarried citizens cannot inherit wealth, and polygamy is lawful. "Be fruitful and multiply," admonished the Old Testament, the Bible of a culture in which sons who could go to war were pure gold— "whoever did not engage in reproducing the race is likened unto one who is shedding blood." Matriarchal cultures, what we know of them, use marriage laws to subdue men, the ancient Egyptian matriarchy led to what the Roman Diodorus called "the hen-pecked men of the Nile." Patriarchal cultures use marriage laws to subdue women: "Your wives are your tillage," wrote Mohammed. Religious cultures modify marriage to ensure homogeneity. Among Christians, Voltaire wrote, "The family is either a little church, a little state, or a little club."

Christianity changed marriage permanently. For the first time, marriage moved away from laws that were meant to protect property or privilege and into the realm of a more spiritual connection. During the Crusades the absence of available men created the connection between love and longing. The first love poetry was written.

American marriage was originally adapted from the British model that A. P. Herbert called "Holy Deadlock" and which Thomas More said was like "reaching into a bag with ninety-nine snakes and one eel." British marriage laws treated women as property, useful for having children, especially sons—the heir and the spare—and keeping house. Wives could be beaten or disposed of as their husbands wished. "The husband and the wife are one, and that one is the man," wrote Sir William Blackstone. Society has changed since then, but marriage has not changed at the same pace.

Marriage has had to adjust to our increased life spans; each of us now lives thirty years longer than we did in the beginning of the twentieth century. It has had to adapt to our new attitude toward our children. Lowered infant mortality rates and a shift in cultural focus have made our children objects of passionate intensity in a way that can be profoundly disruptive to a marriage. The writer Nora Ephron has pointed out that having children is like throwing a hand grenade into a marriage. She is divorced from the father of her children and has been happily married for years to a man with whom she has no children.

Most of all, marriage has had to accommodate the changed status of women. As late as the mid-nineteenth century, women were believed to be inferior beings by men as wise as Ralph Waldo Emerson and Henry James Sr., and it was only in 1920 that women were finally granted the vote. The idea that women might be the equal of men in brainpower as well as in opportunity and earnings is relatively new, and it has wreaked havoc with the institution of marriage as we know it.

If you ask me, the marriage we have now is a nineteenth-century institution trying to adapt to a twenty-first-century world.

In the past four generations of my own family, there have been a variety of different types of marriages. My great-grandfather married a waitress who was suggested by his best friend—she was obedient, puritanical, and happily subordinate. My grandfather married a flamboyant socialite who was as witty as he was brilliant. They fought all the time; it was clear they adored each other. My mother said that the first time she laid eyes on my father as he walked into the office where she worked, she could see that he needed someone to take care of him. His coat didn't fit, and the arms hung down over his hands. On their first date, he had forgotten his wallet, so she paid for dinner. She took care of him all his life.

Born in the 1940s, I have lived through dramatic changes in the relations between men and women. Since my first marriage, even the marriage vows have shifted from solemn statements of eternal constancy to poems written by the participants.

My first husband was a writer and I was happy to be his muse. We married in the 1960s when most of my classmates at college dreamed of nothing more than a satisfactory husband and children and perhaps a suburban home of their own. In my senior year, when I visited the college career counselor, she expressed regret at my single state and offered her condolences on the fact that I had to look for a job. "All our best girls are engaged," she said. In those days, nice women didn't work.

Married at last at the age of twenty-three, grateful to have been saved from the awful fate of being an Old Maid, I thought I had fulfilled my role as a woman. Really, that's what I thought. My husband took over the obligation of supporting me financially; I would never have to work again! I had note cards made on which my own name, first and last, was entirely obscured by my new name, which might as well have been Mrs. Married Person.

For a while, all went well. As a wedding present my husband gave me Craig Claiborne's *The New York Times Cook Book*. The inscription featured a list of his favorite foods by page and the words *Well, what are you waiting for?* I was thrilled. I embraced the care and feeding of my husband as a full-time job. Some of my friends were reading Simone de Beauvoir while I read the instructions for browning chicken and chopping garlic. I learned how to cook chicken baked in sour cream and beef stewed in beer. I thought women's lib, as we called feminism then, was silly. Why would I ever want to have a job? Why would I care how much women got paid? I gave little dinner parties for my husband's friends and colleagues. His boss came for dinner and I made a chocolate soufflé.

We moved to the suburbs. At the end of the day, as the last light slanted across lawns and trees, I would meet my husband at the train station with a pitcher of martinis and a menu of his favorite things, which I had spent the afternoon preparing. We started building a wine cellar and began planning to travel. My husband got a book contract. We traveled. Sometimes the pressure on my husband made him sulky or pushed him over the edge into wild displays of temper. I was delighted to comfort and calm him. He was the creative one; I was the wife. But years went by and my husband couldn't finish his book; as his hope eroded, we fought more. We began to run out of money. I had to find work.

I had been a teacher for a while before getting married, but there were no teaching jobs to be had. Instead I found a job writing announcements on the social page of the local daily newspaper—the *Tarrytown Daily News*. The newspaper had four reporters. Within a few weeks I was covering the police and the schools. I fell in love with journalism, with the excitement of daily deadlines and the thrill of writing about people's lives. I had a voice in the world. People cared about what I wrote. Sometimes they cared so much that they wrote furious letters or showed up at the office with flowers. I worked at a cramped desk next to the composing room where men in grimy aprons waited to set my sentences in oily lead type and thump them into the forms that went downstairs to the presses. Watching the presses run made my heart beat faster.

At first, my husband was thrilled. He would be my teacher, and at the beginning he was able to teach me a lot of what he knew about writing. But the real-life dramas I was covering became more interesting than the drama of my husband's unwritten book. Now I was the writer looking for a muse. Now I was making money, and it seemed infuriatingly unfair that some men made more than women for the same job. When I had a planning board meeting to cover or an important interview, I couldn't cook dinner; much of the time I wasn't even home for dinner. My husband had no interest in cooking. He did not want to meet me at home after work with a pitcher of martinis and a menu of my favorites. He did not want to calm and console me when the pressures of work seemed overwhelming. Without children or a culture of marriage to keep us

together, we grew apart. Both of us fell in love with other people—
he with a younger woman who idolized him, me with a fellow journalist. It was over.

These days, marriage is an emotional contract, a deal. There are
as many kinds of deals as there are marriages. When the deal
changes, with the birth of a child, with the loss of a job or a parent,
or with the inevitable alterations of age, both parties have to adjust
to the new deal. Those who take the attitude that a deal is a deal
will probably not be able to stay married. Life isn't real estate.
What happened in my first marriage was just that. The deal hadn't
just changed; it had been turned upside down.

My second husband was married and I was engaged to be married when we met at a Sunday lunch party in Rockland County. Our
connection was so electrifying that all that didn't seem to matter.
As we spoke, the other people at the party fell away. Time stopped.
It didn't matter that we had made promises that we would now
break; it didn't matter that I was thirty-four and that he was forty-
nine. Only our feelings mattered. By the time all that was sorted
out five years later, we were well acquainted with each other's
worst characteristics. I thought he was too much of a gentleman.
He thought I was too much of a brat. We separated briefly, but
there was no turning back. Our own marriage was built on the
shaky foundation of broken promises, other people's suffering, and
our desperate rationalizations. Then his father died, my father died
after six agonizing months of illness, and I had my first child all
within a year.

The birth of my daughter changed everything forever. The moment I held her sweet self in my arms, I became a different person.
I could feel the old hard shell around my heart begin to melt. I realized that I had never loved anyone before—not my husband, not
my parents, not even the man who was her father. My passion for
my little girl sliced through the web of defenses and poses that had
defined me for decades. What happened next in the marriage? He

would say I betrayed him with other men. I would say he sank into a depression that took him beyond my reach. In trouble, floundering, we tried couples' therapy and then trial separation. We didn't know it yet, but the marriage was over. Within a year we were both married to other people.

Although I have had trouble staying married to a husband, my life has featured many other more successful marriages—I am married to raising my children, so much so that I have strictly curtailed my social life in order to make sure they have the calm guidance and companionship that children seem to need. I am also married to my work, and writing sustains and thrills me. I fell in love with it decades ago when I first went to work for that little newspaper, and I have never stopped loving it. It's easy to work hard at something that gives me a way to say what I need to say, and a way to enlighten others who may feel as I do. "All I have is a voice, to undo the folded lie," Auden wrote. Having that voice always seems like an amazing privilege.

I am still married to my third husband although we haven't lived together in more than a decade. It's hard to explain this soul mate thing; we seemed to be brother and sister, to speak the same language, to have a wealth of common experience beyond anything we had actually shared. When we were together it felt like destiny fulfilled even though he mostly lived in San Francisco and I mostly lived in New York. This passionate connection lasted as long as we were both drinking. Everyone we knew drank. We drank together. Our best moments were often in bars. Looking in the dark mirror behind the bottles I could see our animated reflections; we never ran out of things to say. The jukebox was always playing Beatles songs, the air was perfumed with the smells of sawdust and big dreams, and it was always very late at night. But the time came when I had to stop drinking. I stopped. Living with him seemed to make it hard not to drink. I started drinking again. We had a beautiful son who is now fifteen. When I stopped drinking again two years later, I think we both knew we couldn't live together anymore. We have stayed friends. My son has two parents although he only lives with one of them. When I wrote this my husband was still drinking.

Why didn't I get divorced the third time? When asked, I have plenty of reasons: my husband doesn't show up for meetings and often forgets to hire a lawyer; when I served him with divorce papers charging abandonment, he countersued for custody of our son, and I decided nothing was worth what that would put us through. The real reason is more complicated, I think. When I turned sixty, divorce suddenly began to seem less important; my personal freedom no longer feels like a matter of life and death. Looking backward, I can see that I could have stayed married to any of the men I married. I chose them, and I chose well; they were all good, kind, intelligent men. The things that loomed so large when I was younger (occasional infidelity, sloppiness, depression, ugly words, indebtedness, various emotional disabilities, and even a propensity for unmade beds—issues that seemed to merit divorce) no longer seem as relevant or as earth-shaking as they once did. Looking back, I wonder what all the fuss was about. If at the age of twenty-three I could have seen the world with the wiser eyes and more tolerant heart of the sixty-year-old I am now, my life would have been very different.

IN THE INK OF MY BLOOD
Maria Hinojosa

Back when I was a ten-year-old drama queen, I stood at the end of the long hallway of our apartment in Chicago one spring afternoon and yelled at the top of my lungs at both of my parents. My father had come home for more clean clothes. For the first time in my parents' marriage, they had separated. Actually, it had just been two nights but still that was traumatic for us. Papi was getting ready to leave for a third night when I was possessed by the real-life drama of the moment and the panic of seeing my parents voluntarily separate. I was consumed.

"If you two get a divorce, I will kill myself!" I screamed.

My yelling and my defiance caught me by surprise. Until that moment, I had no idea that I believed so strongly in marriage.

My parents did not get divorced. In fact, they recently celebrated wedding anniversary number fifty-three. So I am no longer surprised that I have this profound tie to marriage. It is an umbilical cord to the rest of my life.

When, as a kid, I would ask my mom what marriage was like (and I asked this question a lot), my mother would always answer the same thing. "Ay, *m'ijita*. Marriage is a wonderful thing, and I love your father. But marriage is a lot of hard work." Inevitably, I would twist up my brow. Love and marriage hard work? I didn't get it. Hard work for me was cleaning my room or studying for a test. What did that have to do with my mother and father's relationship?

The only message I understood was that you were supposed to be married and stay married. That was not only the right thing to do, it was the only thing to do. Within my extended family, I didn't see many other options for grown-ups. I had two aunts who never married. Other than that, it was marriage, and perpetual marriage at that, for everyone. Literally, 'til death do you part.

Now, marriage, in my insanely high-speed day-to-day life, isn't one of those things I sit around and contemplate. I report about it—how gay couples want to get married and how divorce is increasing. In my life I just live it. But I live it in this context: I know that being married and staying married has been in my Mexican family blood for generations. I live it knowing that deep down inside of me there is this thing about marriage in our family. A monogamous couple is considered the natural state of adulthood. Forever. Period.

Staying married in my family is about love. But it's also about not upsetting things. It's about commitment, controlling your passions, and knowing your limits. It's about respect and honesty. But it's also about shying away from risk. It's about friendship and the long haul and seeing others out there who have done it and lasted and still make noble couples. And backward as it may sound, staying married is about not disgracing *la familia*.

There was a time in my rebellious twenties when I excoriated the institution of marriage. From a "left" economic analysis taught by my econ professor at Barnard College, I learned that marriage kept women powerless. In many societies, it was paternalistic and further intensified an economy based on patriarchy. It was an emotional prison that restricted your natural tendency to love many people in your life. Rebelling against marriage was making a truly *gringa* feminist statement for me. Little did I know that nothing could have been further from my traditional Latina heart.

During those years of rebellion, marriage was a point of contention between my family and me. Living with a boyfriend was something I kept to myself. None of my friends were getting married. I rarely went to my cousins' lavish weddings in Mexico. And I am pretty sure that one of the greatest insults I hurled at my father was when I told him I didn't believe in marriage and that he shouldn't expect to see me walk down the aisle in a white—or, for that matter, any color—dress.

But then I got older and I survived a few long-term-but-went-nowhere relationships in my twenties. And just as I was about to turn thirty, I met my future husband, German Perez.

A few months after we met I knew I was going to marry him. A well-known painter and gorgeous man to boot, I became convinced of German's non-*machista*-centeredness when I saw his paintings: fleeting images of multicolored horned angels flying above a bluish night sea, a little ladder to the sky in the corner of the painting. He spoke to my soul like a Caribbean Marc Chagall. Though we were very much in love, neither one of us actually proposed to the other. I think we were just having a regular midweek dinner, and then one of us said something like, "This summer would be a good time to do it." And the other said, "Yeah, and let's do it outdoors." Then we finished eating dinner.

I could tell German was also from the kind of family where we-won't-separate-for-anything marriages existed. Later I learned that his dad had very few nice words and little praise for his mom, and he walked around with a snarl on his face. But she stayed with him until the end. I can only imagine the hell it must be for anyone if they are living in an abusive marriage and can't separate because of the *qué dirans*—the "what will the people say."

As I said before: for some of us, marriage is ingrained.

One afternoon I was rifling through the closet in a PMS mania. It had hit me hard that particular cycle—lasting ten long days— and I was angry at every little thing in the world. But German, my husband, calmly listened to me, his *café con leche* in one hand, his easel in the other, as I started telling him the story of my *abuelita* and her marriage, which was one of the most convoluted things for me to understand as a child.

In my Mexico, there was a rule about marriage that I came to understand. You didn't disrespect *el matrimonio*. Yes, a man could have a *casa grande y una casa chica*, a big house and a little house (for the mistress), and there were *fantasmas*, or phantom marriages, where absolutely everyone played along, and these so-called marriages became one big performance piece. But there was always something untouchable about marriage.

"Imagine this," I tell German, pulling a box of sweaters out of the closet. "My *abuelita* celebrated her fiftieth wedding anniversary with her whole family in attendance, all one hundred fifty of us. She was dressed in an off-white lace-to-the-floor day gown, a hand-sewn veil on her head, a Bible in her hand, and the gold wedding ring on the third finger——and my grandfather was nowhere to be seen."

In a centuries-old Catholic church where we gathered, the priest, in full velvet regalia, looking like a king, was entirely happy to play along with the charade. He blessed my *abuelita*, had her drink wine, take Communion, and kiss each and every one of us, from the six-month-old latest grandchild to her seventy-eight-year-old older brother.

We threw rice on my *abuelita* as she stepped out of the *iglesia* in downtown Mexico City and, escorted by *mi tio gordo* (my uncle, "the fatty"), she made her way into a 1950s shiny jet-black limousine, which dropped her off at a fancy restaurant where eighty family members crammed in and then it wasn't so fancy anymore.

Sitting in the restaurant at the head of the table was my grandfather, looking relaxed and contented. Already half of the day had been devoted to celebrating his marriage to my grandmother for fifty years and yet this was his first appearance. He was sitting there reading the newspaper with his *café con leche* and his cigarette. When my grandmother sat down at his side, he greeted her with a peck on the cheek, as usual. Then everyone just ate and drank like we were all celebrating the happy union of Manuela de Teresa and Hermilo Ojeda. At the end of the night, everyone made their way home, my grandmother to her place and my grandfather to *el lugar donde el duerme*. It was never called my grandpa's house, *su casa*. It was just "the place where he slept."

Three years later my grandfather died. The night before, he took my father and me and showed us "the place where he slept." Only two others in the family had ever seen it. It was a quaint little suburban house outside Mexico City—there was green grass and just a few flowers planted; the window had lace curtains (a hint that a woman lived there). I was happy to finally see it. I assumed he lived there alone. In my thirteen-year-old head, all I knew was that he was still married to my grandmother since they had celebrated their fiftieth wedding anniversary just a few years before.

The next day at the wake, when a group of people walked in, there was a moment of overpowering silence, then muffled sobs, and finally hugs and tears. The other side of my grandfather's life had just walked in. *La casa chica* had moved in to *la casa grande*. There was my grandmother's nemesis, and my mother's half-sisters and my half-cousins who I had no idea existed. Everyone was cordial, *por Dios*, my grandpa was dead. What good did it do for anyone to fight right there, in view of the open casket?

I remember driving from the funeral home to the cemetery for the burial. That's when my older cousin gave me the whole scoop. My dear grandfather had been living a parallel life—the *casa chica* was small in name only. He had a mistress and several more children. I was so sad. But then I was so angry! They had been faking this thing and making fools of little kids like me.

Even so, my grandparents would never divorce because divorce just could not happen. Divorce was simply not in the deck of cards. Divorce was danger, risk, passion, and change. It was unacceptable.

The marriages in my family not only lasted under extreme situations, they sometimes happened under extreme circumstances. When I was six years old, it was not cool to get married when you were already pregnant (like *al chic* marriages in the 2000s). So my cousin married his girlfriend when they were both just sixteen. It was no wonder that fifteen years and two more kids later, when they were just thirty, my cousin and his wife ended up separating and, two years later, to the shame of his whole family, they got a divorce. The first for our entire extended family of over 150.

I saw my cousin back in Mexico when we all got together to celebrate my parents' fiftieth anniversary. We talked about his divorce for the first time, and he told me that to this day, there is a substantial contingent from the rear guard of my family that still pushes for and believes that his marriage can be rekindled! *Qué locura!*

So it goes that precisely in the middle of writing this particular essay about the virtues of marriage, I ended up having a stupid little fight with my husband. It was a nasty row (though we play by ground rules: no personal insults and no swear words) involving issues such as the attack on civil liberties, the recycling lobby, political correctness, and whether putting a plastic carton in the regular garbage is breaking the law. And by the way, who has to deal with the garbage—him or me? I was fuming. Fuming, especially because I was in the middle of writing this essay, and how could I possibly write about the joys of marriage when I wanted to not see my husband for the next eight hours if possible? So I got my stuff together and went for a run in Central Park. The Christo and Jeanne-Claude exhibit of saffron curtains winding through the park was up. It had just snowed. The colors were intense and beautiful. Peoples' faces looked radiant. They were walking through the park in love with life. The adrenaline was pumping through my body as Earth, Wind & Fire's "Reasons" blasted in my ears.

As I was running, feeling protected by the flowing curtains above me, this thought came to me in the crispness of the wind. I stay married because in the middle of a fight, when I can't stand to see my husband, I will run and find joy elsewhere, like here today in Central Park. And I know that after this row, at the end of the day, when I put the fight into perspective, I will have my partner there, next to me, the man who has lived with me for fifteen years and knows me better than anyone. He will be there. For me.

That same day I ran into Jeanne-Claude and Christo as they made a stop at the Great Hill in Central Park, the place where German and I exchanged our vows. I had been forcing myself up one of the steepest hills I had ever run, and at the top of it was a large group of people. I could see the flashes of cameras in the daylight. The crowd had enveloped Jeanne-Claude and Christo, and everyone was just saying thank you, *gracias*, thank you, for your art.

I looked at them and thought: they belong to the extreme marriage club, too.

They must have had some serious fights in their day. They have been married forever, and they work together on everything! They fight and they can't stand each other. But they stay married.

I stay married to my husband because I am committed to the hard work I always knew it would be. And I thank my mom every day for being so brutally honest back when I was just a kid. Because this is work.

But I love my husband. And I love being married. And I love it that my kids can see Mom and Dad argue and later that day we can be hugging, or at least smiling at each other.

I know that in my family staying married may be all about avoiding risk. But one of the things I love most about my husband and partner is that he is so completely open to risk. Don't be afraid to change your life, he tells me. Don't be afraid to lose everything. Live for the moment. Dream it and make it real. And I have seen him do it in his life.

I stay married because this is the one person who understands how to help make me into a better person. When I get consumed by the pettiness of life, my husband will take the step back. Every so often, he will bring up surviving a war, like he did when the United

States invaded the Dominican Republic in 1965. When you live through a war, you live with perspective ingrained in your gut. When the minutiae of my work, the city, and the kids seem to consume me, German knows the right moment to pull me back to earth. I'll be down in the dumps and he will suddenly bring up the big bang theory just to confirm that we are all just tiny specks in the universe.

It's at those moments that I shake myself off and open my eyes *con los pies en la tierra*. With my feet flat on the ground.

Now, I don't know how many, if any, *casa chicas* and *casa grandes* there are in my *familia*. But I know I have cousins who have been married for almost forty years. My sister has been married for twenty-six. My brother who said he didn't believe in the institution got married in Las Vegas on Valentine's Day three years ago. It's deep deep in the ink of my blood.

That ink says, put everything into perspective in your marriage. When you can't stand him, get out of the house. Run. Clean air. Breathe. Music. Adrenaline. Calm.

In my most intimate and tender moments the only person who my heart really hears is my husband. The staying power is knowing that you are ready to dig deeper, to be more humble, to be more open, to peel back even more layers of intimacy. Because neither he nor I have plans to leave our extreme marriage of fifteen years, we better figure out a way to move forward. In love. In respect. In extreme commitment. Not because of *qué diran*. But for the long haul of love.

18,260 BREAKFASTS

Eve LaPlante

"That's not Daddy," my daughter Charlotte, who is eight, informs me, pointing to the wedding photo on my dresser. "He doesn't have a beard." In the photo, David and I stand, hand in hand, on a granite headland in bright sunlight. Visible behind us are brambles, the ocean, and a stone pier. Our smiles look frozen. Fear—panic—plays on our faces.

At our wedding, a third of our lifetimes ago, David was clean-shaven. The David in the photograph is practically a stranger to me, too, as is the younger-looking version of myself, a blushing innocent who looks more like Charlotte than like me now, at middle age.

In fifteen years of marriage, David and I have changed in the usual ways. We've braided together our lives, sharing a bed and tax and mortgage payments, raising children, and, lately, watching our gums start to recede. Every evening after the kids are upstairs, David and I talk together over what have become ritual cups of tea. Since turning forty we share a preprandial cocktail, which we consider anesthetic, once or twice a week. If one of the children asks for a cocktail, we say they can have one when they, too, are past forty with several kids. Raising children, I'm told, can drive couples apart, but our children work like glue. No one could be half as fascinated as David and I are in worrying about, glorying in, and incessantly discussing Charlotte and her siblings.

"So who *is* that guy in the photo?" I ask Charlotte, who ignores me. She doesn't linger over the photo, which is what I would have done as a child. She doesn't need to linger over photos of us, I suppose, because she actually has her father and me.

My parents' wedding photos were not displayed when I was a child, nor did anyone ever show them to me. I was three when Mom and Dad separated and five at their divorce, so by Charlotte's age I had no conscious awareness of them as a couple. To me, their interactions consisted of hot exchanges at the door of Mom's apartment, where I lived, before and after my occasional weekend with Dad. So their wedding photos, when I eventually discovered them, became an obsession.

I must have been eight when I found the packet of photos tucked away inside the cover of Mom's photograph album. Black and white, with the silvery brilliance of old photographs, they were windows on a past that seemed unreal. Mom and Dad were radiant, shining, glowing with expectation. I pored over their images, my heart pounding, searching for a clue as to who I was. But the photos never helped: I couldn't find myself in them. A few years later, while visiting my maternal grandparents, I found some of the same images pasted into a family album with jagged holes replacing my father's face.

"Who's that other guy in the photo?" Charlotte wonders out loud. To one side of the photograph on my dresser is the judge who presided at our wedding, which was held on an Atlantic headland one brilliant September day. The judge, a long-married family friend, started the ceremony by observing, "This is the first wedding I know of that's beginning, literally, on the rocks." Later he described marriage as "the condition for supreme fulfillment."

As a child of divorce, I yearned for marriage, yet the path to its "supreme fulfillment" was a mystery to me. Had I dared to think what marriage really meant, I'd have had to say, marriage is dangerous. It means being embattled and apart, like my parents. The very thing I longed for seemed out of my reach. This quandary was behind some of the panic that still, in the wedding photo, plays on my face.

Fifteen years later, I know what the judge was talking about, although the fulfillment is so layered it's difficult to describe. There's the abiding warmth of waking up each morning beside David, confident that he'll be there to encourage, critique, and even tease me. There's the exhilaration of knowing another person, deeply and without pretense, and similarly being known. As the judge explained, marriage "puts you to the test of accepting one another with all defects revealed, and then having your own weaknesses described as never before." As ordinary as it may seem, David's and my ability to jointly—rather than separately—raise our children thrills me. I savor family life more than I might have if I'd known it as a child. I appreciate special occasions doubly, once because they're fun, and again because they represent the stability I missed. Simply gathering for regular meals as a gang, crowded around the kitchen table, is a delightful contrast to the solitary meals I ate as a girl with Mom or Dad. "Staying together is more important to those of us who come from divorce," a friend in her forties explains. "You really want to work things out."

"The ability to be grateful for comparative happiness," as she puts it, comes up often in conversations with adult children of divorce, who comprise a growing segment of the population. The great wave of divorce in the United States began around 1960, the year before my parents split up. A generation later, during the final decade of the twentieth century, a striking social shift occurred: the number of Americans living in single- or stepparent families surpassed the number in traditional families. Today, one in two new marriages includes at least one child of divorce.

Like many offspring of divorce, I grew up with a poignant sense of loss. Besides the trauma of the breakup and its aftermath, there's the prolonged pain of missing one parent and the security of an intact family. During my teens, I dreamed of a future happy family, but believed my chances of ever attaining one were infinitesimal. I felt inadequate as a potential marital partner; my parents' divorce served as a scar. As a college senior, with little sense of my prospects or of myself, I watched, amazed, as classmates planned weddings as well as careers.

Several years later, I had a series of blind dates that almost turned me off marriage forever. At some point, in hopes of short-circuiting this process, I began trying to figure out what I was looking for in a potential mate. I wanted just one trait, discernible during an initial encounter, that could separate my romantic wheat from my romantic chaff, so to speak. I'd seen in women's magazines descriptions of Ten Traits to Look for in a Future Mate—things like looks, charm, a sense of humor, and financial security—but none of them fit the bill. A pleasing appearance, similar values, and common interests may all be important features in a prospective spouse, but not one of them is as stringent or discerning as what I sought.

Some time passed before I came up with just one question, the answer to which could determine whether to proceed to a second date. That question is: Can you conceive of wanting to wake up every morning and chat with this person over breakfast for fifty years? The time frame arose from the fact that a couple that weds around age thirty can probably look forward to a half century of mornings together. I assumed that the breakfasts my husband and I would consume through the decades would be neither solitary nor silent; this was my hope. I didn't do the math then, but I have now: a fifty-year marriage entails 18,260 breakfasts.

In devising this scheme I was behaving, I believe, like a typical child of divorce. Based on my lengthy if unscientific survey of my peers, we are unlike the children of stable marriages in that we plan for, or rather anticipate, divorce even as we marry. Having learned firsthand that marriage is difficult and precious, we approach commitment with unusual thoughtfulness and practicality.

My scheme may not have been romantic, but it was discriminating. It shrank the number of my dates. Once I met David it allowed us a second date. So far we've been together only fifteen years— that's 5,478 breakfasts—but I remain intrigued by what he may come up with tomorrow over a bowl of cereal and a cup of coffee.

Our marriage is not always easy, of course. We find each other exasperating from time to time, and some of our fights get nasty. Early in our marriage we chose to spend several nights apart, one of us at a hotel, and a few times considered divorce. In our early battles of wills, we kept score, brought up old conflicts, and generally played dirty, as many new couples do. To me, our first few years of marriage felt oddly like reenacting the same years of my parents' lives, during which I was not even present. I became uncharacteristically anxious. I could hear my parents' voices slicing the air and see the worn threshold of the kitchen doorway where I huddled as a toddler to escape their rage. I cannot say where I got this material, for it was certainly not in conscious awareness, but I was somehow compelled to replay scenes from their marriage, perhaps in an effort to defuse their emotional power. It was an odd personal challenge: Can I endure marital conflicts like those of my parents and resolve them in a new way?

For David and me, marriage gets better every year. When my favorite wine critics describe a burgundy as "relaxed yet exciting, familiar yet new, and thoroughly delicious," they could be commenting on our marriage. The pleasures it brings mitigate the frustrations. On Saturday mornings when David and I would like nothing more than to make love, we are blocked by a four-year-old in snowman pajamas, his limbs splayed between us. He, a result of our having made love, is sweet, too, and warm. A few years ago David surprised me by taking up insight meditation, a Buddhist practice. Seeing its calming effect, I began a practice of Christian meditation based on the writings of Saint Ignatius of Loyola. In our tandem journeys, our differences draw us closer.

Marriage is good for my body as well as my soul. I like my physical self more than I did before. David finds me beautiful, which helps me feel beautiful. To be known by him is part of the pleasure: we have nothing to hide. I find every human detail of him delightful, no less so as we age. Our sexual connection improves with each child and each challenge we face. The narrator of the Southern novel *Cold Sassy Tree* calls sex "the sweetening on the ginger cake," which seems just right.

Even with four children, marriage is good for my work. I recall that when I was single and childless, each day stretched out before me. With few obligations to anyone, I often didn't begin writing until the sun was setting. What did I do all day? I have no idea. Now, with my workweek limited to the hours when my children are at school (which has included preschool and part-time family day care), I get much more accomplished. My first book, composed before I had kids, took years to write. My most recent book, begun when our fourth child was less than two years old, emerged in just nine months. During that period, I should add, David did almost all the child care on weekends so that I could write.

This may be the keystone of our marriage: David and I share the work. While he makes more money and works longer hours, we divide the chores. I do more child care during the week, when he has a full-time office job, and he does more child care on the weekend. We divide minor chores by preference: he writes checks; I take care of our cars; he plants in the garden; I rake . . .

The really crucial split involves the two big chores besides child care. David cooks. I clean. That is, David shops for and prepares twenty-one meals each week, while I wash, dry, and put away our clothes, occasionally visit the dry cleaner, and twice a month write a check to a housecleaning crew.

You may think I've got the better deal. I would agree. Producing twenty-five bag lunches weekly, which is only part of David's chore, seems herculean to me. But David would disagree. He actually chose the cooking, back when we first divided the household chores, and I—with an eye to the future—was accommodating enough to agree to clean. He enjoys preparing food, and even when it feels onerous, as it can, he believes eating together at home is healthy and economical. An inventive chef, he scans the Food and Dining pages and keeps a growing list of favorite recipes in a loose-leaf binder he shares with the kids. He tailors meals, producing vegan stir-fries on the evenings when our vegan babysitter stays for dinner. When the children invite friends over, they prepare a menu in advance, requesting his (actually the *Joy of Cooking*'s) chicken cacciatore and "those crunchy potatoes you make." He bakes cakes to order for their birthday parties, oversees their elaborate decorations, and has the agony of watching the giddy guests leave most of their flourless chocolate torte, or whatever was requested, on their plates.

Our arrangement may sound complicated, but it feels simple. One reason it's sustainable is that we each have a separate realm of duty. I never fret about preparing dinner, while David never feels the tug of the stuffed laundry hamper. Dividing the labor is an essential ingredient of our marriage. If I find myself resenting David because he has shirked some chore or other, I remind myself of the delicious meals he routinely prepares. I may even taste one in the midst of my resentment, which might prompt me to do the chore myself.

Another reason this arrangement works, at least for me, is that it's so different from how my parents managed their single lives. Within their separate homes, each was responsible for everything—cooking, cleaning, and child care. The upside of this, from their points of view, was that they could do everything their own way. They took this to divergent extremes, I observed in my time alone with each of them. Meals with Mom occurred at home. Meals with Dad were almost always in restaurants or, at least, out—at the homes of his mother or sister. Mom's dinners—and there were far more of them—were modest, wholesome affairs consisting of eggs, meat, vegetables and fruits (why do I especially remember those that were bruised?), and scarce sugar. Dad gave me cupcakes and candy whenever I wanted them (and sometimes when I didn't), introduced me to delicacies like escargot, and let me taste his mug of beer. Perhaps this makes their divorce seem inevitable.

A happy marriage, it seems to me, is filled with compromises of one sort or another. Now and then, one of us is offered a business trip to someplace wonderful like Ireland or Hawaii. We usually try to bring the whole family along. But if a family trip is not feasible, financially or otherwise, David or I go solo. So far we haven't wanted to fly anywhere together without the kids; a plane crash would orphan them. A while back, when we had three kids under the age of five, David spent several days on his own exploring the churches and piazzas of Rome. Instead of feeling jealous, as I would have if our arrangement were less equitable, I encouraged him to stay.

Not long ago, I had business in England. David urged me to go alone, knowing I'd get more work done. Then, to my amazement, he requested that I travel during February school vacation, the sort of week I admit I dread because of the unrelenting family time. Unlike me, who enjoys combining part-time work with part-time child care, David said that in my absence he would rather go whole hog, spending all day every day with the kids. Naturally, I agreed.

Thick snowflakes were falling on the morning of my flight to London. Taking a trip unnerves me, which may be another legacy of divorce. As a child I hated the long car or, later, bus ride between my parents' homes. Traveling without my family also arouses a certain amount of guilt. While I finished packing, David baked chocolate zucchini bread with the children. As we ate lunch, the five of them discussed all the places they could go and things they could do during the week. Each child announced mealtime preferences: hot dogs for Philip, who's four; veggie burgers for twelve-year-old Rose. Clara, who is ten, produced a chart of the days I would be away, listing each hoped-for activity and meal.

Appropriately, the breakfasts proved most memorable, I would learn later. They had French toast on Monday. David and Charlotte baked blueberry-lemon scones Tuesday morning. Wednesday began with waffles. Homemade beignets and fresh fruit salad were served on Thursday. (Fresh blackberries were on the menu daily, a miracle of international agronomy in February.) The pièce de résistance, on Friday, was a cheese omelet with cinnamon buns, which David prepared the night before, because they require two risings.

I listened quietly as David and our children planned their week without me, feeling myself relax. When the time came to depart for the airport, everyone boarded the minivan to take me to the trolley station near our house. There I kissed each of them, hoisted my bag, and walked across the tracks. I watched the van drive away, David at the wheel, and our children's hands waving in the windows.

Alone in the falling snow, awaiting the trolley that would take me to the airport, I was conscious of having left behind the fear I felt on our wedding day, the fear that persists in the photograph on my dresser. Neither did I feel any guilt about leaving our children at home with David. They would all eagerly await my return. In the meantime, they would be well fed.

THE TWO OF US

Jennifer Heath

He wakes at dawn, sometimes earlier, and after exercising on the front porch in bracing air, he tackles his typewriter. I don't open my eyes until he's left the room. I read or write in bed, hiding, so that I can enjoy the dreamy morning lucidity without interruption.

When he has satisfied his furious morning blast of creativity, he tracks me down. Any sign of movement convinces him that the sociable part of the day has begun. Time to tell me what he's done since he and the sun rose. I cling to the numinous threshold between night and day. When I hear his footsteps on the stairs, I pretend to be asleep under piles of books.

I am jealous of his intense imagination, his passion, his relentless inspiration, his focus. He can write sonnets standing on his head in an outhouse during a tornado.We work at home. I pester him as much as possible. We bicker about whose presence is stronger, more stifling. When he's out of town, I tell myself I'll take advantage of the vast, fresh breathing room to cultivate an unshakable, uninterruptible creative obsession. Instead, I do the laundry and clean closets. The days spent alone, puttering, are delicious. But at night, I cannot sleep.

When I'm out of town, I call him every day.

He is oblivious to noise. His study is next to the kitchen. He works through clatter and chatter. My study is upstairs where I can have absolute princely quiet.

I am in constant turmoil. I need an enemy, a looming crisis, grievances. He has cultivated a peaceful heart.

His realm is downstairs and mine is mostly up. There was a period when it made him feel good to feel oppressed. He liked to complain that this antique house, which I inherited in a divorce, was all mine, that he had merely a pathetic little space on the old back porch and struggled for every inch. This worried me, until one day I noticed that he entertains in the kitchen, uses the living room as a music studio, and calls the dining room his office.

It becomes my turn to be oppressed. To carp about being trapped upstairs and about having to clean around his messes in every room. It was delicious, but eventually the nit-picking got dreary. We lapsed into belligerent acceptance, which, across time without our noticing, morphed into plain acceptance.

He loves to nap. I am terrified of idleness.

He says he's becoming more tolerant and forgiving with age. This is probably true. What once seemed to skewer and make him bleed now rolls off his back. This gives me little leverage to hurt him when I'm inclined to vengeance. Which I am, often.

When I am critical, he rears into a desperate litany of tit for tat, measure for measure, whine for whine. In minutes, we escalate into vicious fights about which of us suffers more from living with the other. In anger, he is a cross between Moses and Rumpelstiltskin.

Enraged, I become a berserker. I go straight for the jugular. I recall decades of minute slights and insults. I become unusually eloquent, articulate. At volumes that would deafen an air-raid siren, I have ordered him hundreds of times to pack up and leave immediately. It it would take a dredge, six cops, and a fire engine to get him out of here.

He still uses a typewriter and is nostalgic about letter-writing. I print or send e-mail messages for him. Now and then, he asks me to look up a Web site that's been brought to his attention. I don't mind, unless I'm feeling put-upon.

When I'm feeling put-upon, I wonder what he would do without me. Either learn to use the computer himself or cut off outside communication, disappear from public view. This would be unbearable. He is outgoing and affable. Women, especially, admire his sweetness, wit, and sparkle. He enjoys attention.

He loves talking on the telephone. He loves gatherings. I am reclusive. I scowl in corners. I am so shy at parties, I inevitably drink far too much.

He underdresses, sometimes in rags. I overdress.

He's shy, too, but whereas I'm self-conscious and self-absorbed, he claims to be fearful of rejection, having grown up as a nature boy in the Illinois woods, far removed from the intellectual circles he now inhabits. He bravely places himself in rejection's way.

I grew up in hotels, with servants and chauffeurs and diplomat parents. He is Motel 8. I am the Plaza.

I don't answer the telephone. I often neglect even to listen to voice messages. Crippled though he is from emphysema and spinal nerve damage, he hobbles full speed to catch the phone before it stops ringing. I roll my eyes at the spectacle.

He lives for the day's mail delivery and is usually disappointed. I forget to look in the mailbox.

I am a spendthrift. He is frugal.

When I am feeling put-upon, I think, Wouldn't it be just too bloody much if I died first and he finally learned to do the things I do for us? If I die first, he'll live happily on eggs, turkey bacon, and bagels and never give my efforts at nutrition, health, and fine cuisine another thought.

He loves supermarkets. I shop in small, expensive grocery stores.

He is sixteen years my senior. He is a senior.

Once upon a time, he drank too much whiskey and beer. I used to remind him to grow up before he grew old. Unfazed, he continues to drink, sipping cheap merlot, while I drink pinot noir. I am not growing up nor will I ever agree to grow old. Mine is a chronic case of arrested development and perpetual adolescence. His huge patience astonishes me, and I exploit it often.

He drives like a Guatemalan cabbie. I am beatific and considerate behind the wheel. At the wheel, I talk constantly to my highway "opponents," with a quiet, dangerous edge to my voice. Police photos that arrive in the mail with speeding tickets reveal that we have the same driving posture, poised over the controls with craned necks, white knuckled, intrepid, pedal to the metal, prepared for any disaster.

He is movie-star handsome. I am plain as a lumpy old chair.

When my Irish mother met him, she snarled, "JesusMaryandJoseph, the fomors have conquered the fairies!" I know what it is to be dwarfed. He would say he is more dwarfed by me than I am by him, and so it would go—tit for tat.

He carries an oxygen tank, wears two pairs of glasses around his neck, and flannel shirts summer, winter, spring, or fall. How can he take the heat? I used to love heat, but these years, the slightest temperature causes me to rent my garments, stand in showers for hours, clip coupons for air conditioners.

He recalls the names, addresses, and phone numbers of everyone he ever knew in childhood and youth. I prefer to forget everyone I ever knew until about the age of forty. He only needs to visit places once and he can find his way back through the murkiest fog or the longest decades. This, I'm sure, is related to his lifelong study of Native Americans, mountain men, and explorers.

He has steered us through traffic jams and unmarked streets around the world. I ride shotgun, encouraging him with made-up verses of "Jack the Navigator" after the old song about "John the Revelator" sung in a scratchy voice, ruined by years of tobacco. He is musical. He sings too loud, silencing everyone else. He calls himself Jack the Noodlegrater.

I express my love of nature by planting elaborate gardens. He does not think of gardens as nature. For many years, he did not hold my labors and the exquisite habitats I created in much regard. This hurt my feelings, but I had the backyard all to myself, which by and large made up for it. When unusual birds visit my garden, I remind him that even if he snubs my effort, the wildlife appreciates it.

He awakens early during the birding season—which for him is all year long—and limps off into the wilderness with his oxygen tank, his binoculars, and his scope.

I hate getting out of bed that early in the morning and become desperately nervous moving at the birder's snail pace, distorting my neck peering into the tops of trees. When I do agree to go birding, I spend the agonized hours squinting and repeating, "Really? Where?" This he has named The Call of the Jenny Bird.

We are each convinced the other is missing a lot.

Soon, however, I may triumph. Soon, he tells me, he will no longer have the sharp eyesight needed for more than backyard birding.

I love museums. I am thoroughly transported by antiquity.

He loves abstract painting and avant-garde film. I try to explain that because I once wrote about visual arts for a living, I have come to mistrust them.

He reads Herman Melville. I read Rafael Sabatini. He reads Charles Olson. I read Natalia Ginzburg. He reads Alice Munro. I read Fatema Mernissi. He reads Terry Tempest Williams. I read Barbara Ehrenreich. He reads Ernest Thompson Seton. I read Jane Wodening. We both adore Thurber and threaten each other with the ticktock of thirteen clocks when we want to be ominous.

When I was a kid, I was girl Captain Blood. He was probably Thoreau.

Despite my mistrust these days of the arts, I will sometimes obligingly accompany him to poetry readings or film showings. I am often transported into bliss. He will occasionally make me happy by

watching a costume drama or reading a novel aloud to me. A quarter of the way through the costume drama, he is snoring. He loves
reading aloud, displaying his gorgeous voice and talent as a performance poet. He's got rhythm. And he does all voices, too. His Miss
Havisham is unforgettable. He reads to me while I paint rooms
or mend clothing. Across the years, what with one room and another needing to be touched up, we've gotten through Dickens and
Stendhal and Trollope, as well as Trollope's mother.

When he reads to me in bed, I fall straight to sleep.

Wherever we go, he carries a legal pad and pens. In restaurants,
in airplanes, in the car on road trips, while waiting for films to begin, we make poems together, establishing rules and passing a
sheet of paper back and forth until the food arrives or the movie
starts.

We have a vast record of our outings, and at his insistence we
made a chapbook of them, too. He keeps every scrap. He types
every word. He troops to the Xerox store daily and copies whatever he's typed—in triplicate. What was once a lovely house has become a repository for cardboard boxes full of papers and notes. He
said, she said. She said, he said, preserved forever on stacks of yellow lined paper.

I am crazy for dancing. I married a crippled man who doesn't
dance. His sister told me that when they were kids and it came time
to attend dancing classes, he stood on a chair in his little suit and
threw tantrums.

Nevertheless, before he became a senior and his back began to
hurt, he was always kind enough to stand on the dance floor with
me, so I wouldn't feel foolish whirling around all alone.

I hate musical theater. He enjoys *My Fair Lady*. When he was a
very young man, fresh out of the Illinois woods, he and his sister
stood in line for hours in New York to get tickets to *My Fair Lady*.
Thus, he is forever loyal to it, as he is to each of his early experiences. *Rigoletto*, for instance, though he is no more a fan of opera
than he really is of musicals.

I adore opera.

His experiences are all precious to him, so that all his life is meaningful. He is sentimental about his youth. I am deeply disloyal to my past. I grew up with privileges that gave me permission to be unappreciative and with memories I'd just as soon discard. This rarely works in my favor.

He says we are "codependent." I do not understand the term. I say we function best as a unit, like bees, and more so as the years pass.

I almost left him when I discovered that his enjoyment of yodeling—and country music—was not a passing interest, but a lifetime study. When I hear yodeling, I wonder if it's too late to call a veterinarian. I'd rather die than admit that although I think yodeling is awful, I actually like that he yodels to locate me. This is how I am rescued, for instance, when I am lost in parking lots. Also, it reminds me of animal parents calling to gather their young.

Children love him. He is serene with them and inspired by them. He stands bravely before them in public-school classrooms teaching poetry. He has changed lives. He has guided hundreds of kids into art. I am intimidated by children.

We have two grandsons. One his. One mine. They bewilder me. He has them wrapped around his heart. They adore him and, more importantly, they mind him.

He is a poet and a professor. He should also have been an attorney. It has taken me at least a decade to find the flaws in his logic. I managed at last when I realized we have had the same single argument for two decades.

I want to win all the arguments, hands down, yet it seems to me unjust, unegalitarian, uncoupled, disloyal, to write about our relationship unless the writing is a collaborative effort. Reading this, he said that I do not understand him. I do not. Nor does he understand me. This is the result of narcissism, which is a result of being human.

I don't believe I chose him. I believe he chose me.

What I have in common with his previous partners is my vulnerability. What he has in common with my previous partners is absolutely nothing.

When we started sleeping together, my small daughter knocked on my bedroom door in the middle of the night, like a disgruntled neighbor, begging us to pipe down. "It sounds like you guys are having a sleepover," she protested. This is because we laugh, giggle, guffaw, chuckle, snicker, hoot, snort, cackle, and chortle until our sides hurt.

We began courting when my daughter was eight. She disapproved of nighttime visits. "It makes you seem slutty, Momma," she prissed, so he simply stayed. He taught her math and how to drive and helped pay for college.

Once when he had been drinking, he told me that he was sure when I became famous I would leave him.

I'm so relieved this has never happened.

Twenty years ago, we met when a friend invited us to supper with our daughters. As often happens, I happily accepted the invitation, then balked when the time came to actually interact with people at a party. The hostess was a dear chum and I was torn. I considered calling in sick, but this seemed rude. Still, I resisted.

I threw the I Ching.

The hexagram read: "It furthers one to eat out."

From Sugar
to Tin

GATHERED

Elizabeth Graver

We got married on a winter day in mid-December—a small wedding, with just a few close friends, some family, our old dog. We had been living together for nearly three years by then. I was thirty-five; Jim was forty-nine. We decorated the town-owned carriage house ourselves, with wooden cross-country skis and a toboggan, a honey extractor filled with bittersweet vines, pine garlands in the rafters, pumpkins and gourds, white lights. I wore a brown velvet dress. Jim wore a cranberry-colored flannel shirt, tuxedo pants, suspenders. The dog, his brown eyes moist, wore a red bandanna around his neck.

When we'd planned our wedding (if what we did can be called "planning," for it took little time and happened easily, though the years leading up to it had their share of hard moments and uncertainty, much stubborn forging through), our decisions had, at first, mostly to do with what it would not be:

No white dress. No suit. No ring exchange. No florist. No DJ or band. No crowd, only a handful of people that both of us together knew extremely well, loved extremely well. No god. No uttering at the ceremony of the word "husband" or the word "wife." No uttering of the word "state."

Here, things began to get a little perplexing. We were getting married, after all, entering an age-old, state-sanctified, legal institution, with all the rights and privileges thereof. We were doing it legally—that was, anyway, the plan. We wanted to try to have a

baby soon. Wouldn't being married simplify things in terms of . . .
what? Guardianship or something? Wills or something? Health insurance? Do we need the piece of paper, we asked each other mildly,
once or twice. Neither of us seemed to think we did, exactly, but
then neither of us seemed quite willing to forgo it either. I was the
one to write the character reference so that our close friend Alex
could be made justice of the peace for that one day in December
and join us in marriage:

Dear Chief of Solemnizations:

I am writing to attest to the high standard of character of
Alexandra Chasin and to ask that you grant her permission to
perform the marriage ceremony of Elizabeth Graver and James
Russell Pingeon. Alexandra Chasin is a person of the highest
character, a warm, loving, deeply moral person who cares enor-
mously about the value of kinship and connection. . . . She has
done vital work in international human rights for gays and lesbians. I can think of no one better suited to perform this marriage ceremony.

Sincerely,
Bridgette Sheridan

Okay, so I wasn't Bridgette Sheridan, but Bridgette was one of
my closest friends, and, being buried under her dissertation at the
time, gave me permission to write the letter in her name. And
maybe it wasn't really necessary to mention the international gay
and lesbian human rights part, but I wanted to, and therein, perhaps, lies the tangled knot of my ambivalence about the whole matter. "Let them stop us because of that!" I remember telling Jim, my
life-partner-to-be: prisoners' rights lawyer, collector of bones and
wild mushrooms, dogsledder, woodcutter, reader, lover, complex
unknown planet, steady long-limbed friend.

"Let them try to stop us!" I said, stomping my foot like the future child of the wife I was quickly on my unradical way to becoming. "Then we'll sue."

This was 1998. It so happened that one of Jim's dearest friends, Beth, was a lesbian, and so was Bridgette, and so was Alex, who would marry us, and then there was my old friend Juda and his partner, John, and Beth's partner, Betsy. After our wedding, Jim's father, eighty years old and Swiss, asked cheerfully if he'd been seated at "zee gay table," and we laughed and said, actually, all the tables were gay tables, because a lot of our closest friends happened to be gay. "Why?" he asked. I remember stopping to wonder, really for the first time. "I don't know," I said truthfully. Perhaps because Jim and I were drawn, each in our own fashion, to the margins of things? Perhaps we liked people who made their own way, or followed their desires, or lived, one way or another, against the grain? But those felt like stretched-for explanations. These were our friends, our dailyness, the human beings who, along with our families, gave light and weight, measure and meaning to our lives.

At our wedding, Beth—a former concert pianist—played the piano, a Beethoven bagatelle, her short, plump fingers filling the room with perfect sound. My sister, Ruth, read a passage by Annie Dillard, who'd been my teacher in college. Then Alex married us.

"We are gathered," she said, in sentences she, Jim, and I had written together a week or two before, "to honor and appreciate many forms of kinship, whether embodied in family, among friends, between lovers, gay or straight, between the people in this room and each of our wider communities. We're also here to mark and celebrate the highly particular form of kinship that Elizabeth and Jim have invented for themselves. . . ."

She spoke, then, of Jim, of me, of the two of us together. I tried to listen, for what she said was beautiful and I had not heard this part before, but there were faces turned toward us, our dog nosing between us; there was my hand clasped in Jim's, my feet suddenly unsteady in what were, for me, high heels. We were about to do this thing that felt, in some ways, terribly particular, specific, as if we had invented it, were choosing it. We had waited long to marry; we were formed already, each of us, not hoping to complete each other, two parts making a whole, so much as to bump along side by side. I was marrying a man who once dragged a dead porpoise up from the beach and buried it so that later he could dig up its bones and reconstruct it. I was marrying a man who cared less than almost anyone I knew about how the world viewed him, about following rules or fitting in. Before I'd met Jim, Juda and I had discussed having a baby together using artificial insemination. Before Jim had met me, he'd talked to Beth about similarly fathering her child. We might, each of us, have ended up in a number of different lives.

And yet and yet and yet. So my wedding dress was brown, so his groom shirt cost twenty bucks, so our marryer was gay. *Très radicale.* We were about to do (for a moment, I floated outside myself: look, a man and woman standing at attention, a two-headed statue, four feet stuck in a cake) the most conventional thing in the world. "Do you choose to live your lives alongside each other in love and friendship?" Alex asked.

I looked at Jim, who was crying, and then I was crying, too, plunged suddenly back inside myself—I had not expected to be, not so abruptly, almost violently. I had expected to cling to a little irony, a little perspective—or at least for stage fright to keep me at a distance in some way. "I'd like to *be* married," I remember Jim saying, after we had decided to spend our lives together. "But I don't want to *get* married." And yet we had planned this event, typed an invitation, and printed it on computer paper scattered with pressed petals. *Jim and Elizabeth invite you to join them at a gathering to celebrate their friends, their families, and their marriage.* Is it a *wedding*? one friend asked, understandably confused. Will there be a *ceremony*? asked Jim's mother. We were lucky in that I don't think anyone particularly cared—or if they did, they didn't tell us so. We're not sure, we said. We're still figuring it out.

In the end, we did do our version of a ceremony. We didn't exchange rings as part of it, but we do wear them: mine is my grandma Becca's Depression-era gold and silver band, Jim's is a silver ring carved with a map of the Concord River. Why this fishing in the grab bag for the pieces that felt alluring enough, or unproblematic enough, to want to take? Because it all *means* something, I suppose. It all means too *many* things, of course: some that are historically exclusionary and entrenched in unequal power structures; others that offer and bear witness, in their best incarnations, to the value of a partner at your side, the making of a home. Love.

I loved the man beside me. I loved his hand in mine, his blue eyes leaking tears, how we had found each other—both of us lonely souls in our ways; how, though he might infuriate me and frustrate me, he never bored me, so that I pictured his mind like an elaborate piece of coral, lacy, swirling, full of turns. We must have suspected that marrying each other before our closest group of family and friends would, in fact, *mean* something, and it turned out that it did. It meant something that was making us cry, that was making our dog whimper in confusion and then making everyone laugh. That "something"—at least the legal part of it—was denied to many of the people in our company, but there they were, crying with us, some of them. Smiling back. Generous. We would take it.

"Do you choose to live your lives alongside each other in love and friendship?"

Yes, I said, he said.

Alex opened her hands toward Jim and me. "Then with the authority vested in me by *you*," she said and widened her arms to contain our family and friends, "and with the power of all of *your* good wishes, I joyfully witness and announce your marriage."

No "by the authority vested *in*," no "State of Massachusetts," though later that week, we would file the paperwork, which sits, a document of record, in the town hall. At our wedding, food and drink. Cake baked by a friend. Toasts, including one made by my mother in Ladino, the language of my Sephardic Jewish grandparents, and one played on the recorder and sung in doggerel by Jim's two cousins and his oldest friend. Afterward, everyone stayed and helped clean up. How tired I was when that night was over. How sapped. How full of limp, exhausted joy. I hadn't expected it, quite—to feel in such a distilled way what I'd known for some time to be true: that this was the human being I wanted to spend my days and nights with, the man I wanted as the father of my children. I hadn't expected, really, to feel different afterward, but I did feel different in the days and months to follow: a little steadier, a little more side by side, less questioning, even though as a married woman, a "wife" with a "husband" (words I continue to stumble over and seldom use), I still drove off into the city to have dinner with my friends alone, I still shut my study door much of the time and showed Jim my writing only at the end, when a piece was nearly done.

"For in marriage a little license, a little independence there must be between people living together day in day out in the same house," writes Virginia Woolf in *Mrs. Dalloway*. Jim gave me, gives me, that, though not in the way of Mr. Dalloway, an upright man of Parliament, for my mate goes off to tangled, wild places when we are apart: the thickets of the woods behind our house; the prisons where he does his work; the rooms inside his mind (his brow furrows, his eyes turn inward), which I can glimpse but never grasp.

Later, he will turn out to be an astonishing father to our two daughters, to have a rare patience with them, a steadfastness and playfulness, an ability to slow down into their child time and listen hard. We will turn out to love parenting together: the walks, the family snuggles, the moment when our older daughter, Chloe, barely three then, picks out a skirt for Jim to wear out to dinner because we've decided to dress up. Here, Daddy, wear this, it's beautiful!—and the skirt was his mother's, who died three weeks before I got pregnant with Chloe—and he puts it on, and we do not laugh because to laugh would be to turn her act of choosing beauty into comedy; to laugh would be to throw the mud of "this is this and that is that" into her upturned face. We go to the restaurant, order food. We do not laugh. Later, we tell the story to friends: it is a joke and not a joke. I will love Jim for being the sort of man who wears his mother's skirt because his daughter picked it out for him, who dances with her in the restaurant when she pulls him by the hand, though he is, he tells me later, suddenly deeply, horribly embarrassed, everyone looking, what are they thinking (this from the man who does not care what people think; and yet how deep these particular currents run, how strong). I, at the table with our baby, Sylvie, am mortified as well, even as I am wobbly with laughter and, somewhere underneath that, moved. Jim's mother's skirt is rayon, long, and flowing. He has a flat belly, narrow hips. In addition to looking ridiculous, he looks good.

Because I love Jim for this and many other things, often I feel as if we are, in fact, making our own kind of family, our own kind of marriage, where our genders, particularly in relation to the emotional and developmental lives of our children, are not the defining fact. Still, let it be said that I, like most of my straight, married women friends with kids, am the one to keep the fridge full. I am the one to make the doctors' appointments and get on the day-care waiting list and find the dance class and comb the secondhand stores for children's clothes and make sure the backpack contains the can of beans for the Food Train, the toilet-paper roll for the bat project, the snow pants and dry socks. I am the one, as well, to pay the electric company when it threatens to turn the power off because Jim has neglected to pay the bill, the one to hire a teenager to move the mailbox after the snowplow has smashed it five times in a row. I am the one to beg my lawyer mate, over and over, every few weeks, for years and years: we need a will, we need a will, we need a will. Oh, I could go on and on (you do, he'd say, go on and on), and when I think of it, a flash of rage comes over me, hot and white and very, very old.

Sometimes I think these imbalances arise because I am, by temperament, more organized, because I love to shop for bargains, because I cannot wait for him to do things in his own good (glacial) time. And sometimes—when I'm bone weary from a day at work, or have no time to write, or am packing for our sixth weekend trip of the summer, or have forgotten something and ended up with a pouting or tearful child—I think it is because he is a man and I am a woman, trained from birth. And then I wonder: What if we were woman and woman, or man and man? Would the roles still solidify, each person hardening into a shape, dried Play-Doh on the sole of your shoe?

On November 18, 2003, the Massachusetts Supreme Judicial Court ruled, by a narrow 4–3 vote, that the law prohibiting same-sex couples from marrying was unconstitutional. On May 17, 2004, the courts began to issue applications for marriage licenses to same-sex couples. I wish I could say that I was there to witness the first gay couples lining up for marriage licenses in my state. I wish I could say that I threw everything aside, drove from my rural suburb to the city, made my way through the crowds to stand at midnight with my friends in front of Cambridge City Hall. Looking back, I wish I'd gone. But I didn't go. I'd been at work all day and hadn't seen my girls. I had a cold, and so did they. And while I felt passionate about the issue, I had, in fact, gotten married when it was a right denied some of my closest friends. Why did I do it? Why have I attended so many weddings where the officiant is a gay friend of the straight couple? Is it like the eunuchs in India who dance and sing at weddings, asked to bless *because* they are outside?

That night, I stayed home and watched people file in and out of the courthouse on the evening news, as the crowd sang "The Star-Spangled Banner" and threw rice. There were, of course, all manner of couples, wearing wedding dresses and tuxedos, jeans and T-shirts, gloss and glitter, leather jackets, brocade shawls. What I remember most is the old couples, the ones who may actually have needed each other's arms to balance themselves as they went up and down the stairs, already married—you could tell, they had been for ages—but now this slip of paper, now this right, and as I watched, I wept. In the days and weeks to follow, my own status as a married person became easier, less laden for me, buoyed by my knowledge that the institution was open to gays and lesbians, at least in my one small, out-of-sync, densely populated blue state. And yet I had taken advantage of that right before I'd known that they would have it, and so my lessening of guilt was spurious, and so the easy answers continued to refuse to come.

Instead, more questions: Would there have been another way to affirm our bond—the same little party, perhaps, even the same ceremony, but without filing the piece of paper? "We're married," we might have said if we felt like it, paper or no paper. Or, "We're partnered," except the word had a coldness to it, a law-firm sound. Or might we have invented our own word, or kept our bond private, silent, since the life of a couple is nearly as private and intricate as one's own inner life and can only truly be witnessed from the inside out?

Ten months after the court decision, Beth and Betsy got married on a stormy September morning in their cottage on Cape Cod. Their dog was there. Ours had died a year before. Our girls—Sylvie at her first wedding ever—were two and four and wore matching flower-girl dresses, purple seersucker with a little flounce (the flower girls were Chloe's idea, not the brides'). Bridgette was there with her partner, Margery. Jim, at Beth's request, wore a skirt. Beth and Betsy wore Japanese silk haori, Beth's a creamy beige

with rose-colored flowers, Betsy's pale blue. They had been together for over sixteen years. Neither of them invited any relatives
to the wedding. Too complicated, they said.

The mood that morning was a tremendously complex mix of
nervousness, hilarity, soberness, cynicism, and elation. The love
between them was not in question, had no need for affirmation.
They were joining a club that had only just recently, and in the
face of vitriolic opposition, deigned to let them in. They were not
going to have a baby. They were well stocked in flatware, vases,
bowls.

All right, so they did want the option of joint health insurance.
And they did want, as women past fifty, to have legal caretaking
rights toward each other in old age. Still, I don't think this was the
whole picture. Through their wisecracks, their faces were at once
nervous and shining. We stood gathered around them, eight adults,
five kids, their dog (their three escape-artist cats were locked in the
bedroom)—the family they had made.

Our friend Joe performed the ceremony. He spoke of Beth, of
Betsy, of the two of them together. And then they exchanged vows,
speaking words they had written together, for each other, in advance.

"I take you forever, my little ball and chain," said Betsy.

"I've taken you this far," said Beth. "I'll take you the rest of the
way."

Joe paused to glance down at the piece of paper he was holding.
Do you promise, do you promise?

Yes, she said, she said.

"In a moment long overdue, and by the power reluctantly vested
in me by the Commonwealth of Massachusetts," Joe said, "I now
pronounce you married."

And so Beth and Betsy joined the institution that Jim and I
had joined, all of us doing it in our own way but doing it—legally,
ceremonially—nonetheless. Why? For myself, I suppose the things

pulling me toward marriage were, in the end, stronger and more powerful than the (also powerful) things pulling me away. In some ways, this does not speak well for me. I wanted the legal and financial benefits of marriage, despite my full and uncomfortable knowledge that these benefits were not available to all. In other ways, though, I think I was pulled toward marriage because, in addition to taking shape in the exclusionary and skeletal language of the law, it lives in flesh-and-blood people gathering with the best intentions for ceremonies across time and continents: red saris, chuppahs, glasses wrapped in linen, chairs lifted aloft, singing, laughter, cake. I am not religious and have few real rituals in my life, but I do tend to cry at weddings, often despite myself, overcome by both the weight and magic of the moment, the stopping to witness, the hopefulness.

Some of this reaction may be rooted in my family history; my parents do marriage well, and my grandparents did too—my maternal ones in an arranged marriage that developed into a sturdy and passionate, if explosive, relationship; my paternal grandparents in a love match that ended too early when my father's father died at thirty-eight. All told, the models I have are pretty good.

But that's not all. Years ago, still single, I visited my Sephardic Jewish relatives in Turkey, and they took me up the Bosporus to the tomb of Telli Baba, Istanbul's patron saint of marriage. There, they handed me a head scarf and had me go into a dark, underground shrine to tie a bit of wire onto a lattice so that a saint—one neither I nor they believed in—might help me find a husband. The place was full of young Muslim women doing the same thing, along with brides in wedding dresses, come back with their grooms to offer thanks. How quaint, I remember thinking, Western, liberated feminist that I was. And yet I took that wire and tied it on, and not simply to please my relatives. So many people have married, for centuries and centuries, across cultures, over time. Where is he, I remember wondering as I climbed the stone steps and stood squinting in the light, feeling oddly relieved and, at the same time, foolish. Where is the man this twist of wire will lead me to? What is he doing right now?

I was thirty then, living alone. While I had a full life in many ways, it was scraped by daily loneliness. I wanted children, had wanted them for as long as I could remember. I wanted to say *"We're* not home right now" on the answering machine. I wanted sturdiness—at least the illusion of sturdiness—in a world that spins fast and is full of loss. Promises. Vows, even, my own matched with another's. Less than a year later, I met Jim. Several years after that, we married. And the world still spins fast, and loneliness still scrapes, but less now, for the house is filled with people breathing, sleeping, waking, touching, talking. I feel terribly lucky to have found this particular mate and had these particular children. To have been granted, through marriage, access to this particular human right.

On November 2, 2004, eleven states passed amendments banning same-sex marriage, and that, of course, was only one part of the national shift further toward the right. The country, I kept hearing on the news, had cast its presidential vote largely on moral grounds. The night of the election, I went to bed before the final results had finished trickling in. I left Jim downstairs by the television and snuck Sylvie, sleeping, from her crib into our bed where I could lie with her, at once my steady comfort and the locus of my fear. For what would this world hold for these children still young enough to think that almost anything was possible—that danger meant needing to hold hands in parking lots and letting someone cut your grapes in half; that the Food Train, like the Little Engine That Could, brought food to anyone who needed it; that you could marry the person you loved?

After Joe pronounced Beth and Betsy married, they kissed and we cheered, as the rain beat down on the skylight and the flowers in a vase on the TV gave off their pinkish orange light. Later, the day cleared and we went to the beach, where we saw, in the parking lot, a gray turtle not much bigger than a quarter making its ancient, resolute way between two cars until Jim scooped it up and moved it—stilled now, a mere clay sculpture of itself—from the asphalt to the sand.

FIRST PERSON PLURAL

Helen Fremont

Commitment

Our marriage is based on a fundamental, irrefutable fact: neither of us can bear the trauma of dating. Our own courtship was excruciatingly long. The general rule of thumb in lesbian relationships is that on the second date you move in together. Donna and I held off cohabitation for nearly two months, which is something like a record in the gay community. Having accomplished this feat together, we are not about to venture out on our own again. This basic fear lies at the heart of our relationship, and offers us a sense of stability and security. We are bound to each other because neither of us has the courage to start over again.

The Dangers of Marriage

Getting married is a little like sticking your feet in cement: it feels sublimely gooey and sensual now, but you know that it's going to feel constricting in time—stabilizing, yes, but dangerously ... well ... *permanent*.

And let's face it: marriage is an act of pure arrogance. You are pretending to lay claim to the future, which is a risky business at best. The gods may not like it. They might feel obliged to prove that *they're* in charge, not you. Common ways for gods to get their

point across would be to kill your spouse for no good reason at all—
by introducing a drunk driver into your lane, or a suicide bomber,
or a grade IV glioblastoma. Something like this happens every day,
and I think it is a pretty simple matter for the gods to arrange for it
happen to you.

And then, of course, there's a statistical reason not to get married:
marriage, as any lawyer will tell you, is the first step to divorce.

The Illegal Marriage

So my wife and I were cautious, and we took both of our weddings seriously. Our first marriage—the illegal one—took place in
1996 in our living room. We planned it ourselves. We invited only as
many people as we could seat at our table with all its leaves added,
once we stacked all the other living-room furniture—the twin love
seats, the television set, and coffee table—out on the deck. Our
guest list was therefore very easy to manage. We invited eight local
friends, plus my second cousin from Italy, plus Donna's foster
brother from Kentucky. Originally, I'd invited my sister, but then
she pissed me off, so I revoked the invitation. A wedding is simply
too important to risk with the presence of immediate family.

The illegal marriage was the one that really mattered to us. We
bought similar white linen dresses and had rings made by a local
goldsmith. I wrote our vows, and Donna planned and cooked an
elaborate menu for our guests. We got nervous and drank champagne afterward.

History Lesson

My wife had been married before—she was what she called a se-
rial monogamist, having been married to a man for ten years (during her twenties), and then having lived with a woman for the next
ten years (there went her thirties). These relationships had ended

badly and therefore she was hardly interested in starting a new one. My history of love was not exactly confidence-inspiring. Until the age of thirty-seven, when I met Donna in my backyard, I had never set up house with anyone. In my twenties, I had gone through the motions of sleeping with boys because that seemed to be what girls did. I had been passionately in love with several of my college and law school roommates, but they were all women, and the Amazing Force of Denial kept me clueless for years. I could not imagine that I might be a pervert or a deviant, so my worshipful feelings must be what all roommates feel for each other. I certainly wasn't queer. My love for these drop-dead gorgeous, sharp-witted women was pure, platonic, and agonizing.

After losing roommate after roommate to their fiancés, I finally decided to get my own fiancé in law school. He was adorable. I'd known him since high school, when we'd flirted and played endurance Ping-Pong for hours, progressing over the years to bicycling and distance running, winter camping and ski mountaineering.

Now, in my third year of law school, we added sex and big American-style breakfasts to our repertoire of activities and accomplishments. I was crazy about him, and he loved me anyway. We announced our engagement to our parents, and then I backed out of the marriage a few weeks later. I had doubts. What, exactly, was love? And why was my sexual attention span so short? I was no longer keen on being a lawyer, either, and I suspected other surprises lurking in my subconscious—that strange corridor where so many of my feelings have permanent lockers.

Sure enough, good old-fashioned introspection (coupled with expensive psychotherapy) led me, within a year, to the epiphany that I was, in fact, a lesbian. For an additional charge, I learned that this was okay. It would take me another five years before I actually tested out my new hunch of homosexuality in the field—I have never been particularly impulsive. And it would be another ten years before I fell for Donna.

Courtship

Donna and I were set up by my neighbors, a gang of opera singers who knew Donna from their day jobs in the health-care industry, where Donna worked. These boys decided to throw a Memorial Day barbecue in my backyard. It was supposed to be a team effort, but they had songs to sing and boys to see, so I ended up doing all the cleaning, grocery shopping, preparing, and cooking, and they invited fifty of their closest friends. One of them was Donna. She walked into my backyard Monday afternoon bearing twenty pounds of potato salad. She was wearing an Indian-print skirt and a little black tank top; her toes were painted a honking red. I was wearing my ratty college crew shirt and a pair of giant industrial-strength canary-yellow rubber gloves, because I was carrying the mildewed grill from the backyard to the kitchen sink.

"Hi," I said, my hands full of greasy grill.

"Hi," she said, tipping the bowl of potato salad in greeting.

I was in love. Immediately after washing the grill I went upstairs and changed into a nicer T-shirt.

The next day I called her for a date and we went out to dinner. She invited me home afterward to meet her cat—an auspicious start, I thought. Her cat was a used cat; Donna had gotten him from the local shelter a few months before. He had already broken every lamp in her apartment. He looked at me with suspicion, but I must have passed the test because Donna accepted my invitation to see the Mark Morris Dance Group the following week. She seemed depressed, however, and cried throughout the performance, so I believed my chances might be dwindling.

But I soldiered on. On the advice of my romance counselors (a couple of friends who had met Donna at the barbecue), I asked her over for dinner. Soon after, she asked me to bring my dog to meet her cat. Fortunately, the two seemed to get along, if not in temperament, at least in color. They're both redheads.

In July, we had dinner at a little jazz restaurant. I cried over the loss of my last girlfriend to cancer; she cried over the loss of her last girlfriend to a younger woman. We shared a container of pocket tissues. Within a month my dog and I moved in with her and her cat. I proposed marriage almost immediately. Two years later, she agreed.

Marriage, Legal-Style

In 2004, everyone was running down to City Hall to register; Massachusetts had legalized same-sex marriages. All our friends were planning their ceremonies, ordering invitations and flowers and dresses and cakes and caterers and musicians. Time was of the essence. There was movement afoot to amend the Constitution to ban same-sex marriages, and our chance to get state recognition was shrinking.

This was both annoying and exhilarating. After all, Donna and I had been married for eight years already, without an ounce of help from the state. Now, in 2004, we had a chance to make our bond legal, albeit at tremendous psychic cost to millions of decent, God-fearing Americans, who considered the sanctity of their own marriages suddenly at risk.

In September, Donna and I went on vacation to Provincetown for a week, and we decided to get married there. Unlike our first marriage at the dinner table, this marriage was a cold, calculated legal move. The week before vacation, we went to get our blood drawn for the medical certificate. It turned out that neither of us had syphilis, and our doctors pronounced us eligible for marriage. We drove to the Cape, checked into our beach cottage, and went to town hall to fill out the application for marriage. The town clerk congratulated us and gave us a list of justices of the peace. We had to wait three days, the legally required cooling-off period, before scheduling the wedding. For a justice of the peace, our innkeeper recommended a friend of his, a Provincetown old-timer who needed the business. I called her up. Judge Millie, as I will call her, was on disability and asked that we pay her in cash, so as not to confuse the authorities. She also pointed out that she was desperately in debt, and that the state-set fees for justices of the peace (seventy-five dollars) didn't begin to cut it. We should feel free to pay whatever additional "donation" we could for her services. We agreed on a time and place. She already had a five o'clock marriage scheduled, but would squeeze us in at four at the rotary in the West End of town, overlooking the marshes. She encouraged us to exchange vows, but very *short ones*.

The wedding was exactly what we'd hoped for. It took less than fifteen minutes. Donna wore a pink cotton skirt and Chinese shoes with beads embroidered in the shape of flowers. I wore white linen slacks and a little red sweater. Judge Millie wore a giant black robe that made her perspire in the bright sun; she smelled of alcohol. Donna and I exchanged two-sentence vows, including promises to be honest with each other, to fail, and to keep trying—goals we believed we could fulfill. There were no witnesses (none are required in Massachusetts), and Judge Millie pronounced us married. Then we took photos of each other, using the disposable camera I'd bought at the drugstore for this purpose. We gave Judge Millie a manila envelope with $150 in tens and twenties, got in our Toyota Corolla, and drove to a clam shack for a soft-serve chocolate ice-cream cone (me) and a glass of white table wine (Donna).

The Certainty of Abandonment and Loss

Throughout our ten-year relationship, Donna and I have been certain that each will be abandoned by the other. Consequently, we remain ever vigilant and . . . well, frankly . . . paranoid.

Perhaps due to a failure of imagination, each of us anticipates the other's betrayal according to a precise transcript of what happened in our previous relationships. Donna's former lover left her for a younger woman, so Donna believes I will inevitably do the same. Never mind that I am not the Babe Magnet that her former lover was. Never mind that I don't have a fraction of her former lover's charm, income, or ability to hold my liquor. Donna is nevertheless certain that every day when I report to the Y for my morning workout, or take the T to my state job defending indigents accused of rape and murder, I will pluck up some sweet young thing, ravish her, and run off to Tahiti. Donna does not confine her fears to the rational.

Neither do I, of course, but I have good reason for my paranoia. My previous lover died of cancer, so I am convinced that Donna will do the same. To prove my theory, Donna came into our relationship with a solid track record of previous bouts of cancer, three abdominal surgeries, six weeks of radiation, and a year of chemotherapy. And sure enough, just to scare the shit out of me, six years into our relationship, Donna had a recurrence. As I had done with my previous lover, I now went to the hospital with Donna, wrung my hands waiting for the surgeon's report, slept in the chair at her bedside for a week, disobeyed the nurses, ate her food, brought her takeout from McDonald's, and planned to kill myself after she died.

For the next ten months, I took Donna to chemotherapy every Monday morning, and we'd cap the day off with a matinee at the multiplex cinema next to the health center. The movies produced in late 2000 and early 2001, by and large, sucked. But we were living our own melodrama, and despite the fact that Donna survived this ordeal, I remain convinced that she will die on me. I believe I'm carcinogenic.

This was the year that made our marriage four-dimensional. It had weight and shape and depth, and now *time*.

Loss, Continued

My wife and I are middle-aged. It is our season of mothers and fathers dying. They are dropping like flies, left and right. They ruled our lives, and now—poof—they're gone.

In the last three years Donna and I have gone to several funerals: her mother's, my father's, her father's. And we have mourned another sort of death—my own. (Just before dying, my father signed a codicil to his will, disowning me and declaring me dead. This had nothing to do with Donna, whom he had liked, or with our relationship, which seemed to amuse him. It had to do with my having written a memoir revealing my Jewish heritage—an identity far more complicated than lesbianism.)

Families are proof that love and loss go hand in hand, but marriage can be a sort of compensation. Donna and I collect our losses and grow closer, like two stitches pulled more tightly together. We fill the gaps for each other, growing into the holes left behind. We double up and increase our resistance; we are twice as brave. We can deny only half as much as we used to as single people. Together we take off into flight and soar over our past and into our future. Our nets are unfurled. Sometimes our nets need mending. You can't do these things alone, or with the people you grew up with; they haunt your imagination. You need a wife for this sort of thing, to leave gravity, to return to earth, to bounce off again.

The Marital Bed

Our lily pad. It sits in the middle of the room, facing the sun. We spend sleepless nights plotting revenge here. We spend hours wondering what went wrong, and then more hours making love, and then more hours floating in our bodies. She tells me her dreams in the morning. We make new ones each night. We snore into each other's ears here, and toss the covers and yank the covers and flop around in the stupidity of sleep. We are most married with our arms and legs flung across each other, unselfconscious, unconscious.

We wash the sheets and make the bed, and now that we are Old Marrieds, we sleep less and spend more time watching the years vanish. The city sizzles outside the window, and we wait until it's safe to wake. We are madly in love, and only the solidity of the days that stretch before and behind us give lie to our sense that we are suspended in midair, that all our intentions amount to nothing but ideas, thin and permeable.

The Daily Grind

My wife and I snap to attention at the buzz of the alarm. We take turns with the hair dryer, the nail clipper, the cuticle scissors. We reach for the nylons and rub lotion on our elbows and begin the day, and then the next day, and the next, and the next. We share a calendar. We share a tube of toothpaste, a bottle of wine, a cold. We share a joke, a fight, a bank account, an apartment, a dog and a cat who consider us divisible. We share doubts about the dog and cat.

She goes to her office, I to mine. And then we call each other in the middle of the day. What's your day like? What are you doing? I miss you. What shall we eat? Who will call the plumber? Who will call our friends? I miss you. Hours go by when we do not think of each other. It happens. I'm sure it happens.

Marriage, the Creature

Ten years in, you realize that marriage is a breathing organism that grows with you. Regardless of what you thought you were raising, you now have a preteen on your hands, a restless, rambunctious ten-year-old marriage that thinks it knows everything, but that still has a lot of surprises left. We're watching this kid grow, and it's got a zillion things up its sleeve, delights and disappointments, and every so often, we feel like slapping it around and taking it to Disneyland. Well, maybe not Disneyland, but Provincetown. Or St. Thomas. Or Pitigliano. Sometimes we are sorry. You never know when you travel with a ten-year-old marriage. Sometimes it gets cranky, but it can be so easily distracted!

The Long Haul

We don't answer the phone. Who goes there? We pull the covers over our heads and wait it out together. We hibernate.

Months go by. Years. We crawl out of bed to see what's new in the world. We double-park and return all the videos and library books and pay all the late fees. We forgive ourselves our trespasses. We eat our daily bread and chocolate. We pray and hold hands. Forever and ever.

PRESERVED IN SALT:
HOW *EMERIL LIVE!* AND EGYPTOLOGY
ARE SAVING MY MARRIAGE

Liza Wieland

My husband cried as he drove away. I could tell this by the fog on his glasses and by the way he held one hand up in front of his face so that we would think he was waving. I stood on the front porch at my parents' house in Atlanta, holding our five-year-old daughter, who stared resolutely over my shoulder at the front door, refusing to look at the disappearing car. Though it was January and bitterly cold, about seventeen degrees, neither my daughter nor I wore shoes. My feet on the wooden slats of the porch were the opaque white of uncooked fish, or alabaster, heavy, dense stone, difficult if not impossible to move.

But move they would, we would. Moving seems to be what we do these days. My husband was returning to our house in eastern North Carolina, to begin a full-time tenure-track teaching job. My daughter and I left later that afternoon for Fresno, California, where I am tenured at the state university and have taught since 1991, where, contractually, I am obligated to finish out the academic year. A small thing, really, we tell each other, a few months' separation. My husband has the dog and the house on the Neuse River near Oriental, North Carolina, the beautiful view, the peace and quiet, the wonderful new friends. I have our daughter, an easy teaching schedule, our old friends, Trader Joe's, relatively inexpensive California wine. "You can do it," our friends said, grimacing. And it's true.

You can do it. You can just split up; couples just split up, and then each half is what it was before, more or less, and alone. Somebody has the kid, somebody else has the dog, the house. Usually somebody doesn't want to split and somebody else does. Often there's another man or another woman or a long history of difficulties. So ours isn't this kind of split, not divorce. And it's not the truly awful split, which is death, when there's just an end, when somebody doesn't ever come home. Or come inside. My husband's father was working in his backyard, and then literally in one stroke, he was gone forever.

In the beginning, what seems like ancient history: January of 1996. When I walked into a classroom at Fresno State to begin teaching an advanced fiction workshop, I noticed an older male student sitting in the front row—older, that is, than most of the rest of that class. This student always raised his hand before speaking, and he volunteered for everything, to turn in the first story of the semester, to write and deliver the first critique, to answer questions, to correct me, which he did with astonishing frequency and gusto, but also with tact. Not the old guy, I groaned inwardly whenever his hand went up, not the old guy again. He never missed a class; he told me he had started college years before and dropped out, but this time he would go the distance. When our daughter asked recently what was the first word her father ever said to me, I knew the answer immediately. He said, "Here." He said it twice a week for five months. It came to sound like a promise, like a vow.

From the earliest days of our marriage, we were trying to figure out where "here" should be. We wanted someplace off the beaten path, water to sail on or walk beside, and quiet in which to write. We spent our summers driving around the country to look for this cheap, quiet place, surveying and sometimes buying sailboats we thought we could live on. The third summer after our daughter was born, we found a house we could afford, in Arapahoe, North Carolina, where there is only one traffic light in the whole county and more registered sailboats than residents. The house is on a gravel road off another gravel road, the middle house of five. The view south is six miles across the river and southeast to the horizon, where the Neuse empties into the Pamlico Sound. The only use you'll have for the word *crowd*, we were told, is to describe the stars on a clear night. We sold our big house in Fresno and transported our possessions across the country, knowing that we would have to spend some more time in California, for a few years, until I could retire. I did not ever imagine that it would be time apart.

In our new life without father, without husband, my daughter and I have established new rituals. Crying is a ritual these days. I am reading to her, for instance, and am moved by the story. My voice breaks; she asks if I'm crying and I admit that I am. She tells me not to do it, but by then it's too late. Or she's tired or hungry and she says, I can't help thinking about Papa, and the floodgates open. She says she knows she'll cry when she sees him again, and then she does it, as if to practice. At night, nearly every night, when I kiss her in the dark, move my lips over her cheek, her face tastes salty. I tell her this makes me think of our wedding and the gospel the priest chose: "You are the salt of the earth." She likes to imagine our wedding, believing, in fact, that she was present in the past and part of her own future, somehow let loose in time.

What is it, she asks me, why do people cry? Why do we cry when we're happy *and* when we're sad or hurt? I tell her what I know or think I know: that the body does not distinguish between emotional and physical pain; the muscles around the lachrymal glands receive a message from the brain, then tighten and squeeze out tears. Tears contain high levels of the hormones ACTH and prolactin, endorphins (which we know are mood-altering and pain-killing), as well as thirty times more manganese than is found in blood, suggesting that human tears can concentrate and remove harmful substances from the body. Prolactin in humans controls fluid balance; by the age of eighteen women have 60 percent more prolactin than men, which may explain why women seem to cry more often. I tell her that sadness—like happiness—is an intense feeling of being alive, of having essence. I try to explain to her my own nonscientific theory: that crying is about weight or heft, that we cry when our bodies feel too light or too heavy to bear or hold on to language.

And yet, there are two men who keep us company. The first is Emeril Lagasse, the popular chef and cooking-show host. The second is Zahi A. Hawass, the eminent Egyptologist, head of Egypt's Supreme Council of Antiquities, director of the Giza Plateau. How is it that in the absence of my beloved, I can be comforted by two middle-aged, portly, slightly balding emcee types? There is little physical resemblance: my husband has a broad chest and colossal biceps; he was recruited to play guard on his college football team. He's built for blocking and for carrying a woman up a flight of stairs. But they remind me of my husband in other ways. For one thing, they're both smart. "Like Papa is," our daughter says. They both love food, or seem to—I don't know this for a fact about Dr. Hawass, but he describes with eagerness ancient Egyptian funeral feasts and the importance of palm wine. They're both demystifiers of experience, purveyors of clarity, and most excellent talkers.

My favorite of Emeril Lagasse's standard phrases these days is "I'll be right back"; given the context of this essay, I probably don't need to explain why. But really I love all his talk: "Pork fat rules." "You could put this on a bumper and it would taste good." "Aw yeah, babe." He has, like my husband, an inclination toward non sequitur. Assembling a gumbo the other night, Emeril said, "This explains why my friend Marcelle wrote that book, *Who's Your Mama, Are You Catholic and Can You Make a Roux?*" Emeril cooks the way my husband does, by smell, by touch, by instinct, like a guy who's never used a recipe, a guy who's not scared of thirty cloves of garlic and most of a bottle of wine dumped into the pot.

All this time, Emeril is, in his own words, "happy, happy, happy." He asks his studio audience "Can you feel the love?" (alas, no; for me the love is three thousand miles away), and when they applaud, he says it again, "Aw yeah, babe." But it's not that Emeril Lagasse's kitchen talk is sexy—in fact, it's not, not at all, or not in the usual way. It's the talk of long marriages, settled marriages, the phrases that reassure us: *Stick around. I don't mind the fat. Stay with it. It's not really that difficult. It just takes a little patience. You don't have to call 911. It's gonna be okay.* There is on his show a kind of cult of the (supposedly unsexy) domestic: Emeril tells us when someone admired or beloved is "in the house." The percussionist Don Gibbs; Hilda, his mother; Coco, who owns the shop where he buys fish.

Emeril's signature ingredient is a mixture of salt and spices called "essence." Look it up, babe. *Esse,* to be. *The permanent as contrasted with the accidental element of being. The individual, real or ultimate nature of a thing, especially as opposed to its existence; the properties or attributes by means of which something can be placed in its proper class or identified as being what it is.* Might all these windy dictionaryisms also describe marriage? *A volatile entity.* Aw yeah, babe. *One that possesses or exhibits a quality in abundance, as if in concentrated form.* And last but not least, *of the essence:* of the utmost importance. How is marriage of the essence? Let me count the ways.

Emeril Lagasse appears to be an instinctive teacher too, as my husband is. He's said of himself, "I love to teach." I've read in several different places that as a chef, as a mentor to chefs, he listens far more than he talks. In all ways, he has a good ear; you can tell by the way he responds to comments from the audience—he hears everything. You can detect an attention to the sizzle, the roil, as much as the presence of other, more seemingly appropriate senses.

My husband, who is exactly Emeril's age, forty-eight, was once a very good clarinet player. "But I've lost the embouchure," he said to me early in our dealings (nothing like a little French to impress the professor). *Embouchure,* to flow into. *The position of the lips, tongue, and teeth in playing a woodwind instrument. To put a mouth on it.* As in taste or kiss. As in talk.

So Emeril Lagasse is saving my marriage. I should say here that *saving* may be too strong a word since my marriage isn't lost or even close. It is, though, quite literally misplaced. I mean something like Emeril's helping to preserve my marriage, to keep it intact, which is the problem; this marriage is not intact. We're living a whole continent apart, though the modern world makes this easier. We talk every evening on the telephone. We e-mail two or three times a day. We have had from the beginning, from that first class in 1996, a romance based on language, on conversation, on words. Sometimes I think I don't know who I am if I'm not talking to this man.

Nefertiti is also a big deal these days. She is, as Emeril would say, in the house. My daughter and I watch a particular DVD over and over: a British Egyptologist, Dr. Joanne Fletcher, proves (at least to my unscientific satisfaction) that a certain wrecked-looking mummy found in the Valley of the Kings (where King Tut's tomb was opened in 1922) is Nefertiti, whose long-necked, achingly beautiful image may be the most famous Egyptian artifact of all. What is most striking about this mummy, to both scholars and the general public, is that the mouth and chest cavity have been deliberately smashed open. Her heart is broken, my daughter said suddenly after what seemed like the eleven-millionth viewing of the video. Dr. Fletcher explains this disfiguring as the work of Nefertiti's enemies, an act that would keep her from communing with the gods and attaining immortality. For if she cannot eat or speak to the dead, identify herself, tell them who she is, she cannot join them.

Dr. Fletcher's staff performs some amazing feats of computerized reconstruction to prove this mummy is in fact the Egyptian queen and, in so doing, gives Nefertiti back her name, locates her in the public, historical sense. The last scenes of the video show a perfectly preserved Nefertiti rising from her funeral bier, driving a chariot to Karnak, the temple she built with her husband, standing in a column of diffused sunlight, and proclaiming herself to the gods.

For my daughter, Egyptology is mostly mummies and curses, and the link between the living and the dead. The living, breathing constant in her obsession with Egyptology is Dr. Zahi Hawass, to whom she refers as the man "in charge of all things ancient." We first met Dr. Hawass in *National Geographic* programs, in his books and videos, in the books and videos of others. Zahi Hawass is, in fact, everywhere, and he has come to seem like a member of the family. When we watched the IMAX movie about the pyramids at Giza, and he was nowhere in evidence, we felt a little lost, bereft, then relieved (*elated* is not too strong a word) to find him in one of the special features, a short subject about the making of the film. We believe we have seen Dr. Hawass in all moods, from all angles. We were watching when he was excavating a tomb in Bahariya and received a mild electric shock from some piece of his lighting equipment and suddenly disappeared from camera view. We two held our breath until he came back to us, lying bemusedly in the dust. We know that he had a heart attack in 1992 just before announcing his discovery of the statues of Inty-Shedu at Giza. We know that he had a childhood fear of the dark, and this fear persisted into young adulthood until he allowed himself to be lowered to the bottom of a Roman well in Kom Abu Billo. We know he went to law school but soon found it wasn't for him. We know he has a son. I suppose we are something of a Zahi Hawass fan club, my daughter and I. He is, as my daughter recently observed, the Emeril of Egyptology, though the spices that inform the talk of Dr. Hawass are myrrh and cassia, and the salt is natron, the divine preservative used in mummification. Extracted from dry riverbeds, natron is heaped upon the eviscerated dead and left for seventy days, after which time the body is washed, wrapped in clean linen, and returned to the family.

We know these things because Zahi Hawass has told us, and I have come to realize his voice reminds me of my husband's. Obviously, I mean tone and timbre rather than accent. Their voices have the same low pitch, the same warmth, not exactly like gravel, more like smooth gray stones in the sun. Their voices are, I must say, *manly*. When I close my eyes and listen to the music of Dr. Hawass's voice, I hear my husband, particularly our first telephone conversation. While I listened, rapt then moved, he explained that though I had told him my home number, he had forgotten part of it. But he knew I was house-sitting for a faculty member, and so he searched through the university directory (all the way to *T*) to find the rest. At the end of this conversation, I said, "I should let you go," and he said, "No."

When I was in middle school—which, as everyone who has survived it knows, is truly a bizarre and seemingly endless middle ground, a suspension between childhood and full-throttle adolescence—the principal was a man named William Stephens. The middle school is now named for him, which should give some sense of his talents as an educator and administrator. It is not an overstatement to say I adored Bill Stephens, from our first dealings in 1971 until his death in 1996. I suppose our earliest encounters were routine, academic, and I don't remember them. I have a grainy photograph of him on a tour bus in Washington, D.C., blowing a tasteful but nevertheless verboten Bazooka bubble gum bubble. What I do remember is asking him to let me give a speech at my eighth-grade honors convocation—for no good reason; I wasn't anywhere near valedictory status. I just wanted to talk publicly, reflect on my recent past. He said yes in a way that made me think he'd already been considering the possibility. Bill Stephens had that gift: he'd already entertained your best ideas about yourself, and he could wait patiently for you to come to these notions on your own. In ninth and tenth grades, I went to his office, and he always put aside whatever he was doing and talked to me while I sat and wept. Sometime during those years he introduced me to Steven Sondheim's *A Little Night Music* and the French writer Antoine de Saint-Exupery. His usual consolation was that it would all be over soon. The afterlife, he said. I would graduate from high school and go to college, and of course he was right.

I saw Bill Stephens every time I returned to Atlanta, from college, from graduate school in New York, from teaching gigs in Pennsylvania, Colorado, and California. We met for lunch or coffee. He occupied a certain place in my heart, a place for which there may well be no language. He was never married and had no children. He was the only person I knew who had gone through a whole life without one or the other of these attachments, and so he was a model of sorts for me. Without his example, I didn't know how it could be done. And so it seems entirely logical to me that within weeks of his death in 1996, I met my husband, and six months later made up my mind to marry him.

What am I talking about here? What does any of this have to do with Emeril Lagasse, Egyptology, and living in this bicoastal marriage? I think part of it is that memory is a kind of endorphin, a painkiller, and that seeing a stretch of causality is consolation. It helps to think about how my husband came into my life, and when. Or maybe I'm talking about immortality, which is essentially the quality of being present when you're really absent—which both my husband and I have to make possible to get through these months.

I have always known exactly when I began to think of my husband as more than just my student. This happened aboard an airplane, on Easter Sunday 1996, flying back to California from Atlanta, where I'd spent spring break with my family. That same week I was part of a panel at the Associated Writing Programs conference, about gender stereotypes in the creative writing classroom. I used Deborah Tannen's business model and talked about the ways women tend to lead groups of people. But bubbling under my assertions about delegation and dynamics were of course sexual politics and issues of power. I began to think about how different it was for a female teacher to become involved with a male student, how traditional gender roles collide with the fact of who's assigning the grade at the end of the class. On the airplane, my not-yet husband, his *essence*, you might say, floated into my mind. The sound of his voice, the vivid yet tasteful shirts he wore, his arms, that he observed the route I took to class and waited about halfway, first with one cup of coffee, then with a second cup, for me. I liked him, I realized. A lot. I was curious. This is what can happen when you're traveling, in the ether, neither here nor there. It felt like the mental equivalent of how and what I could see from the airplane: vastly, extensively, the whole curve of the earth or of experience, ahead and behind. I was suspended, wrapped in my traveling clothes, jubilant, waiting for the new life that would, I suddenly felt sure, come after the end of the semester.

Two and a half months later, after he asked me out for a beer, I was terrifically nervous. Many times that afternoon, I felt I should call and cancel: during our conversations before class and in my office, I had come to know the complexities of this man's life (two daughters, aged eleven and nineteen, a divorce, a failed romance in between, an interest in pursuing graduate work in creative writing), and it seemed like a lot to take on. At thirty-six, I wanted a serious arrangement that would last forever. I was tired of living alone, finally. I didn't want to make a mistake; I had already made enough of them. When I was about to give in to my cold feet, I heard a song on the radio: Sarah McLachlan, that high, pure voice of hers singing to me as I stood poised on the brink of something I knew was huge, momentous, admonishing me not to let my life pass me by. This was as clear a message as I've ever received. I didn't call to cancel, and the rest, as the saying goes, is history. Or the future, actually. The rest is the future.

The meaning of that song and its place in the grand scheme dawns on me now, in the harsh light of my husband's absence: it's about the way the past and the future are woven together, inextricable and sometimes indistinguishable. The real trouble with our separation is that, despite the presence of my daughter, it seems very like my old life, my single life, its loneliness as visceral as hunger. But visceral as in true, pure, *essential*. I lived alone for a long time, without spouse, without children. I found a way to measure that solitary life, make it into something warm and nourishing, make it work, use its lack of distraction to my advantage. I wrote all the time, wrote four books in six years. I had the freedom in which to excavate, get at all that writing.

I need Emeril Lagasse and Zahi Hawass because they remind me daily of the man I really love, and the truth is, I need reminding. Marriage, as we all know, takes time and care, it's here and now. Even a five-year-old child (mine anyway) is not as demanding as a marriage. She's at school or asleep when I work; she doesn't notice when I come to bed at two and get up again at five to go back to work.

But that hunger: to be held in my husband's large arms, to be kissed, to be carried up that flight of stairs. Hunger is why I need Emeril Lagasse now: for the food. Did I mention the food? The lovingly and bountifully plated duck confit nachos, crawfish profiteroles, grilled lamb with red wine reduction, brie and raspberries in puff pastry? I can hardly wait to taste it all. Cooking, though, is making something in order to make it disappear. Enter Dr. Zahi Hawass, the authority on preservation, on bringing the old stuff back, making sure it doesn't disappear again. And enter, at last, the ghost of Bill Stephens. There's a phrase of Saint-Exupery's I've never forgotten: *"l'amour ce n'est pas regarder l'un a l'autre, mais regarder dans la meme direction."* Love is not two people looking at each other, but looking in the same direction. This is finally and irrevocably why I married my husband, why I miss him, why I am still married to him. Because we are looking in the same direction.

We are looking forward to life on the Neuse River in eastern North Carolina, a place in which we will cook and write and sail and live out our days. My husband and I have acquired for ourselves a small house made of cement block and furnished it with our possessions, our small treasures, and like the ancient Egyptians, we are ever mindful of the river's flooding. Right now we live elsewhere until we can live there together forever. The Neuse is brackish; when you drift your fingers in it and bring them to your lips, you taste the same saltiness as tears. When we first cross the river, in New Bern, on our way home but still twenty miles from the house, we can feel the salt in the air and on our faces. *Home*, we say to each other, to our daughter, just the one word. Tears fill our eyes, but our vision is clear.

MURMURS
Audrey Schulman

At my regular medical checkup I mentioned my heart murmur. I'd always imagined my heart's idiosyncrasy as having no more consequence than a drummer adding a stylish *shush* to the *boom-ba* of a drum roll. But now, being in my forties, I thought I should check my assumption.

What kind of murmur? my doctor asked. She explained that one type of murmur was no problem, but research showed the other kind got worse over time.

Biking home from the doctor's, with an appointment for an echocardiogram, I found myself conscious of each thumping beat of my heart. *La Dup Ladup LaDupp.* I found I could now picture with little effort the first of the stabbing pains arcing down my right arm. My body flailing and falling to the ground next to traffic.

What scared me the most about this image was what would happen to my two- and four-year-old sons. This was the kind of mental jump I made a lot, from knowing I was going in for an echocardiogram next Tuesday to imagining my children growing up without a mom. I could imagine this disaster particularly easily since I lost my own mom when I was five—not to death but to a vindictive custody battle. My siblings and I grew up in a tall town house in which we were alone during the day except for a hired woman who hardly ever came down from her top-floor apartment, whom we never turned to in times of need, not when my seven-year-old brother had a chunk of flesh the size of a plum ripped out of his leg by a German shepherd, not the time I stabbed my hand by mistake with a carving knife, not the time I was molested on the subway. Each time something bad happened, we also did not call our dad at work. He was a busy executive and none of us knew his phone number.

The night after my doctor scheduled the echocardiogram, I told my husband about the upcoming appointment. I mentioned it off-hand, faced away, as though discussing groceries or a car repair. Doug didn't like it when I acted fearful about what might happen in the future. This was a tension between us.

Really, Doug said, what will the test show?

If my heart murmur is degenerative or not, I answered. Even the word *degenerative* scared me, a word that camouflaged with soft syllables a death as belabored as though the gasping sufferer had to haul her body toward death at a run.

Doug nodded and moved away. He assumed automatically the results would be fine. He had stated several times that because of my healthy diet, vitamins, and biking, I would outlive him by decades.

He wasn't the kind of person to worry, had been to the doctor only three times in the last decade. He grew up in the suburbs with his mom and dad. Many of his childhood memories concerned playing in the neighborhood pool. With such a past, the future to him was a comfortable place.

At the echocardiogram, the technician placed an ultrasound wand, goopy with Vaseline, against my ribs. *Ka-shush ka-shush ka-shush*, the sound of my pulse filled the room. On the monitor an image appeared. In the midst of a cave-like nook was a valve, a triangle of flesh flapping up and down in the current of invisible blood. *Ka-shush. Ka-Shush.*

I watched closely, with no idea how to read what I saw on the monitor. Was this a damaged muscle clearly flapping its distress in a code I couldn't read, or was this a strong, relatively young heart with one tiny quirk?

Unsure which of the four valves was the one murmuring, the technician moved the wand to examine the next one. She told me many murmurs were developed during childhood fevers. I could picture this, no one noticing I was ill with my mom not around and my dad working more than full-time. So much in my family and in me had been damaged during childhood, it made sense this era would leave its mark on my body, its fingers clenched too tightly around my heart.

I stared at the muscle. Without its continuous work, I would not have my children, my husband, or my life. Without the constant tip-tapping of this tiny toe to a music I couldn't hear, I would have nothing at all.

It beat on and on, working for now in spite of all past insults to it.

A few months ago, I had Doug give our two children a bath. In general, he isn't as careful about their safety as I am. I had to nag him for a year solid before he would fasten the children's car seats properly, taking the time to not only snap the harnesses into the chair between their legs, but to clip the top of the harnesses closed in front of their chests. What, he would say, I'm just driving to the store.

That night, I had a lot of work to do and figured the bath didn't need my supervision. I listened to Doug's progress in the background. The water running, then Doug saying, Oh, you want some bubbles? Hey hey hey, not that much. The kids splashing about, then Doug saying, Sweetie, don't drink that water. I stepped into the bathroom to check. What had been a full bottle of dandruff shampoo was emptied and floating in the suds. Like many people who can imagine disasters in their personal lives, I worried about the environment also, taking the kids to marches against global warming and deforestation. One of the activist alerts I'd read just that morning had listed the most dangerous home beauty products sold in America. Number one on the list had been some dandruff shampoo. Staring at the bottle floating in my children's bath, I couldn't recall the particular name of the shampoo or what the possible results were. Cancer? Skin disease? Neuralgic problems? Whatever it was, my kids' bare butts were sitting in what might be dangerous, my four-year-old was wiping his eyes with a washcloth saturated in it, my two-year-old held a capful of it to his lips.

From my e-mail lists, my fears were continually reinforced with horror stories of chemical poisonings and improper childproof devices. Doug instead read about sports teams and successful business ventures. He looked at our children in the bath and saw innocent bubbles. I saw our kids lolling around in a Superfund site.

I quickly drained the water and dried the children off, explaining the potential danger of the shampoo. In situations like this, I'm not sure what is reasonable to do, what is reality. Not in terms of my own health, or my children's health, or the state of the world. Many of my fears developed when I first became pregnant and realized I would be ultimately responsible for the young life I carried. I'd seen what the best intentions of my parents had done.

It's just shampoo, Doug said. I use it all the time. You're exaggerating the danger. His voice was tight.

Never, I replied. You couldn't pay me to exaggerate, not for a trillion billion gazillion dollars. Exaggerate, me? Ha!

My joke sounded forced and Doug's smile didn't quite reach his eyes.

Three years ago, my friend Lauren mentioned that the most common time for men to have affairs is when their wives are pregnant. She mentioned this casually, as an interesting fact.

My God, I said and rubbed my belly, outsized with my second pregnancy. The child inside kicked as though alarmed.

I considered this fact for weeks, wondering about the way sex for Doug and me had slacked off since having our first child. Exhaustion was what I previously assumed was the cause, as well as our different schedules now that I fell dead asleep at ten thirty and he stayed up until midnight. For the first time, I considered the pretty new woman working at his office and the evenings he returned home late.

Our first baby, Corey, had wrought so many changes in me. Before he was born, I'd always been a gentle and humorous person. Now I was continually in a barely controlled temper from taking care of a demanding two-year-old while heavily pregnant. My body had gained weight and was aging. It would be understandable if Doug found someone attractive who was younger and less angry.

After the kids went to bed, we generally sat in front of the TV with the sound turned off. This was our compromise between his love of the TV and my hatred of it. If he kept the sound down and left it on sports, I didn't find my eyes drawn magnetically toward it. In this way I could cuddle in next to him and read. Before we discovered this solution, we would sit in different rooms, him with his TV, me with my book, and we'd call to each other once an hour or so—How was your day? Did I tell you what Corey did? I miss you—our voices echoing down the hall between us, trying to pull the other closer.

This is also our dynamic in how to deal with the differences between my fears and his confidence. We call across the distance between us, our voices lonely and trying, our push-me-pull-you of love, until we can sometimes work out a solution that pleases neither of us entirely, but both of us more than before. Perhaps this is the secret of every marriage, a way to navigate the friction inherent in long-term intimacy. When it came to planting the backyard, Doug wanted fruit and I wanted flowers. He liked grass and I liked trees. While we were planting it, we fought for real estate, but after five years of growing, the yard has bloomed with both of our loves, an abundant background of peaches and peonies, of paulownia trees and lawn. Sometimes after Doug and I have argued, I go out to the backyard and inhale the lush scent of growing plants. The yard reminds me of what my marriage can be at its best, something richer for all the differences.

One night while he stared at the TV, I asked him about his late evenings at the office. Sitting next to him, in front of the scene of hockey players silently slamming each other into the sideboards, I asked him abruptly if he was having an affair.

No, he said, but . . .

My heart skipped a beat.

Sometimes, he said, I stay late at the office to catnap before coming home. He didn't bother to mention that after a full day of work he had to return to an exhausting two-year-old and a resentful wife. He only said he was tired. He admitted these naps in a voice with which another man might admit an affair.

Hearing his shame, I looked into his eyes. They were what attracted me at first, along with his chest hair. If I placed my nose right in the center of his chest and inhaled deeply, I could pull into my lungs his scent of maple syrup, baking bread, and sperm. I could hold the smell of him there in my body like a balm. He is a quiet man. Unlike me, he is not overly emotional or confessional, just honest. I'd always been able to count on his steadiness. Before him I had a boyfriend to whom I'd say, Do the dishes, do the dishes, do the dishes, and he would forget before I'd finished speaking. Doug, if he says he'll do the dishes, he does the dishes. All those love songs on the radio, all they talk about is that first chemical flush of love. I don't know why they emphasize that part so much. What's more important to me is what comes after those few months of jangly nerves and starry eyes. Does the guy do the dishes, does he respect my work, is he considerate? This is what supports not my feeling of being "in love" but my much more steady feeling of love.

Sitting next to him on the couch that evening, I remembered a study I'd read about how couples perceive their marital conflicts.

Each couple had to pick a fight while being watched and recorded by the study's psychologists. Interviewed afterward, each husband said the fight didn't bother him much at all, pshaw, it was nothing, while each wife wrung her hands, saying it was terrible. The interesting detail is that during the fight, the study showed the sweat glands and pulse of the husband and wife were displaying the same amount of distress.

I am unsure how much Doug might be hiding his own fears, trying to act tough.

I can tell you one story. Six days after Corey's birth, while I was breast-feeding our tiny firstborn and looking down at the side of his head nestled into me, I saw the slightest blue shadow behind one ear. How would a bruise get there, I wondered, and the next day I mentioned it to the pediatrician during the baby's first-week appointment. The doctor bent back the ear to look and then his voice changed. You're taking him to Children's Hospital right now. I'll call ahead for you.

His voice scared me, so I went home instead to pack all the items a day in the hospital might require. I was stalling. The last week had been so filled with doctors and alarm. After two days of labor, Corey had been born with a fever, so they did a spinal tap before he was three hours old to check for meningitis. The next day some doctor botched Corey's circumcision, so his penis looked like a hot dog someone had halfway sawed through. Then two days later I had to take him back to the hospital to check the possibility of his liver failing. With each of these medical emergencies, I coped, I raged and roared and protected, but now, today, I was growing tired. I hadn't slept more than two hours at a time for a week, and the roller coaster of all these emergencies hadn't helped me ride my crashing hormones with anything resembling grace. This morning, I'd wept for forty minutes over the difficulties of trying to assemble a car seat.

Doug, when I called him at work, was quiet. What does the doctor think the bruise is from? he asked.

I don't know. I don't care, I said. I don't want to go in there. It's full of germs. Corey's too young; he hasn't yet built up any antibodies. While talking, I packed diapers and breast pads and everything else I could possibly imagine needing. I was trying not to cry. One problem with crying around Doug was I'd never seen him cry, not once. It made me feel weak.

Do you want me to come along? he asked. I knew he had a lot of work to do, I knew he got tense about work. I looked down at my hands, filled with bottles and wipes, all these items that even after a week of experience I didn't feel I knew how to use. I was just imitating other *real* mothers in the hope that people would be fooled. Hospital, I thought, and the fear was so intense that my vision flickered out for a second, the way a computer will when it overloads. To get pregnant, Doug and I had had to do IVF. This baby was everything. This mewling child was all.

Yes, I said, I want you to come.

We waited all day in the hospital, me wrapping Corey up tightly in his receiving blankets and holding him far from anything he could touch, as though then any germs couldn't get to him, as though with the blankets I could cushion his head now from all past harm. The doctor, when we finally got to see him, looked like some bearded Russian poet. He touched Corey's ear as gently as you'd touch a tropical flower. MRI, he said. You had a difficult birth. We're worried he could have bleeding in the brain.

I was so tired, so tired. I hunched in my seat, staring at my baby, unable to say a word.

And in the MRI room, a gleaming room of white tile and looming machines, the technicians wrapped in towels our baby who was the size of a small cat, and then they covered his body with a lead apron big enough for an adult. His tiny head was placed in the exact center under those attentive machines. Doug and I were told to stand back, away from the radiation. We had to stand back out of the red circle, and as the machines whirred into life and clicked and thunked, our baby began to cry and wiggle his head about in fear.

Immediately, the machines stopped.

They said his head had to stay still, otherwise the image would be too fuzzy to read. They could do nothing if he wasn't still.

And I lost all my strength. For once in my life I had had enough of doctors and hospitals and trying to protect those I loved. All I could do now was stare, mute, half-slumped against a wall, so Doug, he was the one who stepped into the area where the men had told us not to go, the area where there was radiation. Those few times, when I cannot do anymore, this is what he does, he steps forward.

He held out his hand and slid his pinkie gently into the baby's crying mouth, quieting him immediately as Corey started sucking. Doug sang lullabies in a whisper just loud enough to be audible over the machines' busy thunking, and when he turned to me, there were tears streaming down his cheeks.

The technician had me shift onto my side, and she searched with her ultrasound wand along my back for a good viewpoint of the next heart valve. Staring at my heart on the screen, I asked her if she saw anything drastically wrong. She shifted the wand slightly and told me I'd have to wait for the specialist's report.

And so I wait for the experts to decode me, to tell me if there is the rhythm of tragedy encoded in my heart.

I pray each night that the extra drag to my pulse is a perfect syncopation for Doug's even, steady beat. I pray that the rhythm of our combined beat will grow like our garden, richer from all the differences in it, from all the tensions.

Like my heartbeat, when I examine my marriage it seems a living miracle. Working silently on, ignored in the dark, it is the motor that powers the structure of my life.

MY HUSBAND, HIS GIRLFRIEND, HER HUSBAND, MY LOVER, AND OTHERS

Hannah Pine

The assumption is that my marriage is full of danger, full of threat, that it survives against all odds. None of this is the case. In fact, I would venture to say that I am in one of the most wholesome and happy marriages I know. Of course, no marriage is simple, and in it I experience a range of emotions from happy to frustrated to jealous to glad. And indeed, our vision isn't based on any utopian vision, but we think it *has vision* nevertheless.

When Henry and I set out on our path years ago, we had no map to follow for our open marriage—only warnings from others. Yet we persisted, for we thought we were making a good choice, a choice that would teach us more than we could learn from monogamy about generosity and kindness, whether we had affairs or not. So we reserved both the right to have and not to have affairs—that is, affairs are not mandatory, or necessary, for us to enjoy each other's company, to say the least. Yet we agreed: for us, affairs were acceptable, and always would be. This does not mean it always is easy, but it always feels right.

Why? Why am I *still* in an open marriage? Because I still believe it's a good choice. Because I like it.

At core, of course, *I'm still married because I still love being married to my husband.* He's the best person I know, and we have great sex—tender, dirty, lusty, kind.

And truth be told, I have come to believe, in part, that I'm *so blissfully* married because I sometimes do fuck other men. As I said before, I don't *have* to fuck other men. And my husband doesn't *have* to fuck other women. But we can and we have and we will. And in the idea that sex with someone else will not, in any way, constitute a betrayal of our love for each other resides great love and completion and commitment and trust.

To repeat, I feel lucky to count myself among those happily married.

Two weeks ago today I woke up in the arms of a new lover. Light streamed in the tall, antique windows of his wife's office downtown. He took me there because it was okay with her. After all, she'd been sleeping with my husband for a little over a year. I'd met J. the night before at the Veteran's Club, which my husband and I had joined for five dollars this year. At the Veteran's Club, you can still smoke, and cans of beer are a dollar. At one dark edge of the room there's a periscope, and you can look through it to see the rooftops of downtown. You can see his wife's building, in fact.

I'd resisted meeting J. for a while because it just seemed a little bit weird to date the husband of my husband's girlfriend. First of all, I pointed out to my husband—a very kind, very attractive, very smart man—I might not like him. I'm a bit shy and not always fond of people, but perhaps to compensate for this often I act as though I like them more than I do, mainly out of pity. I wanted to avoid this situation because of my husband's affair. If I met J. and didn't like him, but found myself compelled to act like I did . . . it could get complicated. There were others involved besides two—there were four. My husband, his lover, her husband, and me. The math of it did seem to increase the possibility of hurt feelings.

Second of all, wouldn't this make us swingers? Aesthetically, I could embrace the deeply philosophical gesture of the term *open marriage*, but I just couldn't wrap my brain around thinking of myself as a *swinger*.

Third of all, what kind of couple was this—a wife who thought I'd be into her husband? I was completely fine with my husband seeing this woman; the fact that she was in an open marriage was a relief. His affairs are of course always his business—I don't have any say—but in the past, the women who've even slightly gotten off on sleeping with a married man haven't held much appeal. There's a pornography to adultery that repels me. The language of it, the feel: when sneaking around is the thing for a woman, I'm just terribly bored on behalf of my husband.

So from what he said, this married woman sounded gentle, talented, and wise. By chance, I'd met her once on Main Street. She had been exuberantly friendly to me but not in an overly cloying fashion at all. I had liked her. But that didn't mean I wanted to meet her husband, I said. Was this ... what they *did*? So, I am apparently as prejudiced as the rest. Or was, for a few days, as I considered meeting this man.

As it turns out, I do like her husband. A whole lot. Quite to my surprise. And no one's feelings have gotten hurt. We're going to be certain they don't; we can, because we are careful. And so far, feelings have, to the contrary, been very good. We expect that to remain.

How can we be so certain? I only know that over time and with conscious effort we've learned we can do this well. There really aren't any rules in our marriage, though there are essential courtesies and kindnesses. For example, our household is one of never-raised voices (partially, it is our gentle nature, but it is also a choice). This has gone a long way toward our mutual happiness, open marriage or not.

Also, in my marriage, if we want to make plans to see someone else, we are always free to do so. We have autonomy in this decision. Of course, to the degree necessary we consider the timing and appropriateness of any new affair, but we are not beholden to ask permission to have it. This has worked for us because we are always vigilant about paying extra attention to each other—romantically, intellectually, and otherwise. Whether you're in an open marriage or not, I think paying extra-careful attention to your spouse is a must. One of the important aspects of our marriage is constant vigilance, which is actually a treat.

My impression of J. and C.'s marriage is that they also treat each other with the utmost respect and encouragement. They have curfews, particular days of the week on which they may "date." They have different rules for different people with whom they sleep. This seems to work for them and keep their marriage happy. In my marriage, we simply have the affairs when we want, and the rest remains pretty private. This also, for us, contributes to having no hurt feelings. Together we talk about the bigger issues and don't get caught up in the petty details.

For whatever reason, my own affairs have been more intermittent than Henry's. I had a six-year affair in the city where we used to live that was great apart from the fact that the man I'd had it with was, you might say, a little unreliable, albeit fantastic in bed and good for me in other ways, too. I put up with his last-minute phone calls and sudden absences from my life for a lot of reasons, not least that I was really sweet on him and cared to keep him in my life for the long haul. My husband put up with my occasional bad mood about A. not calling me because, by and large, he saw how glowing I was when I got home from seeing A. My husband is hot for me; he likes my glow.

And A. and I are still good friends. And he is friends with my husband, a bit.

The night after our wedding party (my husband's and mine, of course), A. visited the gorgeous suite of our hotel and fucked me on the couch while my husband, exhausted from shenanigans the night of the party, slept in the suite's fancy bedroom. This hadn't been planned, mind you. I didn't plan to fuck another man on the couch of the fancy hotel suite—with a valet who built a roaring fire, for my lover and me!—the second night after my wedding. But I did, and it was great. Who knew?

Does this scare you? Friends have told me it scares them, that they're just *too fragile* to have affairs. This greater claim to emotional vulnerability frustrates me. I'm a pretty sensitive person and most of my friends feel rather protective of me. Are they truly more vulnerable than I am? And this assumption that sex—sex with multiple partners—goes to vulnerability is, at best, deeply and logically flawed. Sex can be emotional, and sex can challenge or comfort our various vulnerabilities, but nothing is given as such: sex can be as meaningless or as excellent as anything else.

My affairs over the years have been good—not overly abundant, sometimes overly decadent, but always thoughtful, never unkind. Once, I got a little too hung up on a guy who treated me poorly, but my husband kindly reminded me how stupid that was. How lucky am I? I get to be married to one of the most attractive and engaging men I've ever met, and also get his advice and support when an affair goes wrong, sometimes over beer and whiskey!

But we don't sit around and talk about our affairs that often; they're our own affairs, as it were. Yet we are strong enough together that if one of us is a little lit up by a new crush, or a little deflated by a lost lover, we can deal—and better than that, we can laugh about it and learn. Once, when I slept with an old friend in a fancy hotel and Henry picked me up at the train station the next morning, I couldn't quite knock the glow off of my face. I had spent hours on the train trying to forget how exciting the night had been—not because I would compare it to any night with Henry (and nights with Henry are pretty damn good), but because it didn't seem fair to my husband to have that terribly distracted "I've had my brains fucked out" look when I greeted him at the station.

"Jesus," he said, when he saw me, rolling his eyes slightly.

"What? What?" I answered, pretending to play dumb. Of course, I made sure to put my hand on his knee as he drove home.

"Whatever," he said, to be coy. In this way, we work. Basically, even if one of us is still warm from another, we very much love each other and are certain to make this known.

I sometimes wonder whether my friends are afraid of open marriage because the married sex they are having is not appealing or frequent enough. I don't know; this is tricky terrain. I think that if you are not in a sexually appealing, or sexually interesting, or at least somewhat sexually satisfying, relationship with your spouse, open marriage is likely not the best idea—at least not until those issues are worked out to the best of your ability.

I'm still happily in an open marriage because sex with my husband is still really hot. I'm not going to go into much detail because the details of other people's sex lives don't really interest me; I find hearing them as tedious as hearing someone's dreams. Suffice it to say that we fuck, and we like it, we enjoy each other's company there.

We have found that having a successful (i.e., interesting and positive) open marriage has taken a lot of careful effort at emotionally open conversation about sex and sexual jealousy. I'm not sure everyone is up to the task. People are fragile in different ways, and some are less able to talk about such matters, even with their spouses.

Again, this is an aspect of our marriage that has evolved over time. In the beginning, our conversations were more heated and anxious. When Henry had his first affair, I'd basically sit the night out, waiting for him to come home, feeling lonely and a little bit threatened. And when he'd get home, he'd be all happy and I'd be all sad, and it was a day or so of cajoling—him telling me he loved me, me telling him I respected his freedom; me admitting my insecurities, him saying the one had nothing to do with the other; and so on. We've had more than a decade to refine such reunions. These days, when Henry comes home from being with C., I am really careful to remind myself not to say the first thing that might come to mind—which might be something stupidly jealous (and I really do believe that jealousy is among the stupidest, most selfish emotions, for its ugly individualism). Because, of course, sometimes we slip, and our small brain in its small range wonders if another person is sexier than we are—even if we know it's not true.

For our open marriage to work, we have become vigilant about not expressing the first thing that might come to mind. We have become patient with ourselves and with each other.

Certainly, I don't think nonmonogamy is for everyone, but apparently monogamy isn't for everyone, either; according to many studies, the estimated number of married couples who will at some point experience an affair is roughly half. The primary difference between—and yes, this is my own unscientific estimate here—roughly 99 percent of these marriages and my own? *We don't lie.* The sex we have is not betrayal.

Popular culture would have you believe that we are ruthless, stupid, bad people. Really, I don't exaggerate here. Let's leave aside the gossip magazines, which use horrifying scare tactics to terrorize married couples everywhere, showing photographs of actors nuzzling actresses on set, while their spouses (or soon-to-be-ex-spouses) are shopping for truly immoral thousand-dollar bags and such. What's hilarious about some of these spreads is that the nuzzling has actually taken place in a scene, as acting. However, we all know that *actors regularly fall for their leading ladies* (and actresses for their leading men). The motivation for headline obsession with this *threat* is clear: if you kiss someone, *even if you think it's not serious,* you will fall in love. A kiss is never just a kiss. A kiss is always more (possibly love) and less (disgusting) than a kiss.

We are afraid. We spend a lot of time in fear.

Popular culture would also have you believe that even *friendships with the opposite sex* are dangerous. Not only is sex dangerous, but friendship is dangerous too. Why? Because friendship with someone of the opposite sex will always lead to sex, and that, my dear, will destroy your marriage. But your marriage is already destroyed by this ugly opinion of you, of your body and its fragile desire.

Even worse, these threats are presented as a defense of marriage and of love.

But sex is not love. Sex can be love, but sex is not always love. I love sex with my husband. I also love him. But if you are in love with someone—your spouse, for example—and you have sex with someone else? This doesn't mean you don't love your spouse. Nor does it mean you *must fall in love with your lover*. Also, you might love your lover, but that's not quite the same thing as being in love with her or with him. Any relationship that is good has the potential for love, even the potential for long and flourishing partnership. Yet it does not mean that you *will be compelled to leave* or must follow that initial sway of unbridled desire that often accompanies the start of an affair. Yes, you want it; yes, you will want it, you'll want to be fucked by him, this new lover of yours, this man who happens to be your husband's lover's husband, who bought you drinks and took you for a walk in the botanical garden—everything dead and decaying in winter, all the frogs sleeping under the mud until spring—and you might think of him at night when you wash the dishes and your son is asleep and your sweet husband reads in the den, that book of poetry he likes with all the *bees* and *light* in it, and you will think of it from time to time while you discuss the presidential election, or the genocide in Rwanda, or how 150,000 children have died in Africa because they *can't afford mosquito nets*.

Dangerous? Affairs? Are you *mad*? Affairs are only as dangerous as you let them be.

An affair constitutes a very private moment between two consenting adults. And that's all. (If you have lost a marriage because of how an affair was conducted or responded to, I am sorry, and I do not mean to hurt your feelings by saying this; mistakes happen, and that's horribly sad. And not every marriage is intended to last; and not every marriage that lasts is a victory.)

Lest my argument seem too strident to you, I'd like to suggest that even among my most intelligent friends, prejudice prevails. I have friends who say they admire my marriage for its openness, and even wish they could have such a marriage. Yet I do experience prejudice from them, and it makes me sad. It does not make me sad for myself. It makes me feel sad for them, and for people in general.

To turn to recent movies, popular among the liberal, intellectual set, many have featured affairs disastrous to marriage. Yes, affairs often have disastrous effects on marriages; this much is obvious, given the divorce statistics in our country and the frequency with which affairs are cited as causal factors. However, must this be the case?

In *Unfaithful*, the writer would have you believe that affairs lead not only to pain, anguish, guilt, remorse, orgasm, and pleasure, but *murder*. In the plodding and bourgeois *Sideways*, the about-to-be-married guy has an affair—a last fling, if you will—before his wedding. The result? He gets beat up by the woman he slept with. (The egregious sexism of this scene itself is appalling: What women would laugh maniacally at a woman being beaten by her lover for lying about being engaged? Am I expected to see this pathetic violence as *sly and ironic*? As funny? And yes, I have a sense of humor, and big.) The movie also takes a *sideways* swipe at swingers, representing them with a clearly lower-class couple living in filth and getting off with grunting, talky hog sex.

Finally, in *Your Friends and Neighbors* (I've deliberately chosen only those artsy films masquerading as *scathing commentaries*), we see two couples entwined ruthlessly. Sex as ugly, sex as lie, sex as manipulation, sex as betrayal, sex as bad. What's bad in such films is the script, which demands repulsion and hatred of the sex act . . . outside marriage.

So even those who consider themselves outsiders to mainstream culture are afraid to question why we persist in thinking marriage *should* mean forsaking all others. This is not rocket science: you can love someone, marry him or her, and fuck someone else. What is not best is to lie to the various involved parties. Can we talk about that?

When I'm going out to see someone, I simply tell my husband, "So I'm supposed to see J. tomorrow night. Is that okay?"

"Sure," Henry might reply.

Then, when I'm getting ready to go out—and yes, this does involve prettying myself up as for a date with my husband—he occupies himself without paying too much attention, out of respect for my privacy, but also out of self-respect, I think. There's a bit of healthy ribbing that goes on, as when I recently washed my favorite pair of jeans the afternoon I was supposed to get a drink with J. "Getting ready for your date?" Henry said. "No! I just needed to do laundry," I answered, blushing furiously. I think this is a far cry from suspicious glances or worse (my husband doesn't have to dig through my jeans pockets to see where I've been—I tell him: we went to the Club). There are no door-slamming scenes when we leave the house.

What, you might ask, is the appropriate departing phrase to use for your husband when you leave for a date? How about, "I won't be home too late, but don't wait up. I love you." Pretty simple. The appropriate response, from the stay-at-home spouse, is generally an exaggeratedly singsong "Have a nice time!" A sense of humor can help.

For the record, we do talk about things seriously. A lot. And I've had great sex in a car and told my husband, and he neither got off on it nor threatened to leave. We don't have the time on this earth to waste with useless arguments about who doesn't love whom, and who has lied, and who has fallen. We love each other; we are sure of each other's love; we know that life will soon end for us, in a matter of years—we're middle-aged, at thirty-six and forty-three.

I reserve the right to be in a marriage that doesn't waste time.

I prefer to think about flowers and birds, to go to my job and do it well, to love my son and my husband, and, when circumstances are right, to fuck other men.

A very talented and exceedingly thoughtful person I know, when told my husband and I were to become parents, said, "I just worry about the child with the open-marriage thing." I heard about this secondhand, and I'm sure she would not dare say this to my face. I suspect that several of my friends have occasional conversations about my marriage where they express similar *concern* for my (and apparently my children's) welfare.

This comment deeply hurt me. That she expressed concern about the welfare of my child should have been a deal-breaker for me in terms of our friendship. She was accusing me—in advance— of being a bad mother because I have sex with men other than my husband. Mind you, this is a woman who would never say, "I just worry about the child with the homosexuality thing"; it would never be acceptable in her intellectual circles.

So why do I remain friends with her? Because I'm happily married, and I feel I can set a good example for her. I take marriage, motherhood, sex, and friendship very seriously indeed.

I've just begun an affair, my first in a very long time, with this man, this husband of my husband's lover. We laugh about it. Apparently, he and his wife (my husband's lover) laugh about it too. "I found you a girlfriend," she sang to him, proud. He tells me this over drinks at the Club, where I partake in an immoral cigarette— something I do only from time to time, because I have that son. (Unlike sex, in which one can partake regularly and safely, partaking in cigarettes regularly cannot be done safely.)

"So, does that make us swingers?" I ask.

"Nah," he says with his ironic smile. "We're just . . . odd. Smart and pretty and odd."

And I look at him, this man I don't know very well yet, and I think, yes, he is pretty and smart. And I like him. And I'd like to fuck him, though I haven't yet. I think that we will. We've made out twice—once downtown, that first night we met, in his wife's office of all places (and with her blessing, because she is cool), and once in my car in a parking garage. Some affairs you want to take slow; this is one, for some reason. I don't want to just fuck him, without knowing him, yet. That's how I am. Or how I have been. This doesn't mean I have terribly involved relationships with my affairs. I do have long friendships in which occasionally sex will take place. These are nice friendships. I like them. I like knowing that I might be able to have affairs with these friends until I'm too old to want them—though I dread the day that happens.

So yes, yes, my marriage is still going strong. Stronger and stronger all the time—how much we learned, for example, from becoming parents and opening ourselves to that different sort of undying devotion and always, ultimately, realizable fear.

Now, I realize I don't say much about the actual marriage here, about my husband and about my son. Marriage is private, you see. What happens between two people, two consenting adults, in the privacy of their own home, is private. My affairs are private too, but since dominant culture seems quite free with its disapproval of adultery, I feel I must stand up against such intolerance.

Please know that my marriage is good. My husband and I do not argue about chores, or money, or sex; we have responsible jobs and are not excessive consumers; and though we are, indeed, members of the middle class, and not just getting by, we are not wealthy by any means. In other words, we have about as much or as little free time as the next privileged person on earth—given that 90 percent of humanity lives in poverty at present, my happy marriage is an embarrassment of riches. My sex life? It's absolutely beside the larger point. Or is it?

That I love my husband, that I am free to love other men, and that I have no designs on my husband's own freedom, all this strikes me as only good—there is no time for frivolous anger.

Yet this will hardly matter to you; you have enough on your mind, don't you, what with the war and the species die-off, or your own domestic situation or struggles. And you have your good marriages too, in which you may or may not have had affairs. And that is fine with me, as long as it is fine with you and your lover, your husband, your wife.

MATCHING LUGGAGE

Karen Propp

He and I sipped our before-dinner drinks at an outdoor café on a temperate evening in June. I was hungry, because we were dining late, and woozy, from the vodka in my glass, and light-headed, because he and I were sparkling new. Already, I loved his smartness and the way he made me feel alive to the world. His eyes misted when he looked at me. "My parents were sparring partners," he said. "They lived at the top of their voices."

I thought he was just trying to say something clever. If you had asked me then what he meant, I might have said that he came from an ambitious, opinionated, and excitable family, and that living at the top of one's voice was fitting for people who hobnobbed with the likes of Moshe Dayan and Golda Meir. Where exactly was "the top of one's voice"? Did it have something to do with opera?

And then our meal came, and the conversation moved on to other topics, and I felt satiated. It was a beautiful night, scented with geraniums. In his clunky Honda, we sped past a park called the Emerald Necklace. We held hands, and so intent were we on the current traveling between his hand and mine that there was no need to talk. He parked in front of my apartment; I invited him in. Whatever he'd meant about how his parents behaved had nothing do with *us*.

But now that he and I have been married almost ten years, I know too well what it is to live at the top of one's voice. The truth is that my husband can become ensnared in a rage so lethal it makes me shake just to be in the same room with him. He yells terrible accusations at me, and I yell equally terrible words back. And yet I love him. Once his anger passes, he is another person—the smart, warm, funny guy I fell for twelve years ago. The father of our child. The person who believed in me when I had nothing but a sheaf of poems and a fourteen-inch television set.

This is not an essay about healthy anger, the cleansing honesty that comes when both people trust each other enough to let their feelings rip. Nor is it a story about feminist-sanctioned rage against centuries-old oppression. It's not even about whether I am or am not a bitch, a role that has become fashionable in certain circles of late. This is a story about an anger that's as bewildering as it is shameful—a hidden emotional spring in which I almost drowned.

My husband comes across, to most people, as a charming, cultivated individual, someone who can explicate philosophers such as Rawls and Habermas, fix broken toys, paddle a canoe, program HTML, and listen empathically to friends in trouble. He knows hundreds of jokes, which he loves to tell. It's not easy to spot his anger. You have to have known him for years and years; you have to be his intimate, and you have to catch it at odd, unlikely moments of close proximity.

My first experience with this unusual form of anger came soon after we'd set up house together. The couch had made it through the door; books were shelved; paintings hung; utility bills taken out in both our names. Though we were not yet married, a sense of permanency was in the air. I was in a blithe mood and cooking spaghetti. Maybe I was humming under my breath, feeling a domestic well-being in cooking for my man. I placed in the sink one of the two colanders he (now we) owned. My hands in oven mitts, I poured the pot of boiling water and cooked pasta into the colander to drain.

Within seconds, my man flew into the kitchen. "What the hell are you doing? Are you crazy? Don't you know anything?"

I turned to him and saw the pulsing blue vein in his neck. "What's wrong?"

In response, he grabbed my arm, and brusquely nudged me so I was again facing the sink.

"Will you look, goddamnit? Will you for once *look* at what you're doing?"

I obeyed. I saw rising steam, and noodles pale as albino snakes. I saw a window, and through that window I saw the amazing Zen garden our neighbors tend. "What's wrong?" I repeated.

He threw up his hands in exasperation. He flung open the cabinet, pulled out the *other* colander, and brandished the metal bowl. "This is the right one. See the difference?"

I shook my head. The two were of similar color and size.

"Feet," said my husband. He tapped the tiny prongs at the bottom of the second colander. "This one has feet. Feet raise the pasta above the water level in the sink and keep it from getting soggy in its own dirty water."

I wanted to cry. At the same time I was flabbergasted. *He was going ballistic over a colander?*

For emphasis, he slammed the footed colander on the counter. Before I had a chance to speak, he continued his reprimand. "How many times have I told you how important it is to use the right tool?"

As he exited the kitchen, he spat over his shoulder: "Dinner is ruined."

The kitchen continued to be an undisputable hot spot in those early years. My husband's anger ignited around serving utensils, coffee beans, garlic cloves, fried eggs, and the refrigerator interior. As his anger increased, so did my sob sessions and my sense of being wronged. The man I had married was turning out to be far different from the one I knew when we were dating. The man whose bachelor apartment shelves sported a generous layer of dust now worried about a penny-sized upholstery stain. The once jocular and generous man now furrowed his brow. In our case, the intimacy, companionship, and security of marriage allowed the nasty parts of his psyche to surface.

Of course, marriage brought me up against my own limitations, too. In my family, the dominant credo was to be agreeable and pleasant. Problems were discussed at length around the kitchen table. Encouraged in my parents' house were a willingness to compromise, feelings of happiness with what you had, and putting others first. (Not a bad set of maxims, I see now.) If this climate also made me clam up, mumble, suppress and censor myself, well, at least no one's feelings were unduly hurt.

As our marriage deepened, so did my husband's anger and my silence. I distanced myself from him. I willed myself numb. He began to target misplaced items—keys, sunglasses, gold pens, airplane tickets—all of which he seemed to be perpetually losing and which kept him in a permanent rage.

And because his rage bewildered and pained me in a visceral way that made me unable to clearly see my situation, "Sorry, sorry, sorry," became my refrain, even when I didn't know why I was apologizing. I had no idea what to say or do. I saw how my husband, too, was burdened by an intense anger that flooded his every cell. I heard his parents' voices in the very rhythm and timbre of his yells. I felt bad for him because I knew that he was frustrated and disappointed with large portions of how his life was turning out. And once an angry phase had passed and my husband recognized his behavior as brutish, he'd often sit with his head in his hands, apologizing to me and saying how ashamed and embarrassed he felt.

During one of our more peaceful furloughs (we did have those, as well as tender moments and makeup sex), I tried to discuss the problem. "It really, really upsets me when you yell."

"I don't yell," he said. "Not much, anyway."

"What about this morning?"

He searched his memory.

"This morning when you yelled at me for leaving the plastic cup on the toaster oven? Remember how you got angry at me for not paying attention? You said that I'd burn the house down and you wouldn't always be here to take care of me?"

He thought for a long minute. Finally: "That wasn't yelling."

"To me it is. You don't know how harsh you sound."

"I'm just trying to get through to you."

"I can't hear you when you yell."

"Why do you keep bringing up my delivery?" Again his voice began to rise. He slapped his knee in frustration. "You never deal with what I'm trying to talk about."

"Not when you start off blaming me."

Round and round we went, warring form against content, two stubborn relationship aestheticians.

I think it was around year five that I fell into a long sulk. A profound sulk, in which I brooded about what neighborhood I would move to and figured out how many more years my car would be operable. I fantasized about nights free from snoring and bathroom sinks free from beard hairs. I began to notice FOR RENT signs and stopped to read the notices in Realtors' windows. I imagined decorating with Provençal textiles, which he pronounced verboten— on the grounds that anything but the harsh, clean lines of the modern is an anachronism after the Bauhaus. I could almost taste the quiet in a place of my own. I would have many friends. He and I would be better friends. Why, we could meet for dinner as often as we liked.

I never acted on any of my fantasies, though. I hoped things would get better. Things did get better—for a while. He got involved with a community where Israeli and Arab children come together in peace. He raised money for our son's preschool, enough to build a fire escape and give the teachers a slightly better salary. At New Year's, he gave my parents a case of fine wine. He read my manuscripts with a cold, clear eye. Our son ran into his arms and shrieked with delight. I stayed put.

And then it was year seven of my marriage. January; single-digit temperatures; snow; early darkness. One weekend all our friends were out of town. We had dragging colds. Our son was five years old and going through an especially cranky spell. In desperation, we decided to see a late-afternoon showing of *Sinbad* at a theater located about five miles from our house.

After the movie, snow was coming down in the fast and heavy flakes that mean rapid accumulation. My husband zipped up his parka, put on his gloves, and bravely set off across the parking lot to get the car. But before two minutes had passed, he was back in the lobby, his beard flecked with white.

"I lost it! My favorite hat! The one you gave me last year!"

"I'm sure it's in the movie theater." I handed my son a juice box. I tried to keep my voice calm.

"My hat in this place? Forget it."

"I'm sure it's here. I'll look."

I found the hat below the seats we'd just vacated. Feeling triumphant and a little smug, I handed the hat to my husband. He looked so grateful to have his hat back, it made me forgive his snappishness.

Driving the few miles home through the storm that night turned out to be treacherous. His head close to the windshield, my husband cursed and spat. And then we were hungry, with nothing to eat in the house but rice and tuna fish.

After our son fell asleep, he and I stood in our chilly living room and screamed at each other.

His face was screwed up, his eyes flashed viciously. On and on he went. No longer was it just my mistakes in handling surface domestic details that set him roaring. Now, it was my entire way of being. I should write faster and about subjects guaranteed to be best sellers (he had suggestions on that account). That I had not done so was, he said, a betrayal. He'd expected so much from me and now he was terribly disappointed. I should be in therapy because of my many unresolved conflicts. Why didn't I go more often to the gym?

It was like being bombed. Already I was tired, cold, and feeling generally beaten down. And now this. I was speechless. I threw myself on the couch, shaking, completely hysterical. Didn't he know me at all? True, he'd supported us financially for the past seven years, during which time I'd undergone infertility treatments, assumed primary caretaking for our baby, helped to bury my mother-in-law, and cared for my husband during his prostate cancer diagnosis and long illness. But now he was treating me like one of his stocks, berating me for being a bad investment.

I slept on the couch that night. The next morning, my husband announced that he, uncharacteristically, would take our son to kindergarten.

"Daddy's taking you to school today," I told my boy as I zipped his snowsuit.

"Not Daddy! I want Mommy!" he cried.

My husband glared at me. *See how you've turned my own son against me?*

I glared back. *What do you expect if you mistreat his mother?*

"You're coming with Daddy," said my husband gruffly.

My child grabbed hold of my leg. He was in tears.

My husband shot me a look. *He knows he can always get his way with you.*

I shot a look back. *You don't know how to treat a child.*

Then he stormed out the front door. "I'm going to start the car."

I knelt until I was eye level with our five-year-old. "Daddy wants his turn to take you to school," I said, trying to keep my voice level. "It isn't fair that I always take you to school. You can show him your cubby. Won't that be fun?"

"I want to go with you."

"Mommy isn't dressed yet. Mommy isn't feeling well today. And I really, really need you to go this time with Daddy."

A few more tears popped out. But he let go of me, put his hand on the door, and started down the front steps.

I looked out the kitchen window. My husband bent fiercely over the car, prying ice from the windshield with a plastic scraper. My son was jumping up and down, demanding a mitten that had fallen in the snow. I knew by the clock that they were already late. After a couple more minutes, my husband screwed his face up and yelled, loud enough for me to hear through the storm window, "You're not cooperating with me! You're completely incompetent!"

I hurried to open the front door. I was still in my nightgown, and my feet were bare. I stuck out my head. "Just get him into the car! His mitten's by the fence!"

I stood there shivering for another couple of minutes until they climbed into the car and backed out of the driveway. When I closed the door, something inside me clicked.

I poured myself another cup of coffee and logged on to the Internet. Sure enough, soon enough, I found a site about verbal abuse. My hands shaking above the keyboard, I checked yes to eighteen out of forty-two items in a list of characteristic abuser behavior. Yes, my partner does ignore my feelings; yes, he walks away without answering me; yes, he tells me I am too sensitive; yes, he rolls his eyes when I talk; yes, he ridicules me and then tells me it's a joke; yes, he seems energized by fighting while fighting exhausts me; yes, yes, yes, he seems to stir up trouble just when we are getting closer, questions my competence, and tries to convince me that he is right and I am wrong.

Taken singly, none of these behaviors seems terribly criminal; even taken together, they are not enough to give a woman a black eye. I checked no to road rage and no to breaking furniture. And yet, reading the list, I was forced to confront a not-so-pretty truth. At times, my husband verbally abuses me.

I scrolled and clicked, looking up the (many) sites devoted to verbal abuse, emotional abuse, and rage, expecting to find that it was now my duty as a self-respecting woman to flee to a shelter for the verbally abused, one with soundproof walls and tape recorders to practice a new, assertive voice. At the very least, I expected to be told I must get my husband to shut up.

Over the next several hours, as I read more, I learned that leaving is only necessary if the abuse becomes physical. I learned something remarkably simple that I had not realized: *the abuser often does not recognize his own behavior as being harmful or hurtful to his partner.* Wasn't this why time after time I became frustrated with my husband? According to him, he was simply speaking his mind, expressing himself, getting things out in the open.

My job, according to the experts, was to make my husband able to *hear* himself. My job was to make him aware. My situation would become dangerous if I found myself *not* expressing my opinions. My long and silent sulks, my retreats, and my brooding fantasies were the worst thing I could do in the face of my husband's anger. If I wished to protect myself and if I had any hope of taming my beast, I had to speak up.

Speak up! Make myself a target to further attack? Invite conflict? Dare to make my small voice heard? The very thought made my stomach contract in fear.

Speak up. Speak up. The phrase hammered in my brain. Why, of course. It was that easy.

I called my husband on the phone.

"I just want to clarify," I said in my sternest voice. "You said this morning that I was completely incompetent. Could you please explain how you reached that conclusion?"

A pause on his end. He cleared his throat. "The ice wasn't coming off. The kiddo was demanding my attention. I was cold."

"And that proves I am incompetent?"

A longer pause. A meeker voice. "Okay. I apologize."

"I am not your punching bag," I said.

"I know," he said.

"Direct your anger somewhere else," I said. "Pick a better target."

"I'll try."

"You sound like your father when you yell like that. Do you realize that?"

"I do?" He seemed genuinely surprised. Then, after a moment's reflection: "I suppose you're right."

It was that easy. I hung up the phone, and the floor below my feet did not cave in. Outside, the snow was still falling. I took a deep breath. It was as if I was suddenly released from the grip of a huge vise. I went into the bathroom and splashed warm water on my wrists and treated my face with every skin product I owned. The face that looked back at me from the mirror looked resolute and clear.

An hour later, I felt a kind of post–speaking-up dread. An irrational dread that anticipated further conflict between him and me. What would he say?

When my husband came home that evening, he hugged me hello and told me he loved me. "I'm sorry," he said. "I've been worried about my health and feeling terrible pressure at work."

I took a deep breath. "Why didn't you just tell me that before?"

"I know. I should've."

"I for one am not going to be silent anymore," I told him. "The rules are going to have to change around here."

"That's good," he said. "That is wonderful."

It's difficult to convey the surprise I felt at his response. Difficult to convey how new it felt to have my assertiveness welcomed.

"I want to give you an apology of action," he said, using a phrase our child had brought home from preschool. "Let me make dinner."

I wasn't sure where this would end up. But I was willing to accept his apology.

He pranced to the kitchen and put on the blue apron I had given him. And all the while I read a storybook with our son in the next room, clattering sounds and pleasing aromas came from the kitchen. That evening, we dined on striped bass, pan-fried with leeks. He set a glass of wine beside my plate.

Was the apology merely part of a pattern of attack and remorse? Was he complimenting me enough to keep me happy, and would he soon go back to criticizing me enough to make me insecure?

Perhaps.

But from that day forward, I continued to practice verbal self-defense.

"You're too sensitive," he said.

"Yes, I am," I said. "Good thing someone around here can feel."

"Can't you take a joke?" he said.

"It's not funny to me," I said.

"You know the one about how many feminists it takes to change a lightbulb?"

I walked out of the room before he could deliver the punch line.

I won't pretend that was the end of our calamities. I can't count how many times he has gone ballistic and then later apologized. Nor can I count how many times I have lost my voice in the marriage and struggled to find it once more. But I've learned not to get afraid when he's upset. I can hear now which parts are his frustration rather than an attack on me. I stand up to him now not only because of the Internet psychologists' advice, but because at some point I realized that my husband and I had brought luggage into our marriage that were a matched set.

Just as he had to learn anger management, my particular challenge has been to learn how to defend myself. I'm convinced that was one of the primal reasons I married my beloved. Entering into conflict was a skill I needed in order to grow up. It helps that I earn my husband's respect when I answer back. He has given me plenty of practice to speak up and hold my own. You could say he's helped me to find my inner bitch. Turns out I can hold my own in the bicker-and-complaint department.

The lessons of my marriage have taught me to find and fight for my place in the world. Before I married, I was often frightened. I was always expecting the big, bad world to turn on me, and I played things safe, took no risks, and frequently shrank from what I wanted or truly believed. I avoided and ran from conflict. I wanted, always, to please. Now, thanks to my husband's training, I can dispute a bill with scam plumbers, negotiate with irate literary agents, wait out tantrumming children, and talk through differences that come up with friends. I can enter into the fray.

Not too long ago, we were packing for a trip to New York City. I'd locked the cat in the bathroom so he wouldn't escape outside while we carried our luggage from the house to the car. The preparations had gone remarkably smoothly. Eyeglasses, cell-phone chargers, water bottles were not lost but rather in their rightful places. I'd cleaned the car of its usual debris, and he'd gone to the library, checked out the audiotapes for Philip Pullman's *The Subtle Knife*; our son, now seven years old, had us hooked on the story. We were looking forward to a family vacation. And then disaster struck. The case I was carrying—his ancient, battered one—split open at the zipper. Out onto the driveway spilled his clean underwear, shirts, shaving lotion. For a moment I felt my body tense: I'd done something wrong and now he would be angry. But the next moment, I caught myself. I had done nothing wrong.

"Don't get upset!" I said before he could even flinch. "This thing is really, really old. And you packed it pretty full."

He came over to me, and I felt a rippling relief go through both our bodies. Together we looked at his belongings strewn on the driveway.

"These things happen," he said. I heard the determination and control in his voice.

"Now you'll have an excuse to go out and buy a new suitcase."

"Yeah." And he bent to pick up the disarray.

And then we were on our way at last, buckled and locked, my husband's stuff zipped tight in his gym bag, fast-forwarding the new cassette tape, and I chanced a look at myself in the car mirror. There I was: hair a mess, bags under the eyes, age spots appearing, chin hairs sprouting. . . . And before I could make my usual disparaging remark, my husband said, "You're beautiful, you know."

When I ask why we are still married, sometimes, the reason seems as simple as the fact that we love each other. We share a history, a home, and a child—none of which I can bear to break, I tell friends when my husband's behavior makes them shudder. Besides, I find my husband as fascinating as he is difficult. He gives me his jokes and cooking and an inexhaustible supply of facts. I give him my laughter and appetite and an inexhaustible supply of patience. I believe in commitment, in seeing things through, in loyalty, and in family. And so does he.

From Paper
to Wood

BEING MR. PACKER

ZZ Packer

Whenever my friend Salvatore calls, he always asks, "So how is Mr. Packer doing?" He knows I've kept my surname, as my husband has kept his—which, by the way, is *not* Packer, but Salvatore has always referred to my husband as Mr. Packer.

The assumption, I suppose, was that I was so intransigently myself that the sheer blast of my personality would emasculate whatever poor soul had consented to marry me. This unfortunate man would live out his life in "wifedom," attending to my needs, taking dictation from me, sharpening my pencils and keeping them at the ready. As a token of my appreciation for all Mr. Packer's efforts, I'd occasionally pat his head and give him one of those dewy sitcom looks of practiced affection.

The joke about "Mr. Packer" started long before I even knew my husband, at the Iowa Writers' Workshop, where I, like Salvatore, hoped to become a writer. So it stood to reason that I'd expect Mr. Packer to turn my books to the proper page while I signed them for my millions of fans. As for cleaning and housework, Salvatore and I had never figured out how that happened. Perhaps in Salvatore's world I had a maid, but as the granddaughter of a domestic, I had unresolved (and not quite logical) arguments against the idea of housekeepers, and preferred to think of Mr. Packer and myself as living in the effortlessly tidy mode of gay men.

I didn't realize it at the time, but this fantasizing about Mr.

Packer was all just a way for both of us to say that neither of us expected me to ever marry. I wasn't opposed to marriage the way some of my white college friends were, nor did I pine after marriage the way some of my black friends did. It all just seemed an irrelevancy. It always surprised me that women thought of it with either fairy-tale haziness or with the stringency of a policy debate; I'd always thought of marriage more like the weather: if certain atmospheric conditions occur, then rain will fall; if not, not. What was the point in hunting after it? Fear of living alone, or worse, with a houseful of cats?

When I did meet "Mr. Packer," and fell for him, it took me utterly by surprise. I was living in San Francisco and was subletting a tiny, closet-sized room in Cole Valley until I could find an apartment. My place was so small that the only activity I did there was sleep.

I read and wrote at cafés instead of in my room, and I went to a local hangout called Finnegan's Wake after the cafés closed. Finnegan's Wake was where I met Mr. Packer; he commented on my pile of books, I sized him up, said a few words in reply, then went back to my reading. But before I knew it, Mr. Packer and I had gotten into a debate about the Korean War (something about the Yalu River). I don't know how the argument ended, but I went back to my reading, and five minutes later, Mr. Packer asked me out.

The first few dates exceeded my low expectations. I didn't date to find a potential husband or even the possibility of a future relationship—I dated to have fun. If someone was kind and intelligent and hanging out with them felt like hanging out with one of my pals, then they were a good date in my book.

But here was someone who was more than a bud I could shoot pool with. Here was someone who was smart, handsome, and had paid his way through college. He could hold forth on any historical topic known to man, and I was grateful that he—unlike other male history buffs—didn't reveal some mad obsession with the Civil War, or a living room filled with his very own replicas of World War II fighter planes.

He possessed an unerring sense of how to tell a story, honed, no doubt, in the air force, which he'd joined as a baby-faced teenager. As someone who'd spent most of her life in one academic setting or another, it felt strange to be suddenly dating someone who'd been in the air force, someone who still spent one weekend a month in the National Guard. It all seemed at odds with his good—though puzzling—career in Silicon Valley as a software marketer. Puzzling because to hear him and his friends "talk computers" was to enter a language free of verbs and scant of any nouns without numbers affixed to them. Also, he loved, as I do, great food, whether it was the highbrow fare at Jardinière or Aqua or the insane and decidedly lowbrow fire-log–sized burritos at El Balazo.

And strangely enough, Mr. Packer *owned* things.

Most of the guys I'd been out with came from the Backpack School of Ownership, the credo of which is that all earthly possessions must be able to fit in a backpack. Relationships with these types, I found out, were subject to the same rigorous rules of compression. There was the guy who so loathed materialistic "normal people" that he lived in a trailer park, despite a pretty well-paying job. But he didn't live in a trailer. He lived in a *shed behind a trailer*. When the trailer-park inspectors visited (who knew such a job existed?), they gave two citations: 1) Fix Steps and 2) Man Out of Shed.

Mr. Packer was a far cry from Mr. Backpacker. It was comforting to date someone who drank wine from wineglasses instead of from jelly jars, who didn't case fast-food restaurants to relieve them of their surplus napkins, ketchup packets, and plastic sporks. Here, finally, was a guy who owned his own vacuum cleaner, which at least filled me with the hope that he'd one day plan on using it.

But what most impressed me about Mr. Packer was his supportiveness. When I landed my first large-circulation magazine publication, he not only bought an embarrassing number of copies, he made his coworkers read the story, resulting in a flood of fan e-mails (touching in their inarticulateness) from the computer geeks and marketing execs who were his coworkers.

It was only a year and one engagement ring later, as I stayed up for four largely sleepless nights to make a deadline for an important contest, that I realized how lucky I had it. He'd gotten only slightly more sleep than I had, but he pinched me when I threatened to doze off, made the coffee, and cooked all the meals (he probably spoon-fed them to me, given that my hands were either furiously typing or pulling out my hair). That's when I understood that Salvatore was right—I was about to marry Mr. Packer.

But the moniker meant something different now, not the uxorious man Salvatore had described (and I myself had begun to believe in), but a man who exulted in my career, as opposed to merely tolerating it. Whereas Mr. Backpacker (himself an aspiring writer) had refused to read one of my stories when it had been published in a small but prestigious journal, Mr. Packer threatened to de-stock the San Francisco bookstores of every publication I'd ever been in. When I was negotiating a book contract, he called every two minutes with advice and encouragement, his excited friends from a few cubicles over yelling their congrats into the phone. With him, I felt as if my writing wasn't a mere hobby, or a collection of wounds to constantly lick before I could face another page; writing began to feel like a career, something to take seriously.

In fact, one of his first gifts to me wasn't roses or chocolate, but a brand-new computer for writing. I couldn't accept such an expensive gift and demanded that he return it. He protested, saying that he bought the computer precisely because he could hear the "straining, spinning disks" of my old hard drive, and pronounced that it would die any second. He extracted a promise that I'd at least save all my files as soon as I got home. I extracted a promise from him that if he refused to take the computer back or give me the receipt so that *I* could take it back, he would accept my monthly cash installments to pay him.

I backed up all my files and was fortunate that I did—my old computer died in a matter of days. He saved the money I repaid him, which contributed, he said, to purchasing the engagement ring.

It is said that every artist needs a wife; I agree and believe this is doubly true of women artists. Though feminism has made great strides in securing women better opportunities in pursuing careers, it still has not erased the stigma of a woman who fulfills herself by means of her art. Male writers get to be crazy, boozers, wedded to their talent and anything that feeds it. It's great if a male writer is a jerk—it says something about his inability to compromise himself or his art; he can be a womanizer or a playboy, and woe be the woman who is expected to tame the wild man in the artist. The woman can play the part of muse—inspiring the male artist to new heights with her beauty, her spiritedness, the essence within her that somehow plays the role of objet d'art and mystical, protean mistress—or she can fulfill the role of wife: pay the bills, clean the house, empty the coffee cups, type or retype manuscripts, soothe the temper when the male genius is stifled or "blocked," understand and brook the infidelities the male artist might have with more muselike beauties and personalities who are always, most assuredly, younger women.

A few women manage to be both wife and muse, a juggling act I can hardly imagine, much less imagine emulating. And if I can't imagine what it must be like to be a midwife to a male writer's creativity, then what allows me to indulge myself, while my spouse acts as midwife for my career? If parity is what we feminists have been after for all this time, isn't expecting anything more than my fair share a bit presumptuous? Or should I take what I can get, noting that Shakespeare's sister—according to Virginia Woolf—would have envied my position?

In Virginia Woolf's *A Room of One's Own*, she recounts how a hypothetical sister of Shakespeare's would have fared were she equipped with the same talent, drive, and ambition as her brother. All these inherent traits, Woolf argues, would have doomed Shakespeare's sister, whereas these same traits—combined with the opportunity to express them—engendered the preeminent literary figure of the Western world. Shakespeare's sister would not have been sent to school, nor would she have been encouraged to write, given that women could not even play roles of women in Elizabethan theater. More likely than not, Shakespeare's sister would have killed herself out of despair, and this, Woolf contends, is why a "room of one's own" is requisite for every woman artist.

If life was hard for Shakespeare's sister, then life was a hundredfold so for a black woman, who, by accident of birth, could not even hope for privileged husbands or fathers to "indulge" them. I constantly remind myself that I'm lucky to have been born in a time in which women, even black women, at least have a chance of pursuing their artistic dreams. But I have to remind myself that just because I'm lucky doesn't mean I'm not deserving. I'm fortunate to have what I have, but this doesn't mean Shakespeare's sister shouldn't have had it too. After many years, I've finally convinced myself that having a husband who's supportive of my artistic career is not an option, but a right.

While I do have a room of my own, I don't have that final requisite for all artists; I do not have a "wife" of my own. Mr. Packer doesn't clean, or at least not enough to make a real difference. And I've left for a month to find that he'd completely forgotten to pay the phone bill, or even notice that the phone had been shut off; was completely oblivious that the inside of the microwave had begun to resemble a modern-art installation, or that the heap of dirty clothes in the corner of the bedroom had grown so gigantic that the dog joyfully burrowed into it as if entering an igloo. As supportive as Mr. Packer is in other ways, he's not a domestic. When I need a break from fulfilling these chores, I take trips to artists' colonies where I can get writing done while someone else feeds me for a while. Mr. Packer shoos me off and wishes me luck.

There was the spring before last, when I picked up a friend from the airport and dropped her off at an artist colony tucked away in the redwood-studded hills of Woodside, just north of Palo Alto. I couldn't help but feel pangs of jealousy as I took the curves of the hillside roads that led back to the main highway; it was as if I were driving through a never-ending cathedral of trees, pillars of light beaming down through the redwoods.

Having grown insanely jealous of my la-di-da friend by the time I hit I-280, I came sulking back home to my husband. *I* wanted those redwoods, *I* wanted that time to write, alone, with no sound but that of twittering birds. There was no doubt about it—I was being bratty about the whole thing. So I tried talking myself out of this artist-colony envy.

Mr. Packer, fortunately, saw things differently. "If that is what you want, just go there and write—you've got two weeks of spring break before you have to teach again." He began to solve the problem the way he solves all problems: he got on the Internet. Within a few minutes he'd found a place for me to write in the Santa Cruz Mountains hamlet of Ben Lomond: a cabin that could be rented out for a mere twenty bucks a night.

And as often as I asked for time away from him, I've asked for him to be by my side more times than I'm sure he wished to be. At one writing festival in New York he gamely chatted up writers, though his interest level in the lit scene is about as tepid as my interest in jokes about his latest XDSOF mainframe. He's woken me up to catch planes when my need for REM sleep let me drowse through alarms, and he's scheduled his own business meetings around my travel schedule.

Perhaps this is what most husbands of women writers do, or what's expected of them to do, but of the cases I know, this behavior is applauded in theory but sorely missing in practice. One of my fellow writers here in the Bay Area is Ann Packer, whose divorce in part had to do with the inability of Ann's "Mr. Packer" to cope with the phenomenal success of her best-selling novel. Another good friend of mine is a poet whose divorce from her husband was precipitated by applying for the same jobs, contests, and awards, always being in competition with each other, if only tangentially. So I know my position is precarious and strangely enviable. It is this type of care and indulgence that has made me grateful, but has also occasionally led me to take for granted the gift of his understanding.

At yet another festival, this time in Jamaica, my husband confessed that there were limits to being Mr. Packer. After a reading, I'd been sequestered to a table with my fellow panelists, signing books and answering questions while he ran errands for me. At some point, one of the festival organizers flagged him down and rudely demanded that he hustle himself back to my table so that he could usher me over to some new event as soon as possible. The rude person had assumed he was my assistant, and when she discovered he was my husband, her face went from shock to embarrassment to bafflement.

Yet another time, while I was covering the Democratic National Convention for a magazine as a fiction writer–cum–neophyte journalist, I got so flustered by acquiring my press pass, cobbling together my story, and getting invited to the places that would provide me access to politicians that I all but neglected my marriage. The day of my biggest coup—meeting and speaking with Hillary Clinton—I lost my cell phone and couldn't call my husband all day. Finally, during a Dukakis reception, I managed to borrow someone's phone.

"Hey," I said once I reached him, "I went to this party—I mean, the *biggest* party, and managed to get some quotes from Hillary."

"Great," he said.

"And guess who else I saw?" I ran down the list of bigwigs he should've been impressed by, but for some reason wasn't.

"Great, honey," he said.

"Where are you?" I asked.

"I'm in Dallas."

When we got disconnected, I wondered if I could have missed him telling me about his trip to Dallas. I called back.

"I might as well tell you now," I said, "I lost the phone. What's our service? Sprint?"

"AT&T," he said, disgusted that I didn't even know.

"How much would it cost to get another phone?"

"Three hundred bucks."

"I thought I left it at the *GQ* party but . . ." I almost launched into who I managed to wrangle at the *GQ* party the previous night, but I could already feel that the silence on the other end wasn't a listening silence.

"Do you remember," he finally said, "what day it is?"

"Yeah . . ." I said. Truly, I'd drawn a blank. His birthday? No? Some important date in history—if so, I couldn't think of what it might be. "Yeah, it's—"

"It's our FUCKING ANNIVERSARY!"

"Our anniversary!" I repeated, full of false, belated joy, but it was obvious I'd forgotten it, for the day, at least, even though just two days before I'd gotten Al Franken to inscribe *Happy Anniversary!* in one of his books for Mr. Packer. Grasping for straws, I told this to Mr. Packer, my only proof that I hadn't really forgotten. "I got Al Franken to sign your book!" I said, lamely. But I could tell he had no idea what I was talking about, nor did he care. I knew I was in deep shit. "But I didn't have my phone!" I pleaded, though I knew more words would only make things worse. "If I'd had my phone I would have *seen* the date—if I'd had my phone I wouldn't have had to look for it! You know my cell phone is the only way I can tell what day it is . . ."

All, of course, was hopeless.

"This is bullshit," he yelled, then hung up.

I tried to call him back, but he refused to pick up.

Then, after I'd spent a while moping in the corner while everyone mobbed Kitty Dukakis for autographs, *he* called back.

"Here's the guy who found your fucking phone," he said. "I was calling you like crazy, worried out of my *goddamned* mind, and this cabdriver guy finally answered."

He brusquely read me the telephone number of the cabdriver who found my cell phone, then promptly hung up again. I tried to call my husband back, just to say thanks, but only after I'd left the Dukakises and the crowds and retrieved my phone did he answer, hours later.

So why are we still married? Especially when my job occasionally necessitates that my husband act as my assistant, my telephone screener, my pickup boy, my iron backbone, my pillow, and my venting machine? Especially when I have to travel, sometimes for weeks or months at a time?

I should not mislead anyone into believing my husband is the saint in our relationship, and that I'm the pampered recipient of his unconditional love and beneficence. In our five years of marriage, I've "done my time," and I do not use the prison jargon lightly. Fishing and sailing are big loves of Mr. Packer's, and though I don't protect my hair at all costs—like many black women—from wind, rain, and any other natural forces that might disturb it, I do not like to be in the water. Mr. Packer, on the other hand, must be in the water every weekend. While I love walking along the beautiful Pacific, or sitting bayside in a great San Francisco restaurant, I do not like being *in* the water, having it churn my stomach and mess with my equilibrium. Within the gulf between his love for the ocean and my indifference to it lies our marriage, and the only way I see to make the marriage work, given his unflagging passion for the stinky, stinky sea, is to take some Dramamine every once in a while, board a boat with him, and shout "Cool!" "Wow!" and "That sure is huge!" at moments that seem appropriate.

And I've attended my share of computer software parties with

Mr. Packer, the most grueling of which being one where everybody shared "a talent." That everyone considered "writing" to be their special talent was especially painful to someone like me, who spent years writing in obscurity and poverty while these near-illiterate Silicon Valley technocrati were amassing millions or gossiping cattily about one another's IPOs. They'd each give me knowing looks as they launched into their poems and/or prose pieces with all the histrionic pride and skill of a bunch of kindergarteners.

And then there was the time I came back from a writers' retreat only to find that Mr. Packer had bought a boat without telling me. Let me clarify. He didn't truly *buy* a boat, because we can't *afford* a boat. Rather, he explained, as he picked me up from the airport, he'd traded some "fungibles" for half a boat. Still, it was quite a shock to find out that my husband had essentially purchased a share of a boat for an amount that could have kept me alive for a whole year in my postcollege days. Though it was great to enter the house and see that he'd gotten rid of his sizable gun collection, it wasn't so nice to come home and see that one of the "fungibles" that went toward paying for the boat was my beloved little egg-shaped Apple computer.

"You sold my computer!" I screamed.

"I *traded* it," he said, as if such a distinction would make me feel better.

"But it was *my* computer—you can't do that!"

"Who bought that computer for you? I did."

"But I didn't tell you to buy it in the first place, and besides, I paid you for that computer. I write on that computer. It's my computer!"

"But I told you I was trading some stuff."

I tried to remember when he'd told me this; he's forever trading something on online community boards like Craigslist or eBay.

"You said you were going to get rid of a bunch of computer stuff," I said.

"So I did."

"A computer," I said, "is not the same as 'computer stuff.' Computer stuff is like broken keyboards and outdated cables and that old CrossPad that never worked. You didn't say you were getting rid of my computer."

(I'll spare readers my screams, his lame attempts to define computer worth and depreciation, and the list of various objects thrown.)

Whenever I see white wives on TV, they always seem demure, saddened by fights. And I can never imagine my white women friends flying into the utter rages that consume me when I'm in the midst of fighting with my husband. Our fights are, strangely enough, the one time I think about race in our marriage, and I wonder if him being a white male—heir to all the privilege that confers—and me being a black female (the supposed diametric opposite of the white male) is just too much under one roof. Neither one of us is yielding. If you were to view us as archetypes, as living roles of race and gender, he, as a white man, is not used to having to yield, and I, a black woman, am so used to being asked to yield, to settle, that I resist it with every fiber of my being.

But I can only view our fights, our relationship, through the prism of sociology for so long. I don't have the patience for grudges, and neither does he. Some writer once commented that every Irish tragedy could be resolved, were it not for the lack of a few pounds. I feel that way about our marriage. Most of our fights are really only squabbles, when you look closely, and most of our squabbles are but petty grievances. When we compare those grievances to the utter lack in our lives without each other, we recognize just how petty we're being.

We got married for love, yet we remain married for the times when love is as apparent and as obvious as the sun rising yet another day, and for all the times when our love seems so distant that we wonder why we bother with each other at all. We got married because we seemed to love the same things, yet we stay married because we respect the same principles. We got married because we were certain the other was the pick of the bunch, and while that's still true, we stay married because we now know that no one else would be able to stand us, and we wouldn't be able to stand anyone else. When we got married we still had some notion that marriage was a union that incorporated "man and wife." Yet we stay married because we see that our roles are always shifting and growing because our world is always shifting and growing; we stay married because he is Mr. Packer when I need him to be, and when he needs the same, I've learned—and am still learning—to be Mrs. Boros.

Monogamy Meltdown

Kamy Wicoff

Growing up I believed two things: that I would get married and stay married for the rest of my life, and that the man I married would not be the first man I ever had sex with. This was not a radical position for a teenage girl to take in San Antonio, Texas, during the 1980s. Our parents were baby boomers, they were getting divorced in droves, and one implied explanation for these breakups (nobody questioned the *institution* of marriage—this was Texas) was that Mr. and Mrs. X had gotten married too young, before they had had the chance to mature, grow, become their adult selves, and oh yes, before they had gotten a chance to have sex with other people. The latter especially applied to Mrs. X, who, having come of age in Texas in the late sixties, probably indulged in the offerings of the sexual revolution about as many times as she got carted off to jail for throwing her body in front of a tank while protesting the Vietnam War.

In light of this, the premarital sex I planned to have with men other than my future husband seemed to be in both of our best interests, crucial to the staying-married-for-the-rest-of-our-lives part of the deal, which would require forsaking all others, etc. By dutifully sowing my oats, growing seasoned and mature, and satisfying my desire to kiss various kinds of lips, I would enable myself to don the white wedding dress when the time came with a feeling of confidence, assuredness, and, above all, contentment.

Knowing exactly how to carry out this plan, of course, was another matter. My mother (who married at twenty in 1968—1958 in East Coast years—with IT'S CHERRY BLOSSOM TIME! written on her honeymoon car in shoe polish) offered this advice: "It's okay to have sex before you get married, but sex is a special, sacred thing, and you should only have it with a man you love, who loves you."

In my twenties I quickly discovered, *however*, that only having sex with a man I loved, who loved me, meant only having sex when I had found the Holy Grail. So I improvised and justified fudging the only-have-sex-with-a-man-you-love rule by telling myself that my adventures would only sweeten—and strengthen—the bond I sought. And while I often ached for that bond as I was buffeted about in the tempest of post–sexual revolution dating, if I were honest I also had to admit (gasp!) that a lot of times I was having *fun*.

I'll never forget the moment I realized that the Holy Grail was on the pillow next to me, and that my quest—and all my conquests—was now supposed to come to an end.

I was twenty-five. I'd been seeing Isaac (whose name I've changed here), who was twenty-eight, for about a year. I knew I was *in love*, and it was extraordinary. But in recent months he had been working so much, I'd hardly seen him. He's in private equity, and at the time his group was doing its first major deal in Japan. This meant eighteen-hour days, six or seven days a week, and enthusiastic participation in all the other events required for the great American pissing contest known as the Macho Investment Banker Olympics.

I, on the other hand, wasn't working at all. I'd quit my job to try my hand at screenwriting. Not working in an office, I was alone a lot. Not working for money, I was feeling insecure. Not having Isaac to talk to, except at night when he came home late and quickly went to sleep, I was feeling abandoned. I started to think: maybe I love Isaac, but maybe I'm not *in love* with Isaac—maybe italics are not happening for us. And it did not seem like a good sign that I was having increasingly hot sexual dreams about Mike, my personal trainer.

Then one night, toward the end of the month, Isaac arrived home late, as usual (11:54 P.M.), and he was wiped out, as usual. He changed out of his suit, and, wearing only his boxer-brief under-wear, approached his side of the bed, picked up his tiny pale blue plastic alarm clock, set it, shook his head, and sighed heavily.

"Ah, another night where I get five hours of sleep," he said, crawling under the covers.

"You say that every night," I pointed out.

"That's because I never get enough sleep," he said, closing his eyes.

"If you wanted more sleep, you'd get a different job," I said. He didn't answer. I cuddled up to him aggressively. "I need to talk to you," I said. "You've been coming home every night at eleven thirty and I haven't even had a chance; you just pass out."

He put his arm around me, pulled me in; he kissed my cheek. I was silent. Coming from me, silence is an alarming, and effective, strategy.

"What's wrong?" he asked, sitting up, concerned. I was about to answer him when he yawned. I sat up too and examined his eyes. They were red. His eyelids were desperate to cover them. "I'm try-ing!" he said. "Talk to me." Okay. *I miss you and I don't care about stupid money, I'm not in this for a Barneys card and a tit job, I want my best friend*—eyelids shut—*and hey!!*—eyelids open—*I don't believe you guys really have to be there all the time*—eyelids shut—*Don't you want to do something more with your life? Don't forget your heart, the things we've said*—eyelids open, he smiles at me. I love him.—*But! you have to have your priorities straight and I shouldn't feel ashamed to feel like this, like I'm a weak dependent woman or something*—eyelids shut—*dammit! listen to me*—eyelids yanked back. After a while, when he peeled his eyelids up, his eye-balls simply followed them, rolling drunkenly up into his head, bob-bing between me and sleep.

"I'm here," he insisted, and grabbed my hand. He made it about ten more minutes. I tried to shove a few more sentences under the closing cargo door of his brain before it sealed for good. No luck, he was out. Bastard.

I turned over, yanked the chain on his fancy lamp, and steamed. I planned my breakup speech. I imagined our parting and our mutual devastation, an exercise not unlike those undertaken in childhood when I'd fantasized about the desperate and unequivocal proofs of love I could elicit from my parents by running away from home. Then, he stirred. I felt his hand on my bare back. I stiffened and softened. He laid his other palm flat across my pillow, on top of my long hair. He folded the tips of his fingers into the strands.

"I know we have to figure this out," he murmured. "I just can't talk about it right now."

"But what if we *can't* figure it out?" I asked.

"That's not possible," he said firmly. Then he squeezed me so tightly that for a minute we fit perfectly together, for our bodies, from head to toe, are almost exactly the same size. And that was when I was seized by a terrible, totally unexpected realization. He was right. I was not going to leave him. Not then, not ever. I couldn't. *It was not possible.* I was *in love*, in italics. Isaac was *the one*.

Was there really going to be, from now on, only *one*?

I couldn't believe this question popped into my head. But it did. It popped in, and then it expanded to fill the space. Because, after all, there was one other condition for my happiness: We were supposed to be monogamous. Totally and entirely, forever. Why didn't somebody tell me when I met Isaac that he was going to be *the one*? If I'd known, I could have prepared! Ordered up one last meal before signing up to eat the same one for the rest of my life!

Women are not supposed to have this problem, of course. And until that moment, I'd played my part: I'd pressured him about commitment, about saying "I love you"; I'd lobbied for the lockdown while he'd ducked and parried. But now he was there—he would never leave me, I knew—and where was I? Unable to fathom the notion that I might never be naked with another man until my body was donated to science. Was it possible that my premarital sex life, rather than ensuring I could eat one meal for life without regret, had instead given me an appetite for the buffet line that I could no longer suppress?

I decided I needed more romance. If I was going to forgo the amorous attentions of new suitors, I thought, shouldn't Isaac play the part of new suitor, all the time? Shouldn't he court me with love letters, flower petals in my glove compartment, chocolate mousse sex trysts, and surprise vacations, as *Cosmo* and *Elle* instruct? I pursued this panacea for a little while, hoping that a burst of romantic heroism from him would exorcise my fears about faithfulness, until one night, irritated and not a little indignant, he spat: "I am not going to go out in the rain and wreck my motorcycle for you, Kamy! That's not who I am. And if that's what you want ..." I flinched, embarrassed and hurt at the same time.

"Don't you know how much I love you?" he asked, pleading, but sure of my answer. I *did* know. I felt the same way about him. So I had to figure something out. I had to understand what my single sex life had been doing for me all these years ... and then hope like hell that I could let it go.

My first task was immediate: I had to figure out how a monogamous, potentially married person would deal with Mike, my personal trainer. Mike was exactly the type of man I couldn't get enough of before I met Isaac: broad-shouldered and sweet, with round, oh-so-sincere blue eyes setting off his close-cropped dark brown hair—a jock with a heart from Saginaw, Michigan, halfheartedly trying to make it as a writer in L.A. When I went into the gym to work out with him, the first thing he always did was stretch me. This meant he put the heels of his hands against my knees, pressed them into my chest, and then pressed his chest against my legs until we were within tonguing distance. *If I could just take him out into the dark alley behind the gym and make out with him one time,* I thought, *I'd get it out of my system!* But I knew I wouldn't.

When my ten prepaid sessions with Mike were up, I didn't buy any more. Instead I went home and told Isaac all about it. This is what a monogamous-for-life person does. Upon further discussion, however, we did agree that those first ten sessions were all right, even if I'd kept them to myself. Nothing had happened. Far more than I wanted to have new naked penises waved around in my face (perhaps later I will be seized by a more purely physical wanderlust), I wanted to be looked at, to be paid attention to, to be wanted . . . and then I wanted to play and tease and bask in that looking and wanting. I wanted, in other words, to be the object of desire. And this was a womanly desire, indeed.

Understanding that I wanted to be wanted by other men more than I wanted to have *sex* with other men did not, alone, get me very far. I suppose I could have simply told myself, at that point, that as long as I always said, "Please look, but don't touch," I could fulfill my perfectly natural desire to be seen as a still-sexy woman in the world with no harm done. But I knew that something deeper and more fundamental lay at the heart of my monogamy panic. I felt threatened by the idea of becoming permanently *taken* in a way that vanity alone didn't sufficiently explain.

It wasn't until I attended a cheesy L.A. party on the beach that I had breakthrough number two.

Isaac was in Tokyo that weekend so I had arranged for an evening out with a group of single, swinging ladies, who also happened to be my best friends. As I got ready I turned up Madonna's *Immaculate Collection*, drank a beer while blow-drying my hair, and put on eyeliner. When we walked into the party everyone stared at us, but everyone stares at everyone who walks into a party in L.A., just long enough to make sure they aren't anybody worth staring at. Things were looking pretty bleak in the flirting department, in fact, until a Calvin Klein model walked over to me and my friend Sarah, looked right at me, and said, "You have sex in your eyes."

I almost choked and was consequently beaten to the punch by Sarah.

She said, "Tell that to her boyfriend."

"How long have they been together?" he asked.

"A year and a half," Sarah said.

What happened next remains a point of controversy. Sarah maintains that aforementioned cute boy simply replied, "A year and a half! She might as well be married," before taking his sex-in-your-eyes rap elsewhere.

But I distinctly heard him say, "A year and half! She might as well be dead."

Being married, and excusing myself from the game of love for the rest of my life, seemed like a kind of death to me. But what kind? Certainly, it had caused me to contemplate the six-feet-under kind, especially when I'd observed hair growing out of Isaac's grandfather's ears and thought, *Am I going to sit across dinner tables from my man until hair starts growing out of his ears . . . and out of my chin?* But I feared another kind of death even more: becoming an invisible woman.

I remembered becoming invisible in the seventh grade, when I went from being a smart, funny, loud personality in my sixth-grade class to being a derided nonentity because I was completely inept at attracting the attentions of boys. That spring, however, when I found myself with a bikini-ready body, there was no question in my mind that my newly developed curves had provided me with the equipment I needed in order to become visible again. And this meant I'd learned how to force the *world* to see me, too. How did every larger-than-life woman in my world, from the popular girls in my class to their popular, made-up mothers, to the actresses and pop icons who were the most prominent examples of powerful women I knew, make themselves visible? They did it by being beautiful. They did it by being *hot*.

When I felt I had complete power over a man, I also felt, whether for a minute or a month, that his power was mine. Possessing *male* power this way had always intoxicated me—and it was the idea of no longer being able to wield male power this way that I feared. Unsurprisingly, the intoxication had never lasted long, and worse, it relied on making a man into a vessel, a tool, and an object to boot, and I could not truly love a man with whom I had this kind of relationship. Which was why it was impossible for me to act out the scenario satisfactorily with Isaac. He was too known, too real to me.

Premarital sex had not just been a search for Mr. Right, or a way of ensuring I acquired the sexual experiences Mrs. X never had. It had become a way of feeling powerful in the world.

Even so, I knew my old habits would be hard to break. Yes, I did a lot of thinking during my monogamy meltdown. Yes, I had a lot of very honest conversations with Isaac. But there was one thing, in all our conversations, that we didn't say. And that was that I had succumbed to weakness (in other words, been unfaithful) several times already, and we both knew it. My weak moments had never taken me much beyond kissing, which had made them easier for us to deal with—I've also been told that this makes the use of the word "unfaithful" sound melodramatic. But the fact that I had never *slept with* anyone else while we'd been together did not make me feel any better. I did not want to be parsing what "is" is. It scared me, and Isaac didn't like it either.

Nothing at all like this had happened for years, not since I'd discovered I was *in love*. But neither that knowledge nor all my soul-searching could dispel my fear—my certainty—that I was doomed to fail at monogamy. I kept this feeling a guilty secret from Isaac. Harboring it, however, was really a way of excusing myself in advance. And just a few months before Isaac asked me to marry him, I failed one more time.

I was living in New York by then, and Isaac hadn't joined me yet—he was still living in L.A., due to move that winter. I was out with a group of people that included a man in his forties, a writer

who was sexy and sought after, as far as I could tell, by several of
the women in the room. He turned his attention to me. They were
charming and formidable. He poured a lot of wine, I drank it, I let
him pour more, and as the evening progressed I was feeling very
doomed, very turned on, and increasingly resolute in my determination to cease all thinking. I felt entitled to some harmless excitement. I didn't want to have to stop, to bow out. After dinner a
smaller group of us went to a bar, and at the end of the evening I
was standing on the sidewalk waiting for a cab, and this man came
outside and kissed me. Having expected him, I kissed him back. I
stopped kissing him as soon as my mind came to me (or as soon as I
was done indulging myself, since the damage had already been
done), got into a cab alone, and went home.

Isaac was due to arrive in New York the next morning. All night
I tossed and turned. It was finally done, I thought. I had confirmed
my worst fears about myself. *I was pathetic and selfish and pathetic and selfish.* I always would be, I always had been. I wondered
how I would tell him. I was going to marry Isaac and then I was going to betray him. I couldn't bear that thought. How could I marry,
knowing that going in?

Isaac came in quietly that morning, slipped off his shoes, and got
into bed with me. He smelled my hair.

"Were you in a bar, sweetie? Were you out partying without
me?" I turned over and told him what happened.

He didn't withdraw. He just listened. He looked troubled. He
touched my face. He didn't say, "I don't care." That would have
made me feel terrible; that would have let me know that he had left
me completely. But somehow it was perfectly obvious to both of us,
lying there in bed, that this was something for us to talk about and
try to figure out *together*. It was a part of the conversation we had
begun, and planned always to continue, about our lives and how to
help each other through. Neither he nor I wanted me behaving the
way I'd behaved the night before. But our faith in each other now

extended so far beyond my last mistake, or his last failing. We were not judging each other that way anymore.

That morning was the morning I finally knew, for the first time in my life, that when the time came I could don the white wedding dress. Finally, I understood: Getting married wasn't going to be about sex, not the way I'd misunderstood it to be, with only my unmarried past to judge it by. Marriage was going to be about something else—something I didn't understand yet, but was beginning to.

I have now been married for nearly five years. I made a leap of faith the day I said, "I do." I married believing that I was giving something up, and I was right. It would have been foolish to think that my sex life with Isaac would be so amazing that I would forget all about longings for others, so fulfilling that monogamy would be effortless, so complete that I would never miss the life I led as a young woman, sexually free. It would have been equally foolish to imagine, of course, that I understood what I was going to get in return for my sacrifice. I married without understanding what it was, because I couldn't possibly.

I know how hard it is to truly integrate sex and love. Our sex lives can get so caught up in fear, power, posturing, and objectification that those things become part of what draws us to sex and what makes sex exciting; they can even become what sex *is*. My sex life with Isaac is private—one of the most precious and rewarding things about it—but I will say this: I now know what it means to have my body and my soul in the same place when I go to bed with a man (when I go to bed with *him*), and I wouldn't give that up for anything.

I'D HAVE TO BE EVEN CRAZIER THAN I AM TO SCREW THIS ONE UP

Meredith Maran

Why am I still married? The implication, of course, is that there are some pretty compelling reasons not to be. I'm all too familiar with that vegetative state of matrimonial ambivalence; it was the bane of my previous marriages. But lucky me. Not this time.

The more pertinent question would be this: Why, after four nearly legal weddings, have I been so happy with Katrine Andrée Simone Thomas that I have never been moved to ask why I'm still married? And by "never" I mean exactly that. Not "hardly ever." Not "only when we're not speaking," but truly, *not ever.*

(Warning: If you're jaded, heartbroken, lonely, mismarried, or averse to country love songs, you're not going to like the answer. Because it's this simple. And this inexplicable.)

Katrine and I belong together. And we know it. Because we were in midlife when we met, because each of us had been painfully partnered before, we knew the first morning we woke up together, and we've known even better each morning since, what only the combo platter of medium-rare common sense with a side of fried relationships could have taught us. How good we've got it. What a miracle it is.

Resist the urge to check my bio. Yes, I'm a New York Jew. And yes, you heard me: I said "miracle." Nothing else could explain the series of fortunate events that brought the two of us together—

Katrine, a French lesbian, thirty-nine, celibate by choice, saving herself for nothing less than *le grand amour*, a believer in angels, socialism, and destiny; me, an American bisexual, forty-five-year-old mother of two, sworn to nonmonogamy, still sifting through the smoldering ruins of two consecutive crashed-and-burned twelve-year marriages (one retro-hetero, one pomo-homo). Nothing less than a miracle could explain the international incident that turned two very distinct "I's" into one merged-and-loving-it "we."

Neither of us expected to find our missing half in a Berkeley boutique on December 18, 1996, although that was exactly what our yenta had in mind. Our mutual friend Devi, undeterred by the challenging commute that an Oakland–St. Denis romance would require, invited Katrine to Berkeley for Christmas and—knowing that I was far more likely to show up for marked-down clothing than for some talked-up French lesbian—summoned us both to her store for an after-hours, private sale.

When they make the movie of our meeting, the opening shot will be slo-mo, the camera panning across the near-empty store as Katrine's eyes first meet mine. The music will swell and the clearance racks will part as we move in wordless unison to the dressing room, where Katrine murmurs—her accent *charmant*, her voice deep with desire—"May I?" then drapes me in black velvet. "Yes. Oh, yes," I gasp, as, boldly yet tenderly, Katrine adjusts my shoulder pads, her fingertips setting fire to my skin. Will the camera catch the buckling of my knees, the heat rising from our bodies, our open-mouthed looks of wonder as we face each other in the floor-to-ceiling mirror, seeing ourselves as a couple for the very first time?

("We belong together," I thought at that moment. And so, as it turned out, did Katrine.)

Three nights later I awoke hours after our first lovemaking to find my body enclosed in Katrine's strong, soft arms, her eyes shining bright as searchlights in the dark. "I found you," she said.

My breath caught in my throat. In the face of such certainty, such *momentousness*, I decided that my "I'll never trust anyone again; I'll never sleep with just one person again" speech—and my career, and my twice-weekly postbreakup therapy, and everything else in my well-scripted, wound-licking life—could wait. For the next three weeks I'd have my Great Romance. Then Katrine would return to France, and I'd return to my previously scheduled programming. Or, possibly not.

And so, for the rest of Katrine's stay in Berkeley, I performed a time-limited, risk-limited, one-time-only experiment as alien to my being as attending midnight Mass. I surrendered to the force field of love. I closed my eyes, opened every other orifice, and let days in Devi's guest bed bleed into blissfully mindless nights. I paid retail for Veuve Clicquot. I whipped up batches of waffles, thrust batter-dipped fingers into my lover's luscious mouth. I breathed in the scents of the private island upon which we had marooned ourselves: Hermès *parfum*, and sex, and fresh-cut narcissus, and high-thread-count pillowcases hung to dry in the sun.

During rare moments alone—driving to the wine shop, peeing preemptively before our next go-round, slipping off to check my messages—I heard my own voice, and my worried friends'. Dream on, they warned me, but remember, it's just a dream. A rebound romance. Don't set yourself up for heartbreak again. We just put you back together after the last one.

"Remember what you told me? You're not ready for a real relationship," said my postbreakup fuck buddy, who felt, quite rightly, that he ought to know.

"You're setting yourself up to crash and burn—again," frowned my twelve-step–schooled friend and neighbor, into whose house I had crawled on mornings I was too grief-stricken to pour my own granola.

"It's the Zoloft," said my brother, who had dropped everything and driven fifty miles, one year earlier, to sit at my bedside on suicide watch. "It makes everything feel good, even when it isn't."

I didn't argue with them. How could I? When I wasn't cooing and panting into Katrine's exquisite ear, I was saying the same things to myself. But then Katrine would beckon me back to bed and wrap me up in the spun-sugar cocoon of us again, and my favorite word, "no"—protector of my psyche, shut-off valve to my soul, emotional emergency brake—would vacate my vocabulary. Yes, I heard myself saying, I'll come to France for three weeks in February. Yes, I'll host your fortieth birthday parties (one in Oakland; one in St. Denis) in April. Yes, I'll go with you to your goddaughter's fifth birthday party in July.

If this is just a dream, I realized two weeks in, it's going to be one hell of a long night. And I seem to be sleeping in silk pajamas, not protective armor.

On the eve of Katrine's departure Devi threw us a party in the twenty-room, leaded-glass, sweeping-views-of–San Francisco Bay mansion where she had been hosting Katrine and therefore that noisy, happy new entity: *us*. The guest list was our first joint venture, half Devi's and Katrine's friends, half mine. I couldn't wait to show off the glamorous stage set of my glamorous affair, my new, gorgeous girlfriend, the new, mellowed-by-love me. As the doorbell began to ring, Katrine and I played dress-up in Devi's costume room, both of us now a full size smaller than we'd been three weeks before. We toasted each other with pre-party flutes of champagne, giggled over a bit of pre-party pot, and descended the wide winding stairway, arm in arm, velvet skirts and newlywed bonhomie flowing.

"Katrine!" called Ananda (not her real name), Katrine's ex-lover, a showstopping beauty I'd seen pictures of but hadn't yet met. I felt the grip of Katrine's arm slacken on mine, felt her attention shift from me to . . . *her*. "I brought some new paintings to show you," Ananda said, her eyes fixed on Katrine's. "Come see." Katrine kissed me lightly, and just like that, they were gone.

And just like that, so was I. Stoned and stun-gunned, I snapped out of the trance I'd been in: three weeks of seeming to be someone far more pliant and trusting than I ever could actually be. A werewolf beneath a full moon, fur sprouting, fangs glistening, saliva dripping, the old me burst forth. Ah! Here I was again, the fighter I'd always been, not the lover I'd been pretending to be. How could I have forgotten? I was the one who chose badly, married quickly, attacked when the misery set in, then wallowed in abandonment, having driven off my abandoner.

But not this time. Not for nothing had I lived a few more years, paid for a few thousand more therapy sessions, learned a few more tricks. This time I was getting out alive. "Good thing I didn't *really* trust her," I snarled silently as I poured wine, sliced baguette, greeted guests. "Good thing she'll be gone tomorrow."

"So where is she, this new love of your life?" a friend asked as I took her coat. "Around here somewhere," I shrugged. God knows *I* wasn't about to go look. I'd been in this movie before. I knew how it ended.

Katrine and I had planned to sleep that night at my house, closer to real life, closer to the airport. At midnight we left the land of make-believe, as I now thought of Devi's castle on the hill, drove down the narrow winding roads to the wide flatland streets below. Neither of us said a word. "Dream over," I growled to myself, jaw clenched, as we pulled up in front of my house. My kids were at their dad's (failed twelve-year marriage number one); the house was the one I'd bought with the woman who'd raised them with me (failed twelve-year marriage number two).

"What's wrong, my love?" Katrine asked as I opened the front door. In the instant before I exploded, a thought flitted across my brain like a butterfly racing to beat out a storm. "Just because this is what you've always done, you don't have to do it now." And then that thought, and all reason, was gone.

"What's *wrong*?" I screamed, slamming the door behind me—the door I'd spent twelve years slamming at someone else, until finally she slammed it at me. "You spent our whole last night together flirting with your ex-girlfriend, and now you're asking me what's *wrong?*"

Katrine sank onto the couch, her eyes wide and glowing in the dark. Claws bared, I waited, poised to pounce. Why wasn't she fighting back? "Don't tell me you don't even know what you *did*," I shouted, flinging my keys across the room. Katrine flinched as they clattered onto the wood floor an inch from her beautiful Italian shoes. I stomped out of the living room. Stomped back in. Katrine wasn't doing her part. Did I have to do *everything* myself? At least my exes knew how to fight. "I knew this would happen," I yelled. "I *knew* it was too good to be true—"

"It is true, Meredith," Katrine said quietly. "You don't have to yell. I'm right here. I'm listening."

Maybe it was the pot, or the wine, or the Zoloft. Maybe it was the way my insides clutched at the sound of Katrine's voice, at the dizzying drift of her perfume in the air. Maybe there is a god or a yenta whose plan was mightier even than my ability to screw it up. Maybe I'd finally spent enough years proving every bad thing there is to believe about myself; the human race; love. Maybe the failure of my self-protectiveness to protect me had made me less willing to go on hauling around the armor.

Whether by the grace of luck, intoxicants, pharmaceuticals, and/or divine intervention, my defenses cracked and tumbled and Katrine's words came through. As clearly as I'd seen the *rightness* of Katrine and me in that dressing room mirror three weeks and a million swooning kisses ago, I saw the choice that was mine, in that moment, to make. There I was, standing in my living room in the dead center of my life, bruised and terrified, with a chance, maybe my last, to love and be loved by someone who actually could—new-age platitudes be damned—*make me happy.* And because I was high or because I was blessed or because I was finally old enough to understand what matters, I took a right turn where always before I'd turned the other way. Instead of freezing over and leaving, I stayed and melted. Instead of yelling and accusing, I dropped into Katrine's arms and wept.

"I'll never leave you, Meredith," Katrine said, and I swear I felt the world tilt on its axis.

There she was, sitting in the same spot on the same couch where my ex had told me, one year ago, that she was leaving me, my kids, our life. How could Katrine know in twenty-one days or twenty-one years that she would love me and stay with me forever? More incredibly still, how could I believe that she would?

What had I learned about Katrine in twenty-one days? That she was smart and funny, hot and sweet; spoke five languages so she could (and promised to) take me anywhere; had started a business in California as a twenty-year-old and so was Berkeley-ready; worked in fashion so she could get it for me wholesale; adored good food, bad kids, fresh flowers, and radical politics; said yes easily and no judiciously; and loved me ferociously. Was that enough to make me believe that we could be together, happily, forever?

Apparently, it was. Because I did. Believe her. Which felt a lot like believing myself. And that, as they say, was that.

Even when I stopped taking the Zoloft, secretly fearing the magic would evaporate along with the serotonin uptake inhibitors: that was still that.

Even when we were apart for weeks at a time. Even when we had to negotiate the logistical, financial, and emotional minefields of wrenching Katrine out of her own country and settling her in mine.

Five months later, on my third trip to France, Katrine woke up one morning and said, "Let's buy wedding rings."

"*D'accord*," said I, the one who always said no.

"And keep them till we're ready to get married."

"*Pourquoi pas?*" I replied.

"We'll have to pay retail," she warned.

"*Pas de problème,*" I said. (Only then, Katrine says now, did she truly know she had me.)

One month later, Katrine packed up her life, and our rings in their velvet box, and moved to Oakland to live with me and my raging teenage son. She got a job in a small, hip San Francisco fashion studio. I wrote a book. She drove me to the hospital where my son was handcuffed to a gurney, to juvenile court where he was handcuffed to a chair. We made pan after pan of lasagna, prayed, and cried together when our dearest friend got cancer and, six years later, died. We went to church together when my son found God and, five years later, got well. I wrote another book. Katrine became a landscaper. I flew to Brittany for her father's funeral. She stood in line and bought a copy of my book at every one of my readings.

Five years later, we were reading the paper in bed. "It's 02/02/02," I said. "A good day for couples. Let's get married today."

"*D'accord,*" Katrine said.

"In bed. Naked. Just the oh-two of us."

"*Parfait.*"

"With Veuve Clicquot."

"*Naturellement.*"

The vows we read to each other as we finally exchanged rings that night at 20:02:02 proved to be our first, but not our last. We got married again one year later, before friends and family, this time with our clothes on and officiated by my no-longer-raging, now–Baptist preacher son. Again when we registered as California domestic partners, and again in France, where we applied for le Pacte Civil de Solidarité. We made a date to make it legal—at San Francisco City Hall on April 9, 2004—but the gay-marriage roulette wheel stopped before it landed on our number. Next time we're in Massachusetts, British Columbia, or Denmark, we'll probably get married there, too.

What amazes me is not that it took Katrine and me five years to

decide on the right time, right place; or that once we started getting married we couldn't seem to stop; or how solidly married we
managed to make ourselves while the marriage wars raged around
us and the world's opinion of our right to love each other shifted
and slipped beneath our feet. What's surprising is that a person
who used to launch screaming fights about which movie to see or
whose turn it was to clear the table (that would be me) could go
through five years of conversations about when, where, and how to
get married without exchanging a single harsh word.

Why am I still married? Because, as it turns out, just like the
worst intention, the best intention has the power to make itself
come true.

All the years I spent loving from sickness, not in health, thrash-
ing around in relationships that were equal parts pain and pleasure
(on the better days), all I wanted was the same things every lover
wants: for it to be good, and for it to last forever. Like love, marriage, and the baby carriage, I thought, one led to the other, and
only in that order.

But when Katrine said, "I'm never going to leave you," three
weeks after we met, I saw that being brave and crazy and certain
enough to say "I want it to last forever" is not just an end point to
hope to get to. It's a great beginning. Making the one big decision at
the outset made all our small decisions exactly that: small. Slamming the door on ambivalence with its endless, erosive judging and
appraising left the werewolf outside, howling at the moon.

"We're lucky, huh?" Katrine says often to me. "And we know it,"
I say.

Note to cynics: I know what you're thinking. I still speak that
language, too. Separately and together, Katrine and I worry that
we're being dangerously naive, arrogant, smug. Why should we be
able to dodge the bullet when so many around us are falling down
wounded or dead? Good marriage notwithstanding, I'm still the

sick fuck (as Tony Soprano would say) I've always been. Katrine is still the sweet sick fuck she'll always be. She smokes cigarettes, and I really wish she wouldn't. I make plans without consulting her, and she really wishes I wouldn't. She's opinionated (French, after all), I'm self-centered (Jewish, as I have mentioned). She leaves the light on in the closet. I leave drawers not quite closed. We fuss at each other, rarely. We fight—about three times a year, by current calculations, and always with our hearts in the right place (open). Never again (and by "never" I mean exactly that. Not "hardly ever," but truly, *not ever)* since that night in what is now our living room has either of us slammed a door, raised a voice, or thrown a set of keys.

Why am I still married? Because I've got less than half of my lifetime left, and I'd rather turn the closet light off myself than waste a minute of how good it is, being married to Katrine.

"I just wish I'd found you twenty years sooner," Katrine says often.

"No you don't," I always say. "I wasn't ready. I would have ruined it." She shakes her head, thinks I'm drawing a happy face on the one sad thing about us: that we had to live so much of our lives without each other. But I know better.

Each morning of each day of each of the eight years we've spent together, Katrine has called me back to bed. "Just for five minutes," she says, coaxing me away from the e-mails I'm answering, the book I'm writing, the papers I'm shuffling.

"Isn't this good, baby?" she asks me then, rolling me around in our high-thread-count sheets in her soft, strong arms.

"Yes," I answer. "This is good."

OF RIVERS AND LOVE

Diana Abu-Jaber

Do we know whom we're meant to love? Is it possible that certain people really are meant for each other, and is it possible to discern such a thing consciously, deliberately, purposively?

Sometimes when I think about the way my husband and I came together, I think we came together despite ourselves, knowing better, trying not to.

We met under the flickering, unfiltered ray of a computer screen. I'd always hated computers; they were the enemy. This one was especially bad—the disk drive was loud as a vacuum cleaner. It roared at me from the middle of my desk, from the center of my new office at Portland State University. I'd tried to ignore the thing as much as possible. I've always written my books longhand, but suddenly it was 1996 and it was time for me to move beyond the word processor's realm of glorified typing, into the three dimensions of the Internet.

Well, I was trying. I was thirty-five but it seemed like I still hadn't figured out a damn thing. I'd resigned from a good tenure-track job at my previous university, running from a bad boss, escaping to a new city, a new school, and a stack of unpaid bills. Everything seems to spin around the pivot of that year—a year of trying to grow up, to pay the student loans, to see if I was really a writer of novels or if my first novel would be my only novel. There was so much at stake. So I was trying really, really hard.

Did I mention that I was also running from marriage? Seven years and it hadn't worked. When I was still married, I'd convinced myself that I'd figured love out at least. But I hadn't. I'd married a friend from graduate school, and after all these years we didn't have a thing to say to each other. I didn't have one single bit of any of it figured out, and I was thirty-five and I had to try again. Harder this time. The whole idea of trying again scared me to death.

At the moment, though, I was just trying to pay back all the debts that had spilled out of my dissolving marriage, so I took whatever jobs presented themselves. Portland State was the first. But there were private workshops, speaking gigs, all sort of pieces to the puzzle that was money. And then I was offered a crack at something new. A small private college was starting up something unheard of (by me) at the time—an online degree program.

It sounded perfect: a class that you could teach from your home computer while sitting around in hair curlers and fuzzy slippers; a glorified version of the stuff-envelopes-from-home gig—my perfect job!

When the kind program administrators asked if I knew HTML, I laughed in my most breezy, carefree manner and said, "Of course!" The truth was, I'd never heard of HTML. I didn't know what it was, and when they sent me the start-up packet, I took one look at the registration form for the software and burst into tears.

That's where Scott came in. Turns out that there were all sorts of well-meaning professors like myself out there who assumed that HTML just required a little on-the-job practice to pick up. The college was forced to hire a consultant to go around training us hopeless cases in how to use a computer.

"You can do it," Scott said. "You've just got to relax a little and take it in."

"It's too complicated," I whimpered. "It's like *math*."

"No," he said and smiled. "It's not so hard, you're just not that interested."

* * *

It's a little strange to think of oneself as a hopeless case at thirty-five. I'd spent my life studying and teaching novels, poetry, theater, film—at the center of which resided grand themes of romantic love and passion. Yet here I was, divorced. It seemed that I had gleaned just enough information to go out into the world and make myself unhappy.

I'd grown up in a traditional immigrant household where the nicest thing you could say about dating was that it was forbidden. My father, an immigrant from Jordan, had always hoped to be the one to select my future husband—preferably from a pool of my many available cousins. Which is partly why I left the house at sixteen. Not that I had anything against arranged marriage, in theory. I had several relatives who were formally paired with their spouses. All of them were still married—to varying degrees of success—but most appeared to be quite content.

But my father had courted my mother as a young swain all on his own in the New World. To me, their marriage was the height and breadth of romance because it was all so unexpected. They didn't even speak the same language. Their families, customs, and religions were as different as could be, and they reached across that dividing line and held on tight.

And that was what I wanted.

While my father instructed me that a good girl never does anything as silly and frivolous and potentially disreputable as "falling in love," I was learning about courtship from Jane Austen, mystery from Jean Rhys, and eros from James Baldwin. I also learned about obsession from Ingmar Bergman and flights of transport from Marc Chagall and Martha Graham. But in all that time, I didn't learn how to decorate a house, cook a lasagna, or make a bed in cooperation with another person. I read the classics, I got a Ph.D. in literature, but none of that heady education taught me about plain and simple love, about the ordinary garden variety way of compromise and endurance, about love without a central crisis point or denouement, about the love of sharing home and bed and time—our singular precious time on earth.

I'm not certain I would've ever learned it, either, if I hadn't eventually met this guy in a flannel shirt who could program computers and read rivers and who seemed to know, somehow, that we were meant for each other. As I think I've mentioned before, I didn't know much of anything. Once I'd escaped the confines of my parents' home, my social life sprang into being and included all sorts of guys—or at least that's what I thought as I went out on a series of dates with boys in stovepipe jeans and black T-shirts, boys who carried around paperbacks with titles like *Of Grammatology*, *Les Fleurs du Mal*, and *Tender Is the Night* in their back pockets, boys who sipped espresso in the rear of the café as they debated the relative merits of Peter Greenaway versus Atom Egoyan, boys who lived indoors like me, over a glass of chardonnay and a plate of mesclun and radicchio. This was the life I craved: to be an intellectual, an artist, a free thinker, to live the cosseted life of the mind, a life of rarefied, expert, and delicate pleasures—passive pleasures, best entertained within the darkened box of a theater or cinema, or the small circle of light thrown upon the top of a desk.

Nothing—nothing—in that college life or beyond prepared me for the fact that when I turned thirty-six, I'd attempt wading, chest-deep, into a frigid, ropy river. But there I was, swathed shoulders to booties in neoprene waders, balancing—just barely— on ice-slick river rocks and trying to duplicate the peculiar slashing motion Scott was making with his fishing rod.

I'd never been particularly afraid of water per se—as long as I was admiring it from a beach chair—but wading rivers was another matter entirely. The water had an immense, bone-chilling force, and the special gripping felt bottoms of my boots still seemed precarious and unreliable: I was terrified of being swept into the whirling depths.

"Don't fight it," Scott said. "Try to become part of the river."

This was his real calling. When he wasn't writing about or talking about computers, he worked as a fly-fishing instructor. While all the other men I had been involved with had known all sorts of subtle, specialized things about ideas, Scott was the first one I'd ever met who could make or do things.

Our courtship over the keyboard had evolved so gradually, at first I wasn't even sure it was happening. After a few early computer training sessions that disintegrated into (my) panic, Scott began designing, posting, and organizing my online class for me. I realized, only after we started meeting at his apartment over plates of grapes and brie, that he was no longer trying to teach me anything to do with HTML, and he even eventually began discouraging my feeble questions on the topic. In the matter of teaching this Internet class, I became completely dependent on Scott, thus necessitating that we saw each other week after week.

Still, I hesitated to think of Scott as anything more than a good buddy. He was capable and competent, but was that sexy? *Sexy* was Heathcliff, smoldering on the moors—or in the back of a seminar room. Scott balanced his checkbook; Heathcliff would never balance his checkbook—he wouldn't bother with FDIC-insured banking at all. Heathcliff was the sort to inherit a trust fund or, even better, go bankrupt and be thrown in debtor's prison—now *that*'s sexy! And Scott was good-natured, not given to tantrums, not a wisp of glowering or smirking or smoldering in sight. My friends and I called him F. Scott—the *F.* stood for "Fun." Could I really fall in love with someone named Fun Scotty?

After we gave up on HTML, our courtship developed—as so many must—as a sort of mutual training exercise. There was a real learning curve here—Scott was a whole new world to me. He was open to great food and wine but winced when I proposed attending poetry readings, and he fell asleep inside of ten minutes, his head slumped backward, at a lecture on Lacanian psychoanalysis. For me, the first crisis came when we attended a special screening and critical analysis of Antonioni's classic *L'Avventura*, one of my favorite films.

"A total bunch of baloney," F. Scott announced afterward.

I was flabbergasted. "How can you say that? It's an incredible film—the imagery, the subtext, the depth of characterization . . ."

He shrugged. "It was boring. Okay, the boat part was pretty good, but then it just dragged on. What a pointless ending. And then that whole lecture afterward! People should be able to enjoy a movie right away. Anything that needs to be explained to you by a bunch of experts is failed art. I mean, that's if you ask me . . ."

"But that's what I do for a *living*—I teach, I help people to appreciate art."

He shook his head. "Maybe, but what you really are is a writer."

I gaped. Impossible! How could I love anyone who didn't love Antonioni?

After our crisis on a dreary, rain-soaked Friday, the following Saturday was clear and bright. Portland sparkled like a newly rinsed glass. Scott and I walked to a big outdoor courtyard and fountain near my apartment. He was carrying his nine-weight rod and his reel; he was going to show me how to cast.

We came to the vast, modernist fountain, constructed of big flat irregularly shaped slabs of cement and flowing panes of water. Scott threaded the line through the rod and held it up in one hand. "It's really simple," he said. "Keep your wrist straight and cast in a forward motion like this." He cradled me between his arms in the old, suggestive golf-instructor pose, and I happily pressed into the warmth of him. I considered playing the Clueless Ingenue, just to prolong the moment, but discovered I didn't have to act very much at all. Casting was hard!

"No, relax, you're trying to control too much. Just watch me for a second."

With that, he lifted and snapped the rod with a single stroke: the line rose overhead, described a miraculous airborne, serpentine *S*. And for a moment, he was Indiana Jones, cracking his magnificent whip, dashing and exotic and desperately sexy.

Thus ensued what is now close to a decade of mutual appreciation and bafflement: we are not the same person! How did this happen? There are times when our differences are the greatest single problem in our relationship, like the sabbatical year I wanted us to spend in Manhattan and Scott wanted us to go to the Virgin Islands. (We compromised and split the year between locations.) There are times when I believe that I literally cannot listen to one more word about sailing or kayaking. And if Scott ever feels this way about my rambling about books or writing—well, he's usually too discreet to let on.

A close friend recently underwent a crisis in her own relationship. Matilde and Josh (not their real names) also had a seemingly mismatched union—she was a painter and professor of art; he was a chemical engineer—but they had a funny, easy, happy marriage. Then after years of relative contentment, Matilde fell in love with another visual artist who'd come to guest-teach at her university that year. Their affair was intense and all-consuming, and Matilde was racked with guilt and confusion. She confessed to Josh, hoping, I suppose, that his reaction would decide everything. But instead of leaving—or berating—her, Josh told her that he loved her and that she would have to make a choice between them.

"I love Josh, but sometimes I think I don't know if I've ever really *loved* him," she said to me, lowering her voice. "It's so hard to admit something like that, even after suspecting it for so many years. I'm an artist in my very fiber, and I need someone who can speak to the deepest parts of me. I need poetry in my life. I want more than friendship—I want electricity."

At the end of the year, she left Josh and moved away with her lover. She wrote to me from Mexico a year later: she thinks she made a terrible mistake.

Of course, whenever a friend does something giddy, exciting, and romantic, there's always the temptation to look at our dependable old partners and muse: Hmmm ... is there sufficient poetry here? In fact, when's the last time I saw him reading or writing poetry?

But when we're not arguing about Italian films of the 1950s, then it seems clear that Scott and I not only instruct each other, we enlarge each other, we lead each other into places and ways of being and seeing that we've never experienced before. We're not teenagers, growing into a mutual curve together, but because we came together as adults, we bring more to the table. Every time I agree, grudgingly, to try something as alien as snorkeling, inevitably, one of my girlfriends will say: you're so lucky—my husband never wants to do anything new.

And at times (not every time), when I find myself tramping through a gorgeous piney field, I think, I *am* lucky.

The best part turns out to be that Scott and I recognize deeper truths and needs in each other that we have lost sight of in ourselves. I encouraged Scott to leave his stultifying corporate computer job and go freelance, to help him find more time for rivers. And he has helped me see how vital my writing is to my happiness, my sense of self, and has helped me find the ways to make writing foremost in my life, to find the courage and determination to pursue it.

So there I was, slipping and quavering and quaking in the middle of the Deschutes River in eastern Oregon. I wasn't feeling lucky or happy, but I was feeling determined. It was my third fly-fishing outing with Scott, and I'd been making my wobbly uncertain cast for hours. I wanted to catch something—anything—just once, just to know that I could do it. And yet, I wasn't entirely convinced that

I wanted to—the whole system of catch-and-release fishing seemed counterintuitive. You didn't kill the poor fish, only hooked them, pulled them out of the water to admire, then let them go, saving the fish's life but probably making it very unhappy in the process. Some of his fishing buddies jokingly referred to this as "torture and release."

I made my feeble casts, forgetting to do important things like strip the line or mend it or any of the other operations that separate a plunker (me) from a real fly-fisher (Scott). I was freezing, defeated, and generally miserable, wondering why I'd let myself be led into such a pointless and unpromising enterprise. Meanwhile, Scott, slightly upriver, was hooking fish after fish. Eventually, he drifted my way. "Come on, you can do it," he coached. "You've got a great cast—you've just got to fish with confidence."

It was the same piece of advice he'd given me regarding my writing career. Years had passed since I'd published my first novel, and I was working on the second with equal amounts of excitement and dread—I wasn't sure if I could really write another novel or get it published. When I confided these fears to him, Scott responded: fish with confidence. When you approach any task with this attitude, he said, it makes a real difference. Believe that you can catch the fish, he said, and you will.

I was tired, I was hungry, I was ready to reevaluate this whole love and fly-fishing business, but Scott stood next to me in the roaring water and nodded. I closed my eyes while the frigid water churned around me, shut everything else out, and imagined the fish rising to my hook. *I will catch a fish*, I thought. I snapped my rod back with the clean, chopping motion Scott had taught me, and for once the line did what it was supposed to do, snaking through the air, landing soft as a kiss.

Almost instantly there was a tug—playful, almost coquettish—on the other end. I didn't believe it—I was certain I was snagged on a hidden rock somewhere and I pulled back, trying to free it. The line sparked and tightened and turned alive, electric. I felt that I was in direct communication with an ancient, alien life form. "Scotty?" my voice quailed over the roaring water.

"Reel it in!" he shouted, catching my excitement. "Don't let the line go slack. Nice and easy."

And then in all that swirling water, rising like some sort of bright secret from the center of the world, I saw my fish. It soared up at me as I spooled the reel, a gleaming silvery being that I'd tricked and summoned on a fly that Scott had just tied for me that morning.

I held it in my hands just for a second, felt the mystery of its hidden working body as it stared back at me, then dipped it in the water, and it swam between my fingers, elusive as a dream. We laughed, clinging to each other in the wild water; I felt safe, warm, and steady. I felt at that moment that anything was possible. Even writing books, even falling for a fisherman. "Let's go in," Scott said. "I'm starving." He offered to let me pick the movie again that night, in honor of my fish.

But I had already turned back to the river.

MARRYING OUT OF HISTORY
Nell Casey

When my sister Maud was three, a chubby girl with determined eyes and pixie bangs, she stormed over to my parents and said, "Who will be my husband? I want to meet him. I want him here *right now*." I made the same demand throughout my twenties. I didn't have the patience or the confidence or the cynicism—whatever it takes—to allow my fortune to unfold naturally. I wanted marriage and all the attendant fantasies the institution brought with it—the stamp of normalcy, a second go-round on family (since the first had left me spooked), a chance to fly the noncommittal coop, finally escaping the paranoid, whispering no-man's-land of single life—and I wanted it, like the toddler Maud, *right now*.

And, though, even to me, this setup sounds as if it would be guaranteed a disastrous end—something Henry James might have plotted, along the lines of a hasty marriage to a flimsy character who could never deliver on these promises—I found a more generous fate instead. I met my future husband when I was twenty-three years old. He was a guest at my cousin's birthday party. We talked for all of ten minutes, during which he struck me as handsome and brash, which naturally sent my youthful, masochistic heart aflutter. Still, it took us another four years, spent in an exquisitely careful friendship, before we actually confessed there was something between us, which is to say we finally decided to risk falling in love. This saintly pace, I should admit, had nothing to do with me.

At the time, I was in the habit of throwing myself foolishly into relationships—*Who will be my husband? I want him here right now!*—with my eyes closed and my arms thrust forward like some kind of insistent sleepwalker. But my future husband, Jesse, set the slow and measured stride of our relationship, and I, taken with his cool demeanor, followed suit. "Thank you," I whispered when Jesse finally kissed me at the front door of my West Village apartment building that night. "Thank you," Jesse still whispers, now seven years later, both teasing me for my dramatic gratitude and flattering himself with the purity with which I drank him up that night.

It's an unfashionable view, to love marriage. It sounds eager or naive or like a lie. Perhaps this is because it's a view that belongs mostly to the young or newly betrothed, whom I, for better or for worse (as they say in marriage), represent in this collection. I understand that love sometimes turns out to be more of a willful fantasy, an elaborate projection of all that you believe it *should* offer, which can fade away after jostling between familiarity and disappointment for too long. But I don't think that will be the case with Jesse and me. So I'll take this positive view of marriage on wholeheartedly, if only to provide a time capsule of sorts filled with all the galloping confidence of a thirty-four-year-old, happily married woman. Let this be a love song then. To marriage, to my husband.

My own parents' marriage, which began as a glittering romance between two attractive, quick-witted writers from socially ambitious families, ended mostly in disaster. As I understand, it started with my father mistaking my mother for someone else at a debutante ball in Washington, D.C. He placed a hand on her elbow from behind and leaned in close only to say another woman's name. By the time he'd realized his mistake, and my mother had turned around, it was too late for him to correct himself. Thankfully, she laughed at the mix-up and they struck up a conversation. This exchange led to a speedy six-month courtship that led to their living together for a year, which led, finally, to a proposal of marriage from my father, shyly offered as if it were just a casual suggestion—*hey maybe we should get married, what do you think?*—as they lay in bed together one morning in their house in Iowa.

It's strange (and dreamy too, as if I can suddenly peer into their young, unknowing hearts) to consider the hopeful start of my parents' marriage when their relationship is so defined by its end in my mind. My father has always objected to my describing our family as "dysfunctional," and I suppose now I can see his problem with it. It's a dismissive word, ugly and narrow, unwilling to account for the vast array of experiences shared by a family, painful *and* nurturing. I realize this is also how I've always viewed my parents' marriage. Simply as dysfunctional. Unhappy. Destructive. Bad. Without a fair sense of the kaleidoscope of emotions that make up a marriage over the years, even one that ends.

I am trying to imagine the ways that my mother and my father once fit together: his dazzling intellect, her sharp humor; his boyish insecurities about his looks, her angular beauty; his appreciation of odd behavior, her driven eccentricity; his jittery sense of intimacy, her rising to that challenge. Still, a kind of glamorous doom seems to lurk even in these pairings, so I wonder if it's impossible for me to separate the beginning from the end. Knowing them now as I do, as an adult, twenty-five years after their divorce, I can only see the ways they so clearly *don't* fit: his competitive streak, her alert defensiveness when challenged; his rule-oriented sense of romance, her renegade couplings; his emotional shyness, her near-religious commitment to compassion. It's probably always a little unfair when a child looks back on her parents' lives, not having been there, at least not consciously, for much of it and yet still drawing these dramatic conclusions from the shadowy scenes perceived through the scrim of childhood memory.

It's unclear to me who brought my parents' marriage to a halt finally, who said the clichéd phrase, "I want a divorce." (Do people say it differently now, out of respect for their own lives, to keep such a sacred disaster from sounding like a scene from *Days of our Lives*?) I do know I started to suspect that things weren't quite the way they were supposed to be when my parents began frequently retreating into the study for hours at a time. And I can vividly recall the afternoon, right down to the dust mites dancing in the single beam of sunlight that sliced the air before us, when my mother sat my sister and me down to say that she and my father had decided to go to couples' counseling. A rather sophisticated announcement, I realize now, for a nine- and eleven-year-old. Was she trying to soften the inevitable blow, as she must have suspected by then that they were going to separate? Within the year, my mother did indeed tell us of their plans to live apart—maybe by then she was even using the word "divorce"—and my only question, through deep gasping sobs, was: "Well, why did you even give birth to me if you were going to do this?"

In the end, my mother left with another woman. She confessed to an affair with a close friend of both my mother and father named Alice, who had been, until then, engaged to Ben (not their real names), another close friend of my parents. The two couples had once been a comfortable foursome, going to movies and dinner and hanging out at our house often. This sexy plot twist—one that has been mulled over quite a bit by our family, especially by my father, who finally exorcised the ghost by writing a novel about it—came to obscure, in its constant mythic retelling, the more meaningful problem of my parents' marital collapse for me. Which is not to say my mother's lesbianism was an irrelevant event in my life. On the contrary, it made me feel, with burning adolescent shame, that our family had spiraled into a realm of unrecoverable eccentricity. I yearned for "normal" with the same intensity that most teenagers hurl themselves into nipple-pierced rebellion. But I later came to understand that this particular detail finally amounted to little more than a distraction in the larger narrative of my parents' breakup. My mother's shifting sexuality was, after all was said and done, another circumstance among the confusing many that brought on the most defining part of the story for me: the end itself. This was the end of family as I had known it.

In the postdivorce era of our family, there were many discombobulated years of joint custody ("two weeks/two weeks," as we came to describe it), dark and temporary apartments, blustery tantrums, and, from my young perspective, hideous new alliances forged between my mother and Alice as well as my father and his new, young wife. My sister and I shuttled back and forth between these two households, inventing a willy-nilly sort of intimacy with my parents and the cast of characters they had recently introduced, though mostly I raged against the absurdity of it all. I was furious about the "boundarilessness"—a word I can only guess I picked up from the gentle but ineffective therapist my mother took me to see when I was twelve—with which my parents conducted their newly separate lives. It took many years for our two families to find steady footing, much less unselfconscious routine. My stepmother, Ros, who, at thirty, was four years younger than I am today when she married my father, had a difficult time navigating her own new relationship while simultaneously finding her place in relation to her two unhappy stepdaughters. Ros and I fought often and with gusto. We mainly clashed about the mundane details of keeping the house in order—changing the kitty litter and cleaning my room—but, honestly, we were in a turf battle. She wanted to make a home of her own, and I, seeing her authoritatively and actively undo the house I'd grown up in, fought to keep her from erasing our history. In the meantime, only barely beginning my own teenaged sexual awakening, I was horrified by my mother's drifting between the genders, leaving Alice for a time to date a man and then eventually pairing up with Alice again for twenty years. In time, as I entered my own young adulthood, I would develop sympathy, and even a sense of humor, for the pioneering complexity of my mother's life then, but at ten and thirteen and even eighteen years old, I could only see her behavior as an assault on what might have been a normal life—*oh how I deeply believed normal was the answer!*—for me, for our family. In my youth, I had a simple, Jerry Falwell–like reaction to the chaos of it all: we were living in sin, a shameful aberration of family life.

We each inherit our own legacy of marriage, defining ourselves with or against our own parents' marriage. In this sense, children are given the chance to do the finishing work of an earlier generation, studying their parents' past and then making their way into the future. This doesn't always guarantee brighter outcomes. My own parents, for example, were determined not to imitate their parents. My mother wanted a deeper intimacy than she saw in her mother and father's marriage. She didn't really feel that they *knew* each other. Although they were a wonderful match physically, sharp and elegant, they didn't seem to take each other seriously as partners. Her father would stifle her mother's attempts to talk about the world, cutting her off with a condescending remark. My grandmother, wounded and unruly, would often roll her eyes and murmur under her breath, "Men are such tragic babies." And so my mother, in an effort to make romance more egalitarian in her life and in her time, chose a husband who seemed more open to women. But my father, only one generation away from the man who cut his wife off from speaking her mind, turned out to have his own limits in this regard. He would never have shut my mother down in such an open display; in fact, he would have likely outwardly appreciated her standout wit and intelligence, but there was also a quieter sense of disapproval at work. And what was an eye-rolling response in the fifties became an affair with a woman in the seventies. In the end, I think my parents may also have been a little too in love with their own eccentric story. Like some kind of emotional

Minotaur, they were one-half self-mythologizing, one-half earnestly aching to pull their marriage back to a safe place. Finally unable to contain their bursting and opposing emotions, my parents' marriage blew apart.

And so I begin the next chapter, armed with their defeat but also with a strong sense of idealism. I do not believe the happiness I have found with Jesse is simply love as redemption, or retribution for an unhappy childhood, but I do believe my sturdy sense of commitment sprang, in part, from the wreck of my parents' marriage. I still carry the past with me, worrying in irrational ways that seem to date back to my young suspicions that something was wrong in our house, that something was about to go terribly wrong. There is no sense in trying to banish those emotions, rooted as strongly as they are in my history, but here also is a new chance, and I am going to take it.

What does it mean to have a marriage that gives you back some of the joy you lost in childhood? "You learned from us," my mother once offered. "You shaped yourself against the grain of our unhappiness." I tend to think of it more as luck, as if I whirled around the dance floor a little recklessly and somehow ended up in the arms of the right man at the end of the night. But, truthfully, I think my happiness is made up of some unknowable combination—as unknowable as love itself—of work and circumstance. It has to do with my own strong desire to level a shaky sense of family and the joyous luck of meeting someone who so deeply suits me. Perhaps my own modern childhood crisis has sent me backward, back beyond the cynicism of recent times, seeking marriage in an old-fashioned sense.

I would like to describe Jesse for you—his excellent forehead and distinguished face—and the meaning he has brought to my life. I could tell you the stories that make up the very marrow of our marriage: the ways he's helped me truly know myself or his devoted love of soul music or the way that emotional subtlety and outrageous humor reside together so comfortably in his personality. I could tell you that our love reassures me, draws me out, and steadies me on the beam. Or I could simply recount the time Jesse, not long after meeting my mother for the first time, suddenly broke the reserve between them by dancing ahead of us across a busy street in Manhattan, kicking his leg out to the side and singing, "I've got the rhythm of the city in me!" But then I'd be trying to convince you of something that is mine alone to know. There is no way to explain the reason for why someone walks into a room and wakes up your most primal dreams.

I was seated next to a well-known painter at a dinner party the other night. He is in his midsixties and has been married for thirty-eight years. When I asked him what stayed the same, what essential bit made his marriage last, he grasped uncomfortably for the answer. "She's still my best friend," he said and then slightly grimaced at his own corny offering. "We amuse each other. We have a shared interest in our children." His eyes closed and fluttered as he concentrated, searching for meaning. "A long marriage can sometimes feel like life imprisonment," he said, suddenly opening his eyes again. "But love also changes again and again and again over the years. Don't expect that what you have now will be what you have down the road. You won't even recognize why you first fell in love." He shrugged, offering one last possibility, "And some people are just lifers."

I felt torn. I respected the words of an intelligent man who has been married decades longer than me. I tried to weave his weary appreciation into our future, imagining Jesse and me one day feeling the same way. And I also shrugged his words off with the impishness of a teenager. I am impatient with those who resist marriage after having chosen it, who don't endorse it wholeheartedly. Why not *love* love? Why let time wear it down? *That won't happen to us*, I thought.

Perhaps my determination and optimism won't carry me effortlessly into the future. I may have to learn to loosen my grip, to embrace an Andy Goldsworthy model of love: let nature have its way and let our creation disappear before building a new one up again. My gratefulness for having healed the wounds of the past may get harder to summon, and I'll have to face the coming days, naked and unpredictable, making it up along the way. We might have to draw on strengths we can't be sure we have, or face the frightening truths about ourselves that longtime intimacy can so often demand.

Or maybe we'll just be happy lifers.

Still, I go forward with the only reason the institution of marriage has survived all these many centuries: hope.

AUTHOR BIOGRAPHIES

Diana Abu-Jaber is the author of the memoir *The Language of Baklava* and the novels *Crescent* and *Arabian Jazz*. Her many honors include a PEN Center Award for Literary Fiction and fellowships from the Fulbright Center and the National Endowment for the Arts. She teaches at Portland State University and lives part-time in Miami.

Kathleen Aguero's poetry collections include *Daughter Of, Thirsty Day*, and *The Real Weather*. She has edited several anthologies, teaches at Pine Manor College, and was a Visiting Research Associate at the Brandeis University Women's Studies Research Center.

Julia Alvarez is the author of five novels, including best-selling, award-winning *In the Time of the Butterflies* and *How the Garcia Girls Lost Their Accents*, the essay collection *Something to Declare*, five books of poetry, and four books for young readers. Her articles have appeared in the *New York Times, Elle*, and *O, The Oprah Magazine*.

Anne Bernays's ninth novel is *Trophy House*. She has published two works of nonfiction: *The Language of Names*, written with husband Justin Kaplan, and *What If?*, written with Pamela Painter. Her articles and essays have appeared in *The Nation*, the *New York Times, Town & Country*, and *Sports Illustrated*.

Nell Casey edited *Unholy Ghost: Writers on Depression,* a national best seller. She was a Carter Center journalism fellow in 2000–2001. Her work has appeared in *Elle, Mirabella,* Salon.com, *Self,* and the *New York Times Book Review.*

Susan Cheever, the best-selling author of twelve books, including five novels, four memoirs, and a biography of Alcoholics Anonymous cofounder Bill Wilson, is a National Book Critics Circle Award nominee and Boston Globe Winship Medal winner. She writes for *Newsday* and teaches in the Bennington College MFA program.

Susan Dworkin was a longtime contributing editor of *Ms.* magazine. She is author of *The Nazi Officer's Wife: How One Jewish Woman Survived the Holocaust* and *Miss America, 1945: Bess Myerson and the Year That Changed Our Lives,* as well as *Stolen Goods,* a novel; the Peabody Award–winning TV documentary *She's Nobody's Baby: American Women in the 20th Century* and numerous plays.

Helen Fremont is the author of the national best seller *After Long Silence,* a memoir. Her stories and essays have appeared in *Prize Stories: The O. Henry Awards, Ploughshares, The Harvard Review,* and *The Marlboro Review.* She works as a public defender.

Elizabeth Graver is the author of *Unravelling* and *The Honey Thief,* both of which were New York Times Notable Books. *Awake,* her third novel, was published in 2004. Her work has been included in *The Best American Short Stories, The Best American Essays,* and *Prize Stories: The O. Henry Awards.*

Jennifer Heath is an activist, award-winning journalist, and longtime art critic who has lived and worked all over the globe. Her books include *A House White with Sorrow: Ballad to Afghanistan,*

Black Velvet: The Art We Love to Hate, On the Edge of Dream: The Women of Celtic Myth and Legend, and *The Scimitar and the Veil: Extraordinary Women of Islam.*

Maria Hinojosa is the senior correspondent for *NOW* on PBS TV and the host of NPR's *Latino USA.* She authored a memoir, *Raising Raul: An Adventure Raising Myself and My Son,* and the book *Crews: Gang Members Talk to Maria Hinojosa. Working Mother* magazine named her one of the "25 Most Influential Working Mothers in America," and three times *Hispanic Business* named her as one of the hundred most influential Latinos in the United States.

Erica Jong is the author of eight novels, including *Fear of Flying, Fanny: Being the True History of the Adventures of Fanny Hackabout-Jones, Shylock's Daughter, Inventing Memory,* and *Sappho's Leap.* Her other books include the nonfiction works *Fear of Fifty: A Midlife Memoir, What Do Women Want?* and six volumes of poetry.

Eve LaPlante is the author of *American Jezebel: The Uncommon Life of Anne Hutchinson* and *Seized.* Her articles have appeared in *The Atlantic Monthly* and the *New York Times.* She is working on a biography of her sixth great-grandfather Samuel Sewall, the Salem witch judge.

Aimee Liu authored the novels *Flash House, Cloud Mountain,* and *Face,* and a memoir, *Solitaire.* She is a contributor to the anthologies *My California* and *Meeting Across the River* and has coauthored seven books of nonfiction on medical and psychological topics. She is a past president of PEN USA.

Meredith Maran is the author of nine books of nonfiction, including *Notes from an Incomplete Revolution: Real Life Since Feminism* and, most recently, *50 Ways to Support Lesbian and Gay Equality.*

She has written for *Brides, Mademoiselle, Self, Tikkun, Utne,* and Salon.com.

Bharati Mukherjee won the National Book Critics Circle Award for *The Middleman and Other Stories.* She is the author of seven novels, including *The Tree Bride, Desirable Daughters, The Holder of the World,* and *Jasmine*; two short-story collections; and two books of nonfiction coauthored with her husband, Clark Blaise. She teaches at UC Berkeley.

ZZ Packer's stories have appeared in *The New Yorker, Harper's, Story, Ploughshares, Zoetrope,* and *The Best American Short Stories 2000* and *2003.* Her collection, *Drinking Coffee Elsewhere,* was a New York Times Notable Book, a Commonwealth Book Award winner, and a PEN/Faulkner Award finalist. She is a recent winner of a Guggenheim Fellowship.

Marge Piercy's newest novel is *Sex Wars.* She has written more than thirty-eight books, including novels, poetry, a play, and a collection of essays, all with a focus on women's lives and social issues. Her numerous awards include the Paterson Poetry Prize and the Arthur C. Clarke Award for *He, She and It.*

Hannah Pine (a pseudonym) first appeared in *The Bitch in the House: 26 Women Tell the Truth About Sex, Solitude, Work, Motherhood, and Marriage.* Her husband wrote for *The Bastard on the Couch: 27 Men Try Really Hard to Explain Their Feelings About Love, Loss, Fatherhood, and Freedom.* Essays by both Pines have been published in *Elle.*

Audrey Schulman is the author of three novels: *The Cage, Swimming with Jonah,* and *A House Named Brazil.* Her books have been translated into eleven languages, and her articles have been published in *Ms.* magazine, *Grist,* and *Hope.*

Kamy Wicoff's first book, *I Do but I Don't*, will be published in spring 2006. She has written for Salon.com and spent five years as a television journalist in Los Angeles. She lives in New York City.

Liza Wieland is the author of two novels, *The Names of the Lost* and *Bombshell*, and two short-story collections, *You Can Sleep While I Drive* and *Discovering America*, as well as a volume of poems, *Near Alcatraz*. Her work has been awarded two Pushcart Prizes, an NEA fellowship, and a fellowship from the North Carolina Arts Council.

ACKNOWLEDGMENTS

Heartfelt thanks go to those who made this book possible: our stellar agent, Neeti Madan at Sterling Lord Literistic, who worked tirelessly every step of the way to assure our book's safekeeping and to make this book a reality; our editor and publisher, Laureen Rowland at Hudson Street Press, whose wisdom, humor, and sharp eye helped us hone the manuscript into the book it has become. Thanks also to Kate Prentice at Sterling Lord, to Hudson Street Press's Danielle Friedman and Elizabeth Keenan, and to Penguin's Sabila Kahn for creative ideas and dedicated work, each of who found her own way to connect with *Why I'm* Still *Married*.

To our friends who encouraged and cajoled us, lent their support, or read our personal essays, we thank Pam and Harry Bernard, Barbara Helfgott-Hyatt, Pagan Kennedy, Tehila Leiberman, Susan Mahler, Sandra Goroff-Mailly, Shela Pearl, Lauren Slater, Priscilla Sneff, Rickie Solinger, Taylor Stoehr, and Sondra Upham. To our parents and siblings, who taught us much about marriage through their lifelong commitments. To all the husbands and wives who appear in these pages, without whom we could never have compiled this book. We thank you for your willingness to put your marriage under glass, to allow us to learn from your truths and for the eagerness to consider the question of why you're still married on a deeply personal level. And especially, we thank Roger and Bob, our two helpmates, lovers, and witty husbands who stood by us, stood up to us, and contributed to our belief that being married is about "more happily than not," and that staying married matters.

About the Editors

Karen Propp is the author of two memoirs: *In Sickness & in Health: A Love Story* and *The Pregnancy Project: Encounters with Reproductive Therapy*. Her essays, poetry, and reviews have appeared in *The Women's Review of Books*, *Lilith*, and *Ploughshares*, and she has won several grants from the Massachusetts Cultural Council. She lives in Cambridge with her husband and son.

Jean Trounstine, author, activist, and professor, published *Shakespeare Behind Bars: The Power of Drama in a Women's Prison*, based on her award-winning work directing plays behind bars. She has been featured on NPR and the *Today* show and has written for the *Boston Globe* and *Working Woman* magazine. She coedited *Finding a Voice* and *Changing Lives Through Literature* and has published a collection of poetry, *Almost Home Free*. She and her husband live in Tewksbury, Massachusetts.